BLACK HAMMER ™

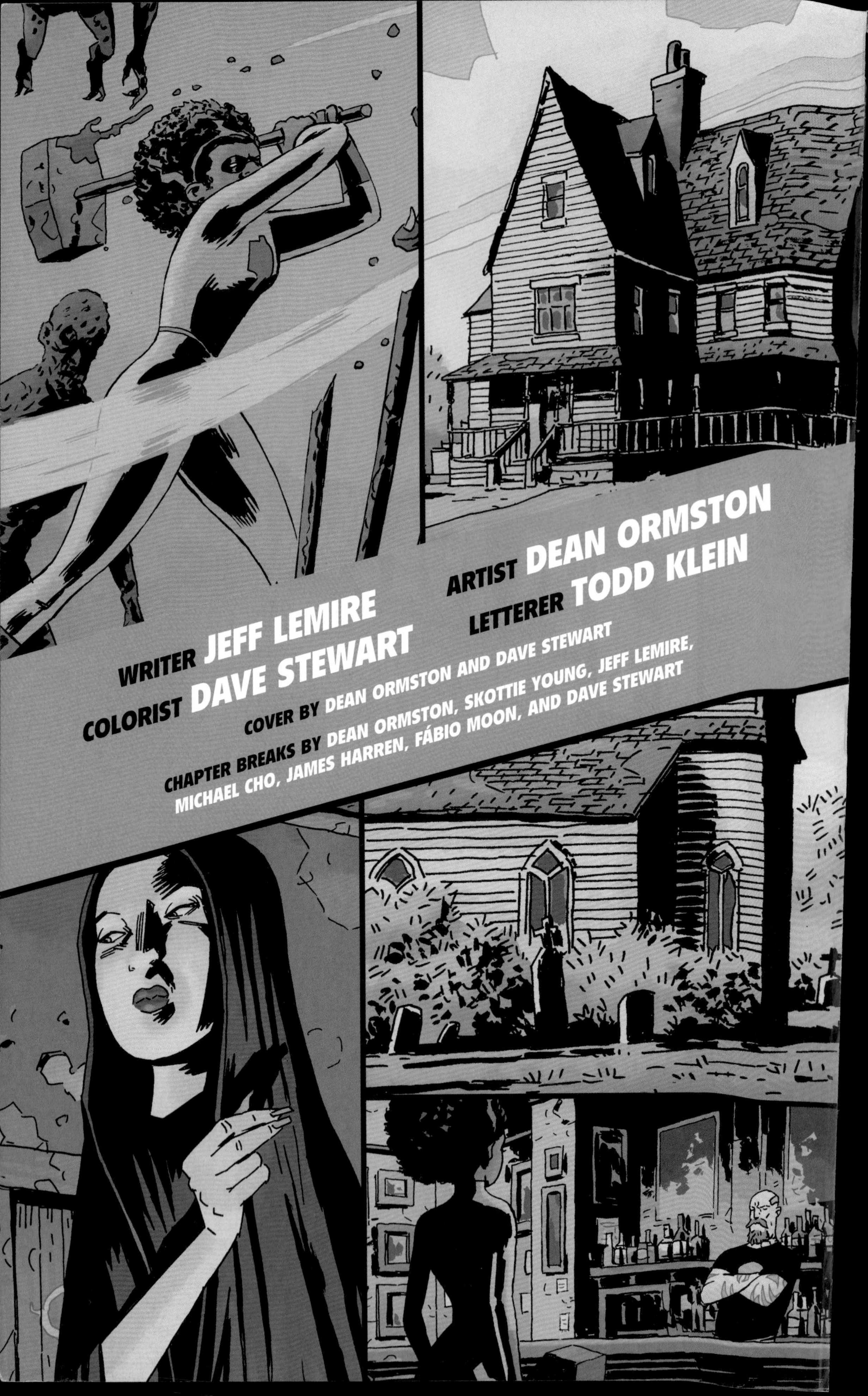

WRITER JEFF LEMIRE
ARTIST DEAN ORMSTON
COLORIST DAVE STEWART
LETTERER TODD KLEIN
COVER BY DEAN ORMSTON AND DAVE STEWART
CHAPTER BREAKS BY DEAN ORMSTON, SKOTTIE YOUNG, JEFF LEMIRE, MICHAEL CHO, JAMES HARREN, FÁBIO MOON, AND DAVE STEWART

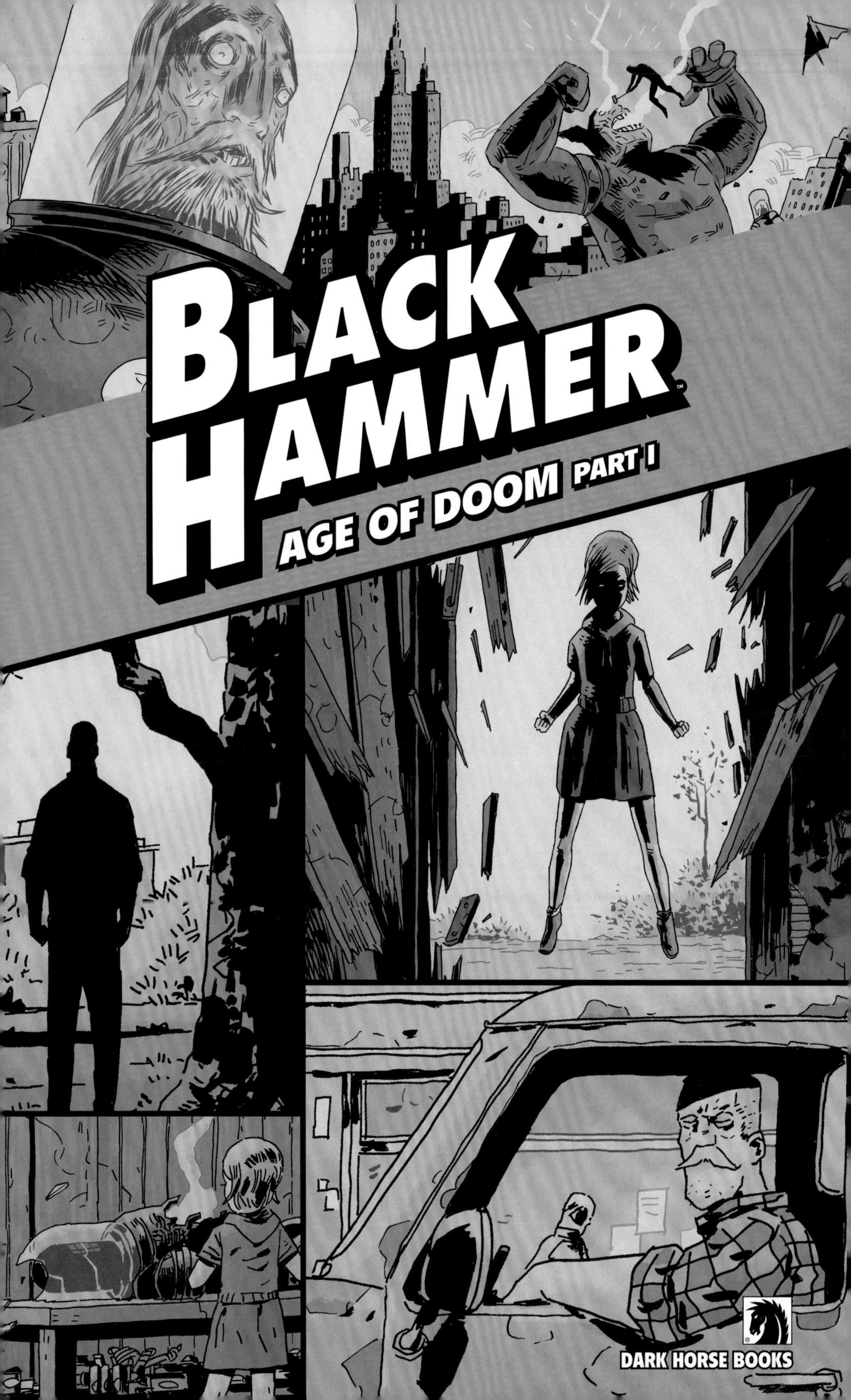
BLACK HAMMER™
AGE OF DOOM PART I
DARK HORSE BOOKS

PRESIDENT AND PUBLISHER **MIKE RICHARDSON**	**DESIGNER** **ETHAN KIMBERLING**
EDITOR **DANIEL CHABON**	**DIGITAL ART TECHNICIAN** **JOSIE CHRISTENSEN**
ASSISTANT EDITOR **BRETT ISRAEL**	

BLACK HAMMER CREATED BY JEFF LEMIRE AND DEAN ORMSTON

BLACK HAMMER: AGE OF DOOM PART I

Black Hammer: Age of Doom™ © 2018, 2019 171 Studios, Inc., and Dean Ormston. Dark Horse Books® and the Dark Horse logo are registered trademarks of Dark Horse Comics, Inc. All rights reserved. No portion of this publication may be reproduced or transmitted, in any form or by any means, without the express written permission of Dark Horse Comics, Inc. Names, characters, places, and incidents featured in this publication either are the product of the author's imagination or are used fictitiously. Any resemblance to actual persons (living or dead), events, institutions, or locales, without satiric intent, is coincidental.

Collects issues #1–#5 of the Dark Horse Comics series Black Hammer: Age of Doom.

Library of Congress Cataloging-in-Publication Data

Names: Lemire, Jeff, writer. | Ormston, Dean, artist. | Stewart, Dave, colourist. | Klein, Todd, letterer.
Title: Age of doom. Part I / writer, Jeff Lemire ; artist, Dean Ormston ; colorist, Dave Stewart ; letterer, Todd Klein ; cover by Dean Ormston and Dave Stewart.
Description: First edition. | Milwaukie, OR : Dark Horse Books, January 2019. | Series: Black Hammer ; Volume 3 | "Collects issues #1-#5 of the Dark Horse Comics series Black Hammer: Age of Doom."
Identifiers: LCCN 2018033423 | ISBN 9781506703893 (paperback)
Subjects: LCSH: Comic books, strips, etc. | BISAC: COMICS & GRAPHIC NOVELS / Superheroes.
Classification: LCC PN6728.B51926 L36 2019 | DDC 741.5/973--dc23
LC record available at https://lccn.loc.gov/2018033423

Published by
Dark Horse Books
A division of Dark Horse Comics, Inc.
10956 SE Main Street
Milwaukie, OR 97222

DarkHorse.com

To find a comics shop in your area, visit comicshoplocator.com

First edition: January 2019
ISBN 978-1-50670-389-3

10 9 8 7 6 5 4 3 2 1
Printed in China

NEIL HANKERSON Executive Vice President TOM WEDDLE Chief Financial Officer RANDY STRADLEY Vice President of Publishing NICK McWHORTER Chief Business Development Officer DALE LaFOUNTAIN Chief Information Officer MATT PARKINSON Vice President of Marketing CARA NIECE Vice President of Production and Scheduling MARK BERNARDI Vice President of Book Trade and Digital Sales KEN LIZZI General Counsel DAVE MARSHALL Editor in Chief DAVEY ESTRADA Editorial Director CHRIS WARNER Senior Books Editor CARY GRAZZINI Director of Specialty Projects LIA RIBACCHI Art Director VANESSA TODD-HOLMES Director of Print Purchasing MATT DRYER Director of Digital Art and Prepress MICHAEL GOMBOS Director of International Publishing and Licensing KARI YADRO Director of Custom Programs KARI TORSON Director of International Licensing

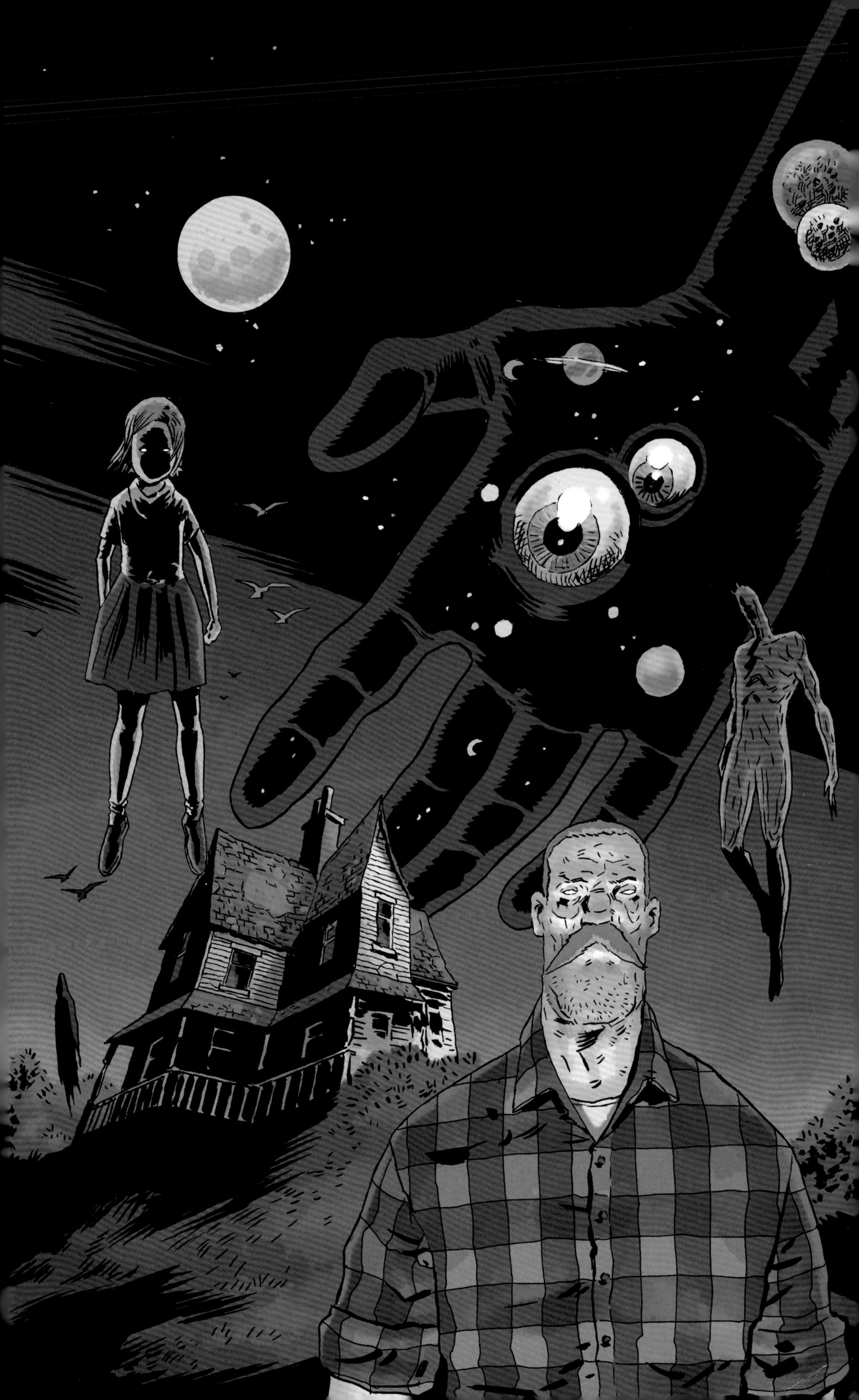

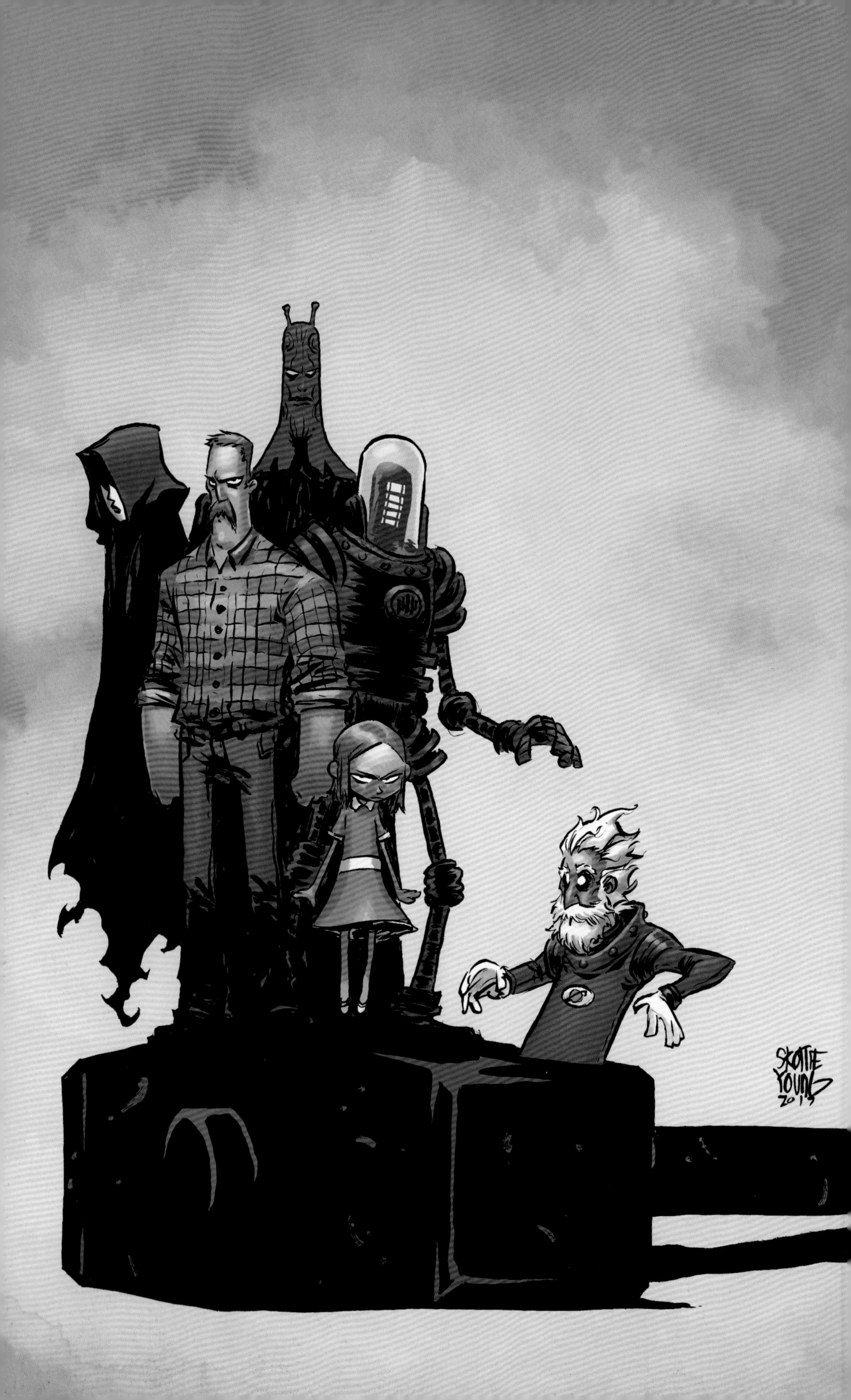
SKOTTIE YOUNG

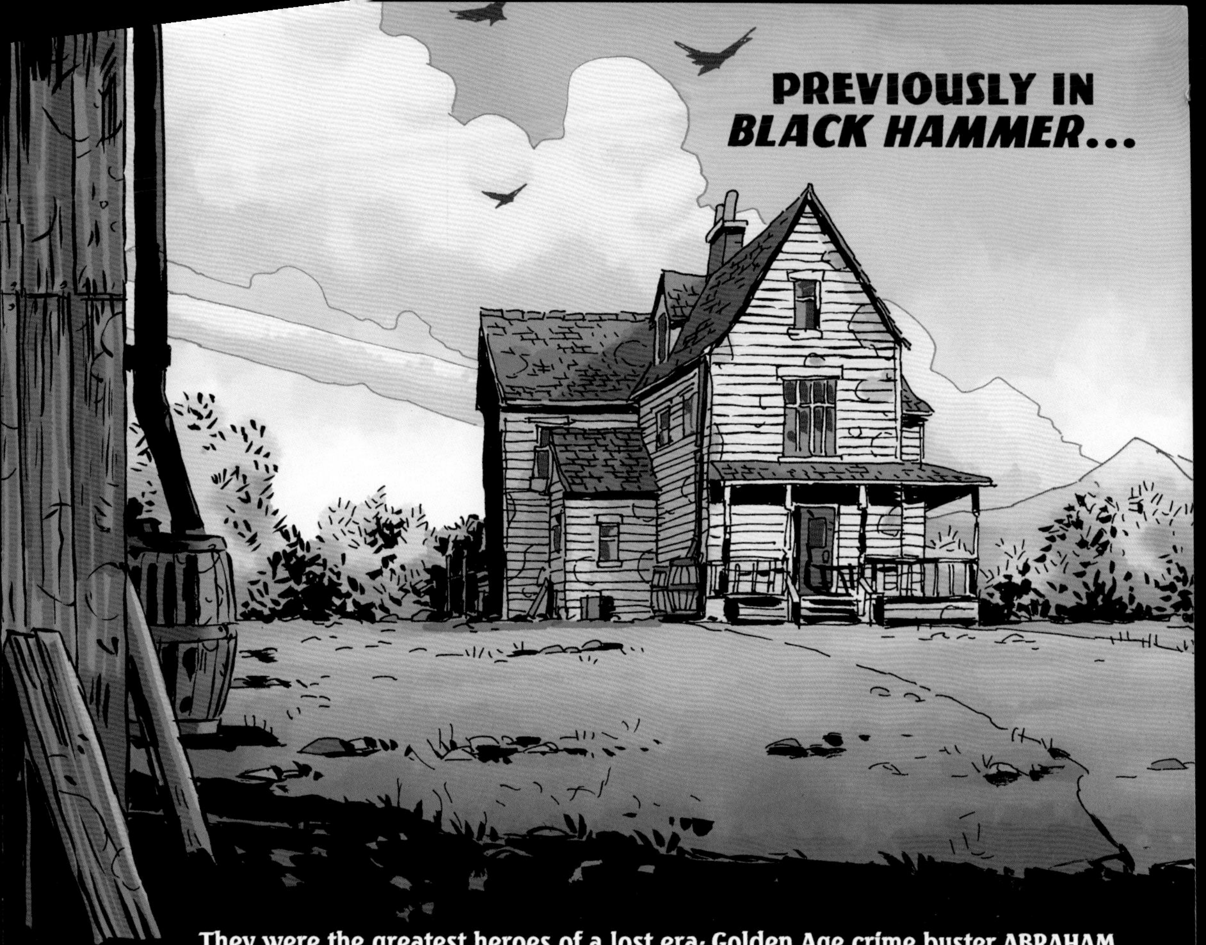

PREVIOUSLY IN *BLACK HAMMER...*

They were the greatest heroes of a lost era: Golden Age crime buster ABRAHAM SLAM, interstellar adventurer COL. WEIRD and his robot sidekick TALKY-WALKY, BARBALIEN warlord from Mars, GOLDEN GAIL, America's super-sweetheart, MADAME DRAGONFLY, mistress of the macabre, and BLACK HAMMER, invincible champion of the streets.

Ten years ago the greatest heroes of Spiral City battled a near-omnipotent cosmic despot named ANTI-GOD and, in destroying the evil entity and saving the world, the heroes seemingly died as well.

But, unbeknownst to anyone, these colorful superheroes found themselves mysteriously transported to a farm in a small, quiet town... a world where superheroes don't exist.

Soon after, the greatest among them, the powerful BLACK HAMMER, tried to leave the town's perimeter and was horribly killed by unknown and awful forces. The heroes were trapped. They had no choice but to do their best to hide their true identities and to live on the farm, and in the small town, as a strange surrogate family, all the while trying to solve the mystery of where they were and how they could get home.

Meanwhile, back in Spiral City, the daughter of Black Hammer, an inquisitive and determined young woman named LUCY WEBER, never gave up hope of finding her father and the other heroes. Nearly ten years after he disappeared, Lucy finally picked up his trail and suddenly, unbelievably, she too found herself on the farm. But mysterious MADAME DRAGONFLY cast a spell, making Lucy forget how she had gotten there or anything else she had learned.

Lucy tried to live with the others on the farm and make the best of it, but she could not stop searching for the truth. And that quest led her to pick up her father's cosmic hammer. Upon grasping the powerful weapon, Lucy Weber was transformed into

THE ALL-NEW BLACK HAMMER!

Facing the other stunned heroes, Lucy declared...

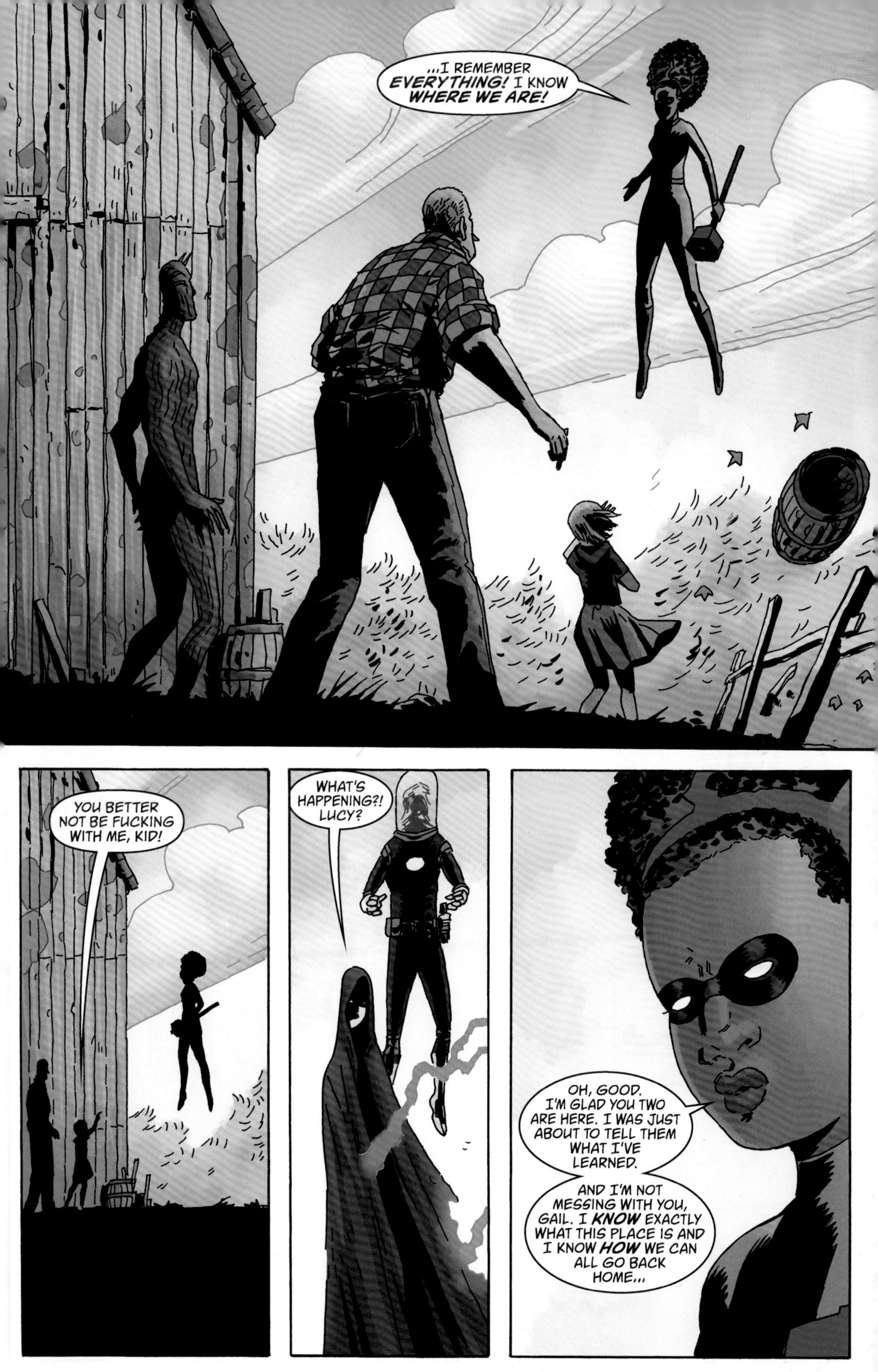
...I REMEMBER EVERYTHING! I KNOW WHERE WE ARE!
YOU BETTER NOT BE FUCKING WITH ME, KID!
WHAT'S HAPPENING?! LUCY?
OH, GOOD. I'M GLAD YOU TWO ARE HERE. I WAS JUST ABOUT TO TELL THEM WHAT I'VE LEARNED.
AND I'M NOT MESSING WITH YOU, GAIL. I KNOW EXACTLY WHAT THIS PLACE IS AND I KNOW HOW WE CAN ALL GO BACK HOME...

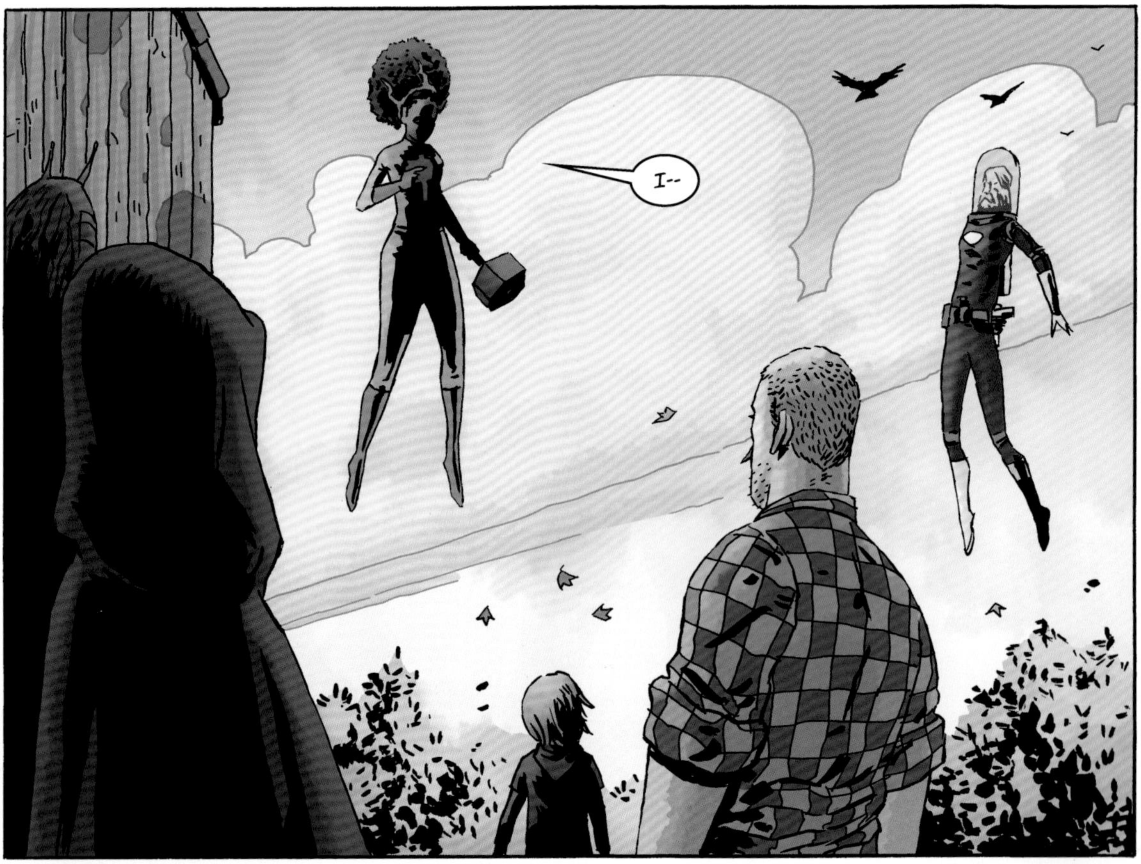
I--

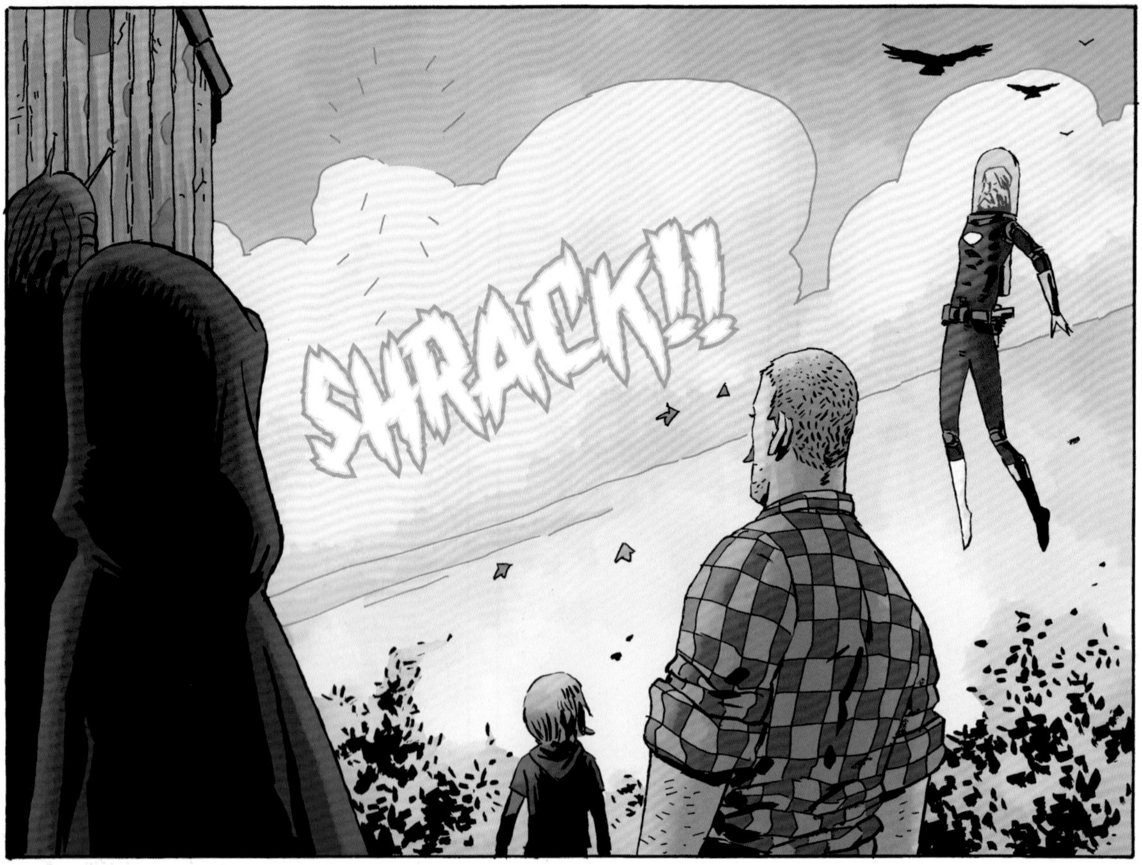
SHRACK!!

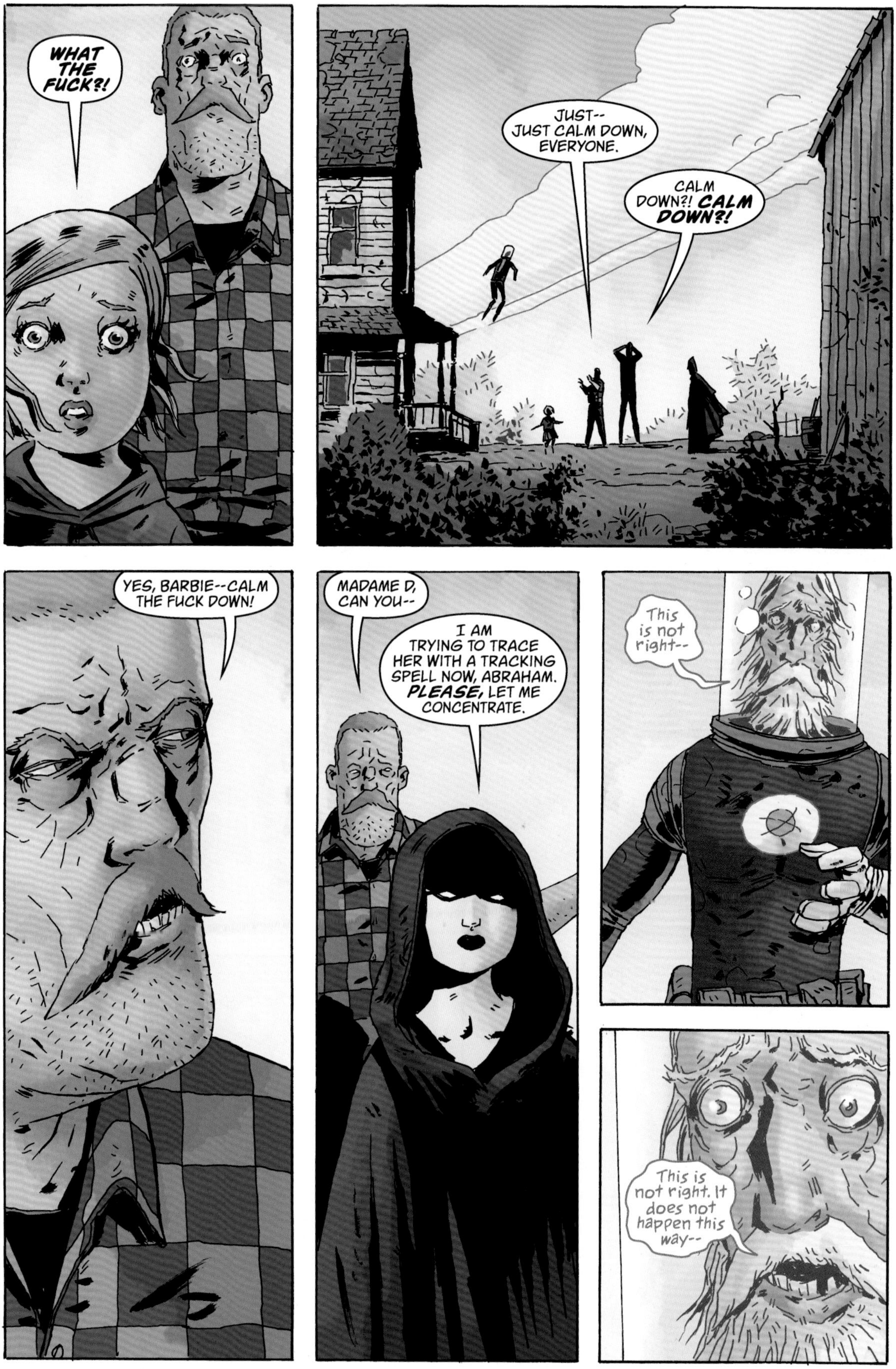
WHAT THE FUCK?!
JUST-- JUST CALM DOWN, EVERYONE.
CALM DOWN?! CALM DOWN?!
YES, BARBIE--CALM THE FUCK DOWN!
MADAME D, CAN YOU--
I AM TRYING TO TRACE HER WITH A TRACKING SPELL NOW, ABRAHAM. PLEASE, LET ME CONCENTRATE.
This is not right--
This is not right. It does not happen this way--

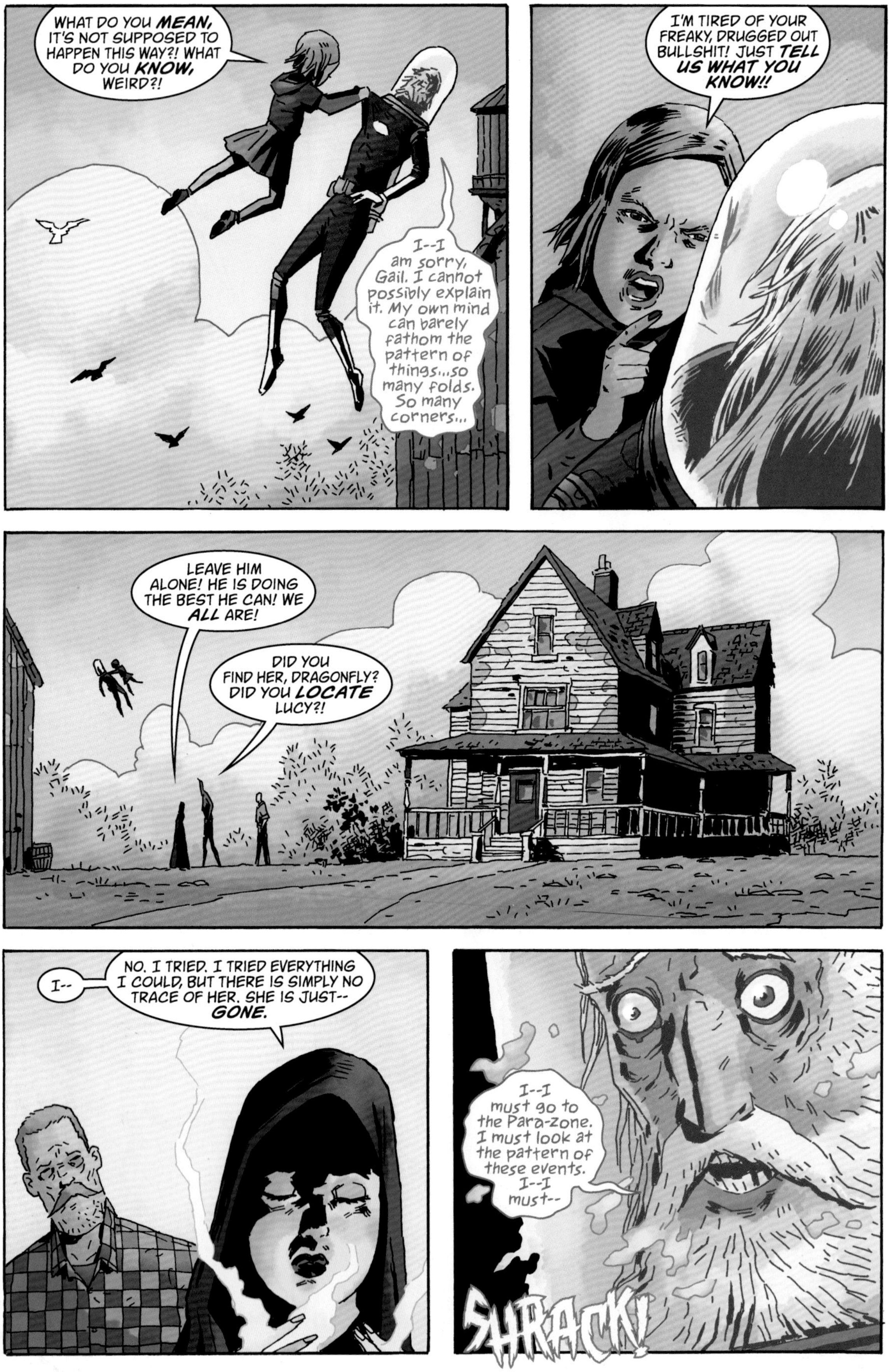
WHAT DO YOU MEAN, IT'S NOT SUPPOSED TO HAPPEN THIS WAY?! WHAT DO YOU KNOW, WEIRD?!
I--I am sorry, Gail. I cannot possibly explain it. My own mind can barely fathom the pattern of things...so many folds. So many corners...
I'M TIRED OF YOUR FREAKY, DRUGGED OUT BULLSHIT! JUST TELL US WHAT YOU KNOW!!
LEAVE HIM ALONE! HE IS DOING THE BEST HE CAN! WE ALL ARE!
DID YOU FIND HER, DRAGONFLY? DID YOU LOCATE LUCY?!
I--
NO. I TRIED. I TRIED EVERYTHING I COULD, BUT THERE IS SIMPLY NO TRACE OF HER. SHE IS JUST-- GONE.
I--I must go to the Para-zone. I must look at the pattern of these events. I--I must--
SHRACK!

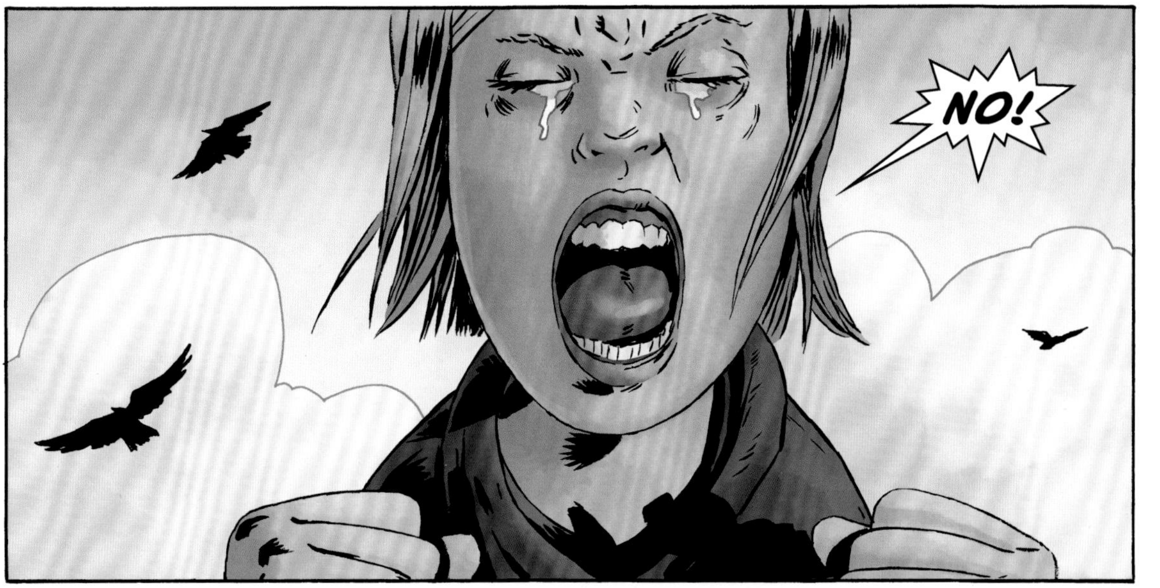
NO!

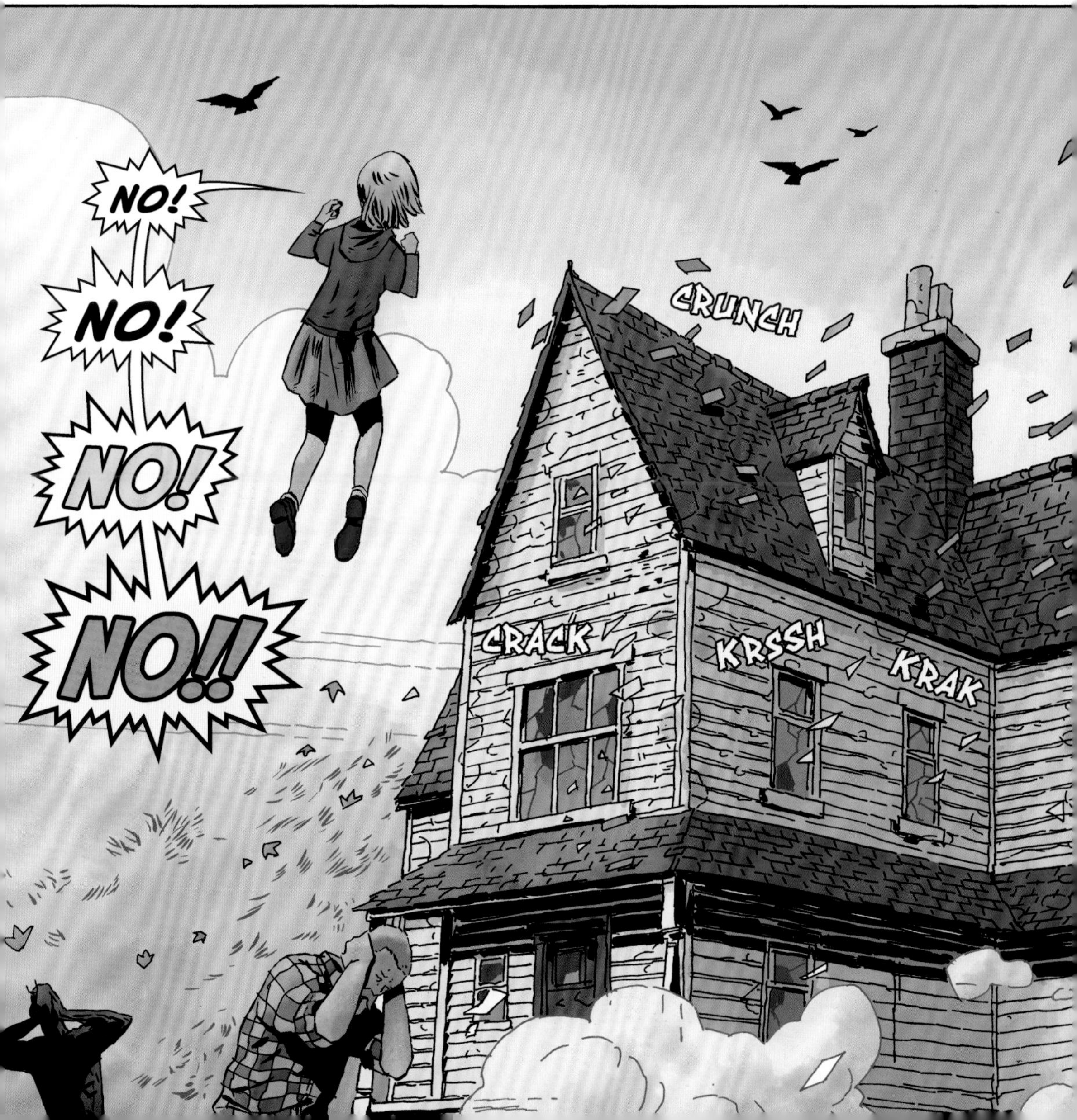
NO!
NO!
NO!
NO!!
CRUNCH
CRACK
KRSSH
KRAK

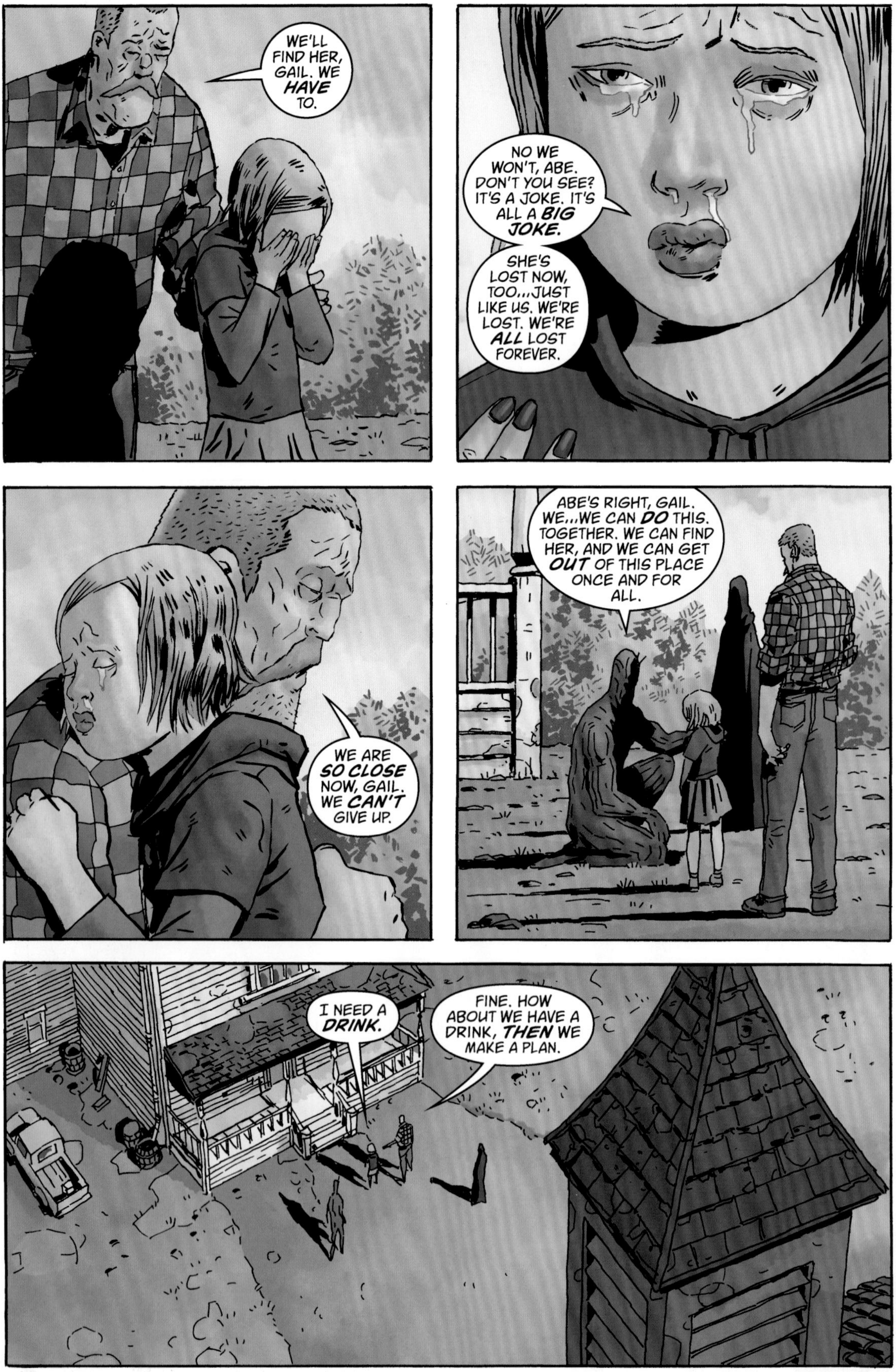
WE'LL FIND HER, GAIL. WE *HAVE* TO.
NO WE WON'T, ABE. DON'T YOU SEE? IT'S A JOKE. IT'S ALL A ***BIG JOKE.***
SHE'S LOST NOW, TOO...JUST LIKE US. WE'RE LOST. WE'RE ***ALL*** LOST FOREVER.
WE ARE ***SO CLOSE*** NOW, GAIL. WE ***CAN'T*** GIVE UP.
ABE'S RIGHT, GAIL. WE...WE CAN ***DO*** THIS. TOGETHER. WE CAN FIND HER, AND WE CAN GET ***OUT*** OF THIS PLACE ONCE AND FOR ALL.
I NEED A ***DRINK.***
FINE. HOW ABOUT WE HAVE A DRINK, ***THEN*** WE MAKE A PLAN.

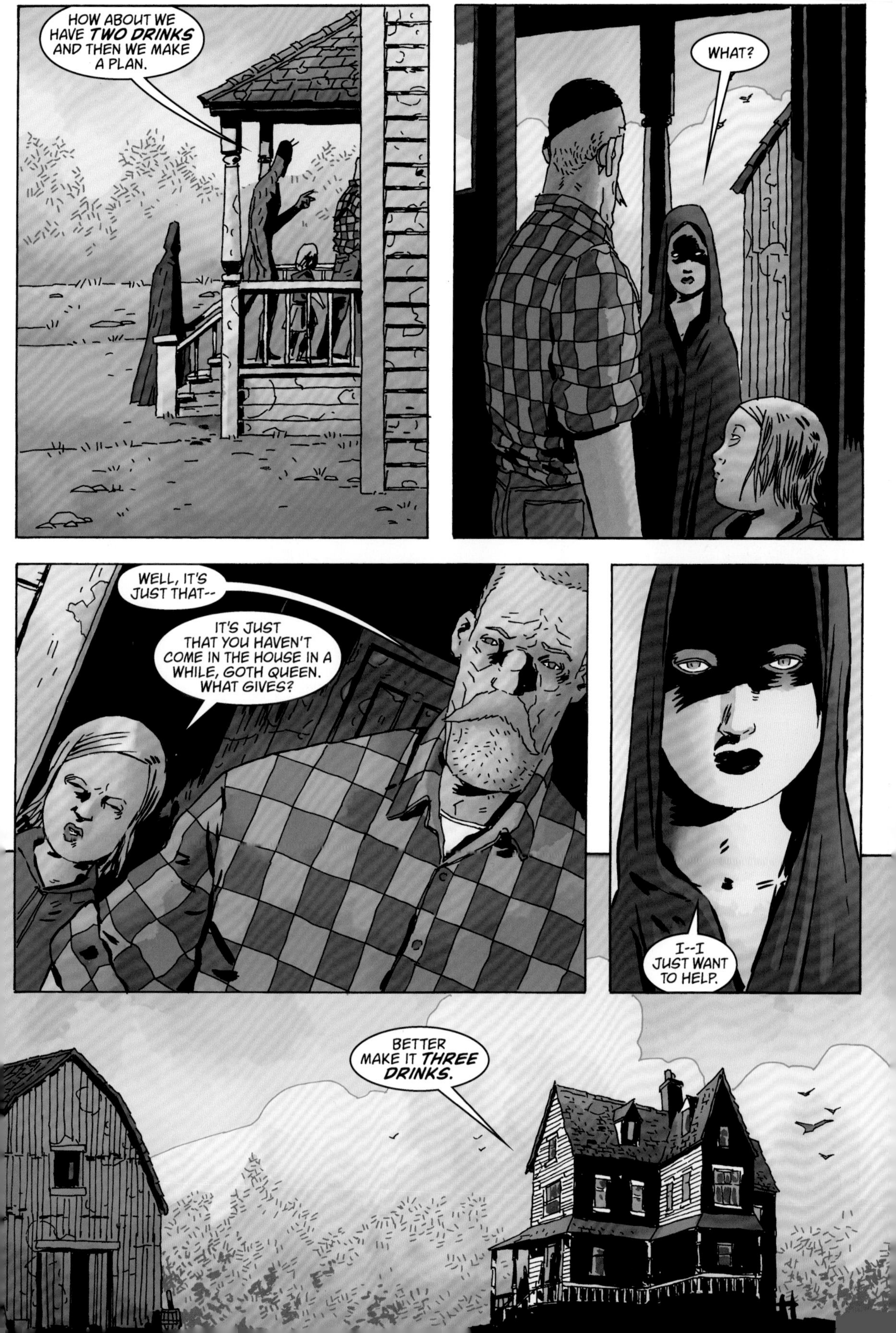
HOW ABOUT WE HAVE **TWO DRINKS** AND THEN WE MAKE A PLAN.
WHAT?
WELL, IT'S JUST THAT--
IT'S JUST THAT YOU HAVEN'T COME IN THE HOUSE IN A WHILE, GOTH QUEEN. WHAT GIVES?
I--I JUST WANT TO HELP.
BETTER MAKE IT **THREE DRINKS.**

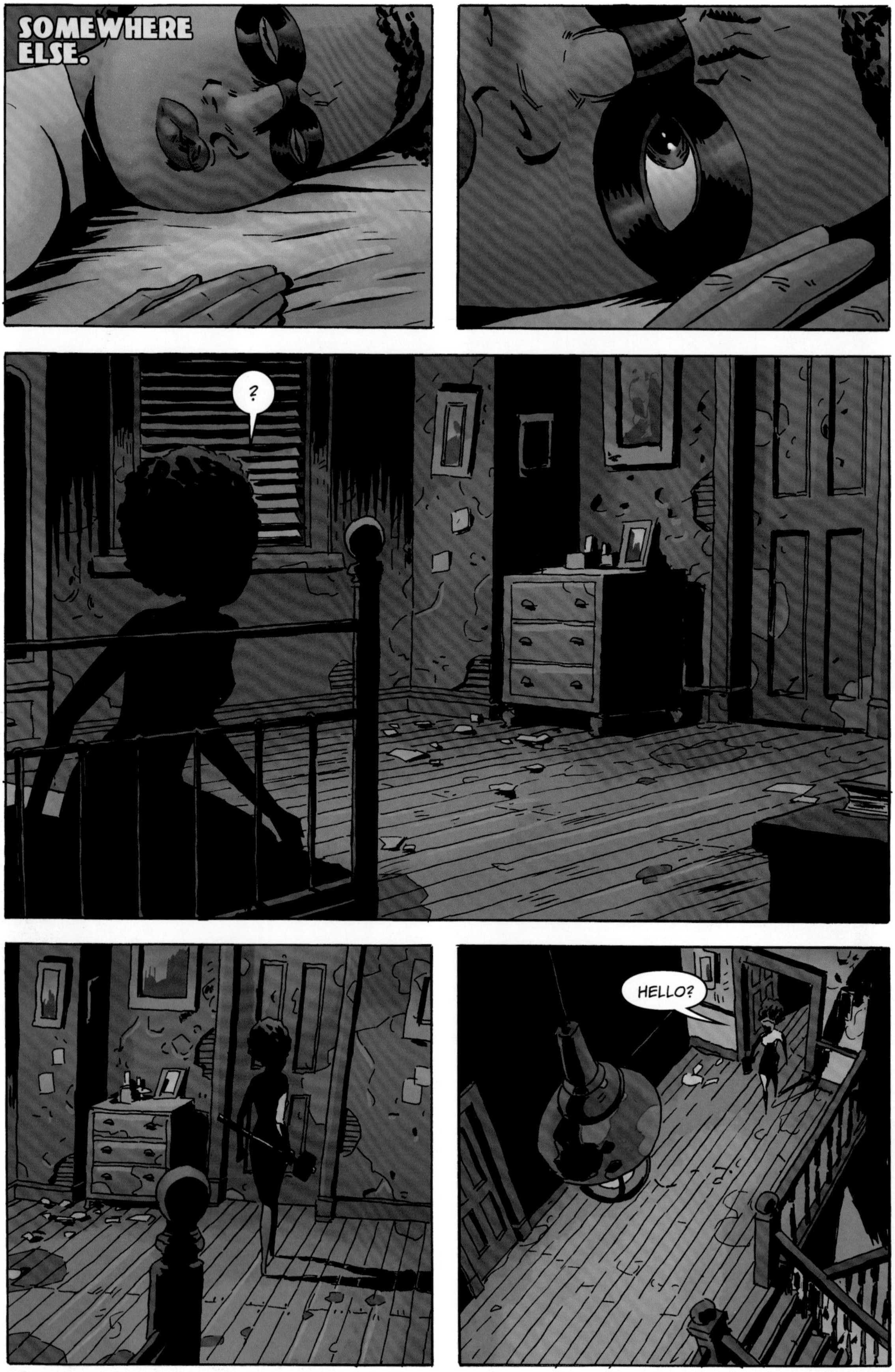
SOMEWHERE ELSE.
?
HELLO?

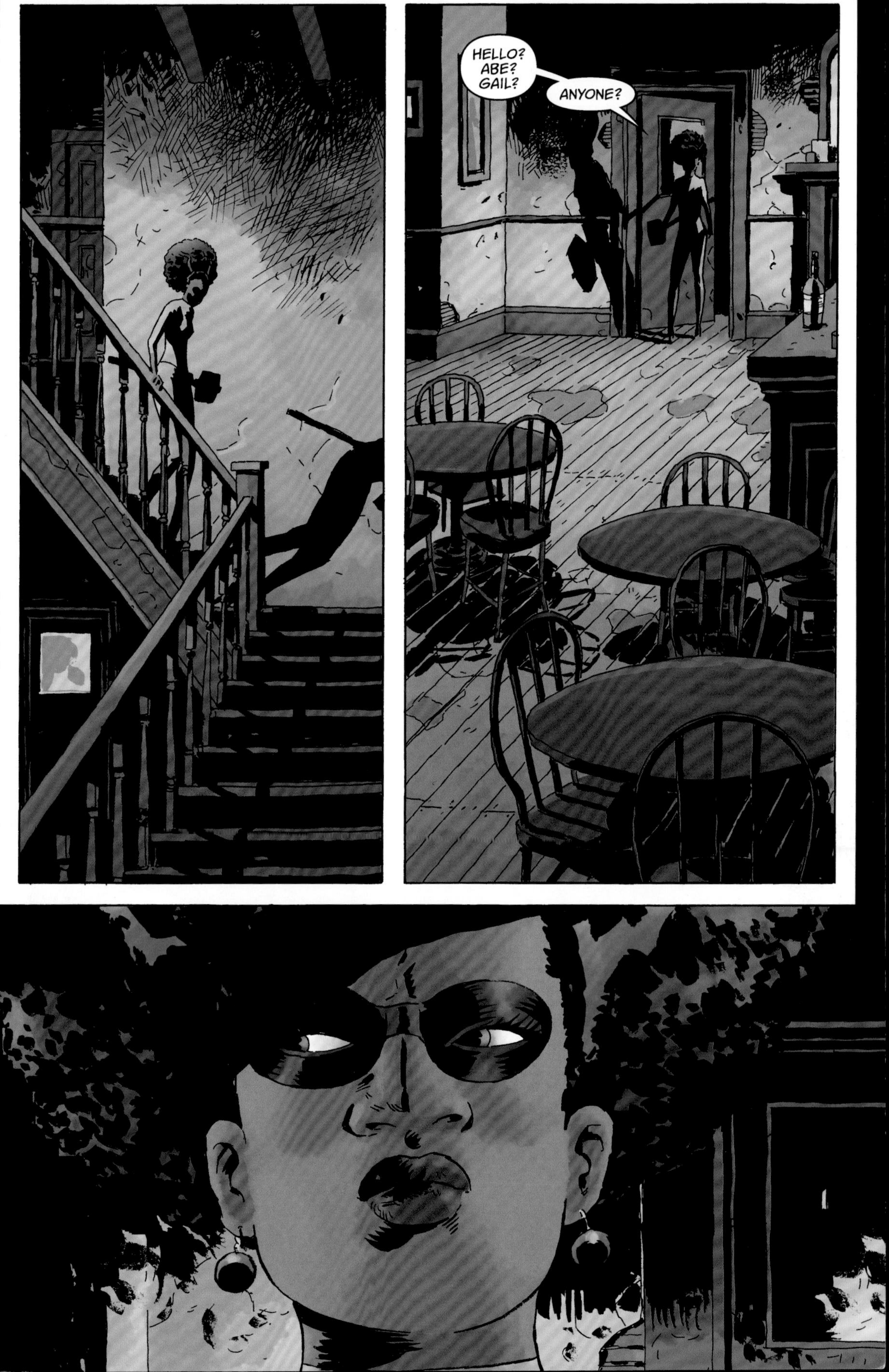
HELLO? ABE? GAIL?
ANYONE?

HEY, YOU'RE LATE!

EXCUSE ME?

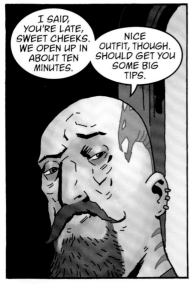

I SAID, YOU'RE LATE, SWEET CHEEKS. WE OPEN UP IN ABOUT TEN MINUTES.

NICE OUTFIT, THOUGH. SHOULD GET YOU SOME BIG TIPS.

WHO THE HELL ARE YOU?

WHOEVER YOU WANT ME TO BE.

WHAT IS THIS PLACE? WHERE ARE ABE AND THE OTHERS?

THIS IS THE ANTEROOM, DARLIN'. AND I DON'T KNOW ANY "ABE," BUT I DO KNOW PLENTY OF OTHERS.

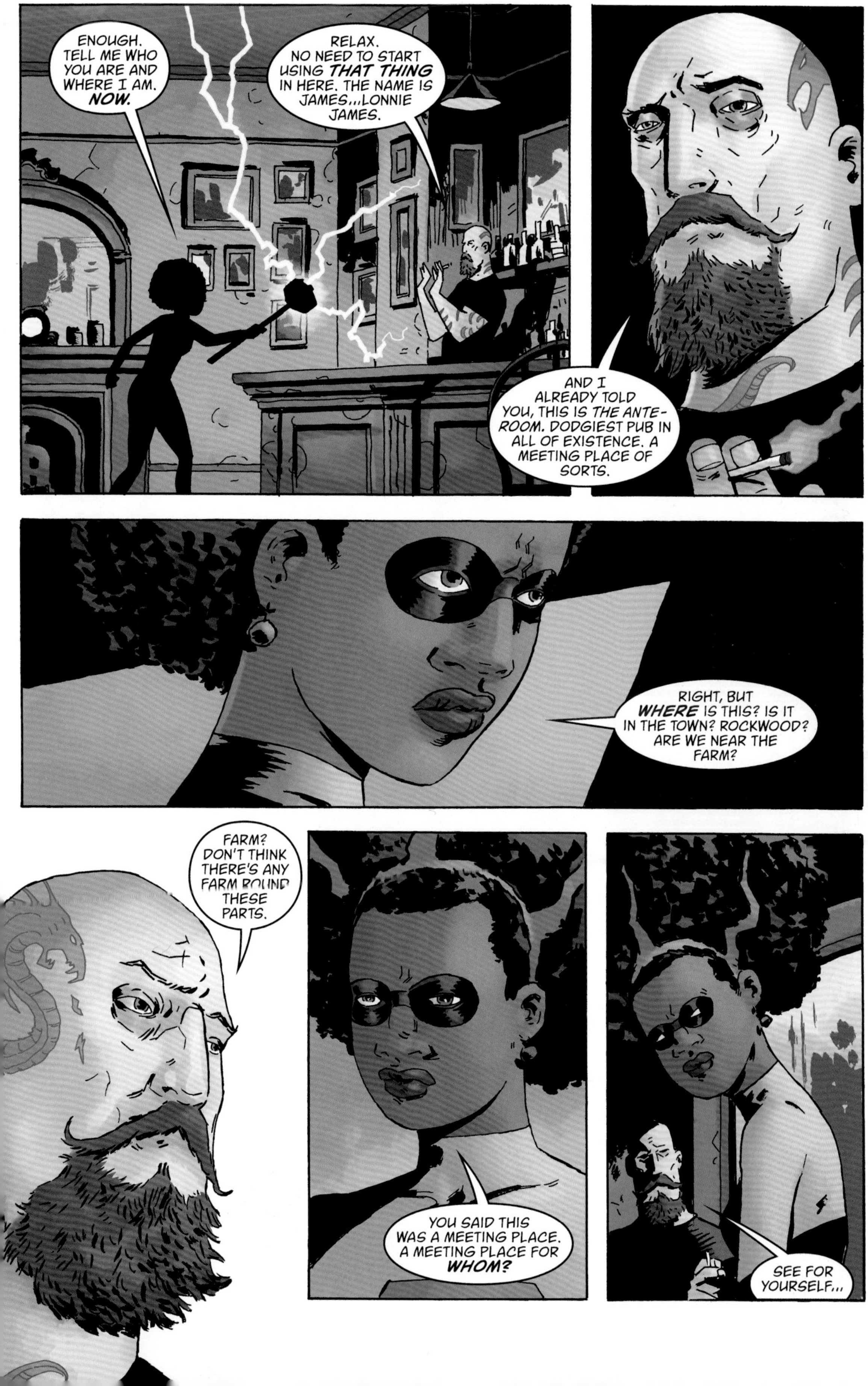
ENOUGH. TELL ME WHO YOU ARE AND WHERE I AM. NOW.
RELAX. NO NEED TO START USING THAT THING IN HERE. THE NAME IS JAMES...LONNIE JAMES.
AND I ALREADY TOLD YOU, THIS IS THE ANTE-ROOM. DODGIEST PUB IN ALL OF EXISTENCE. A MEETING PLACE OF SORTS.
RIGHT, BUT WHERE IS THIS? IS IT IN THE TOWN? ROCKWOOD? ARE WE NEAR THE FARM?
FARM? DON'T THINK THERE'S ANY FARM ROUND THESE PARTS.
YOU SAID THIS WAS A MEETING PLACE. A MEETING PLACE FOR WHOM?
SEE FOR YOURSELF...

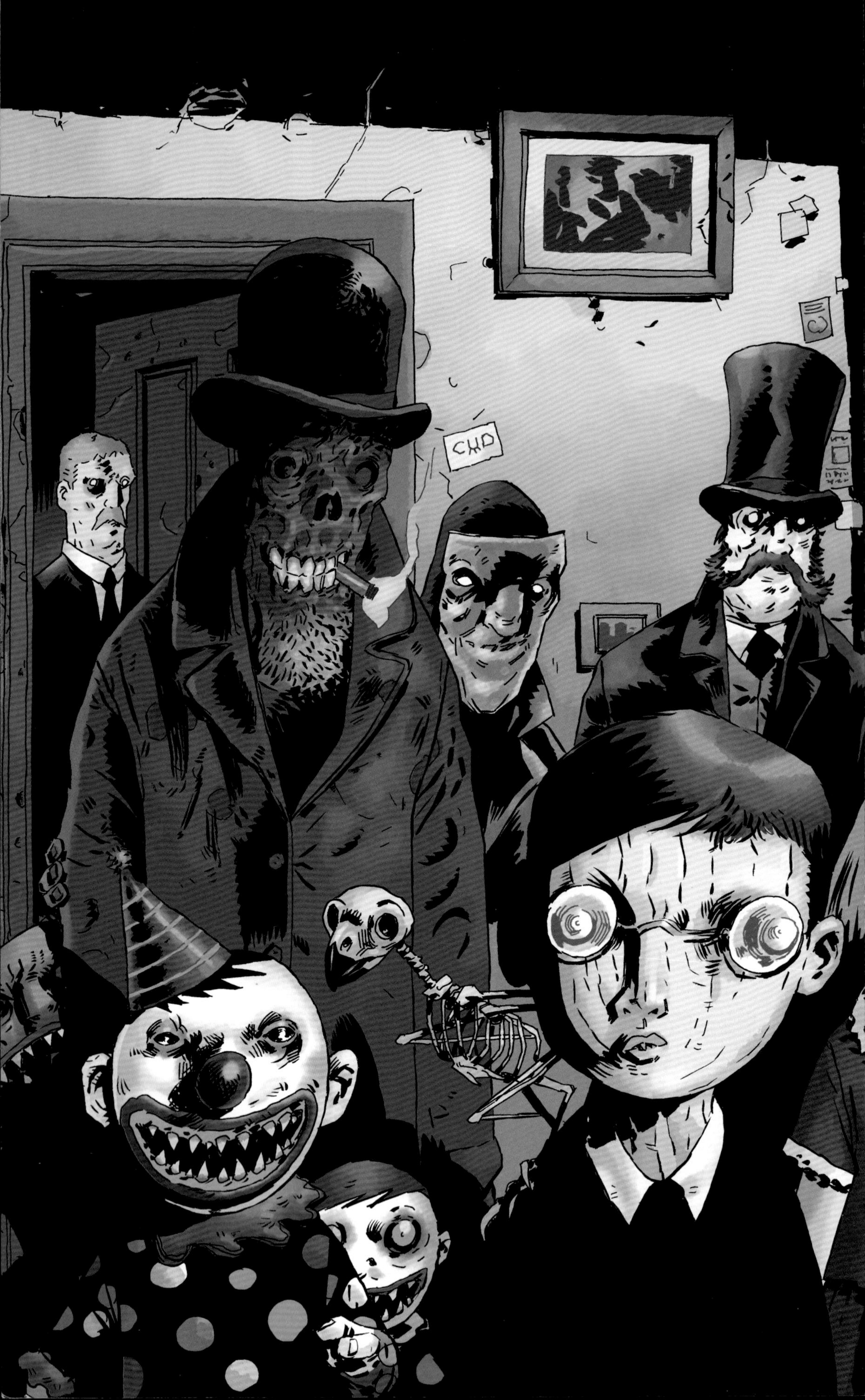

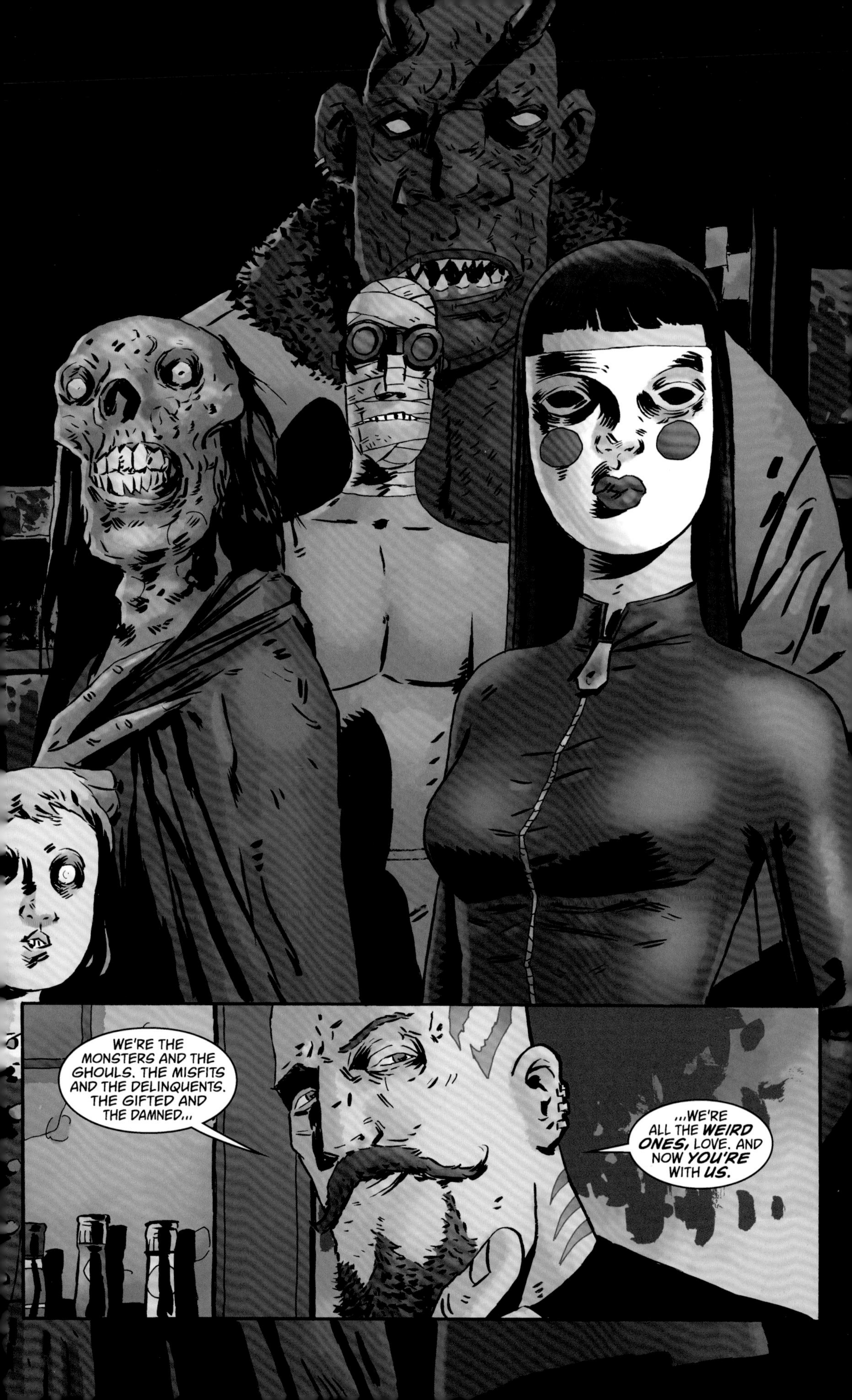
WE'RE THE MONSTERS AND THE GHOULS. THE MISFITS AND THE DELINQUENTS. THE GIFTED AND THE DAMNED...
...WE'RE ALL THE WEIRD ONES, LOVE. AND NOW YOU'RE WITH US.

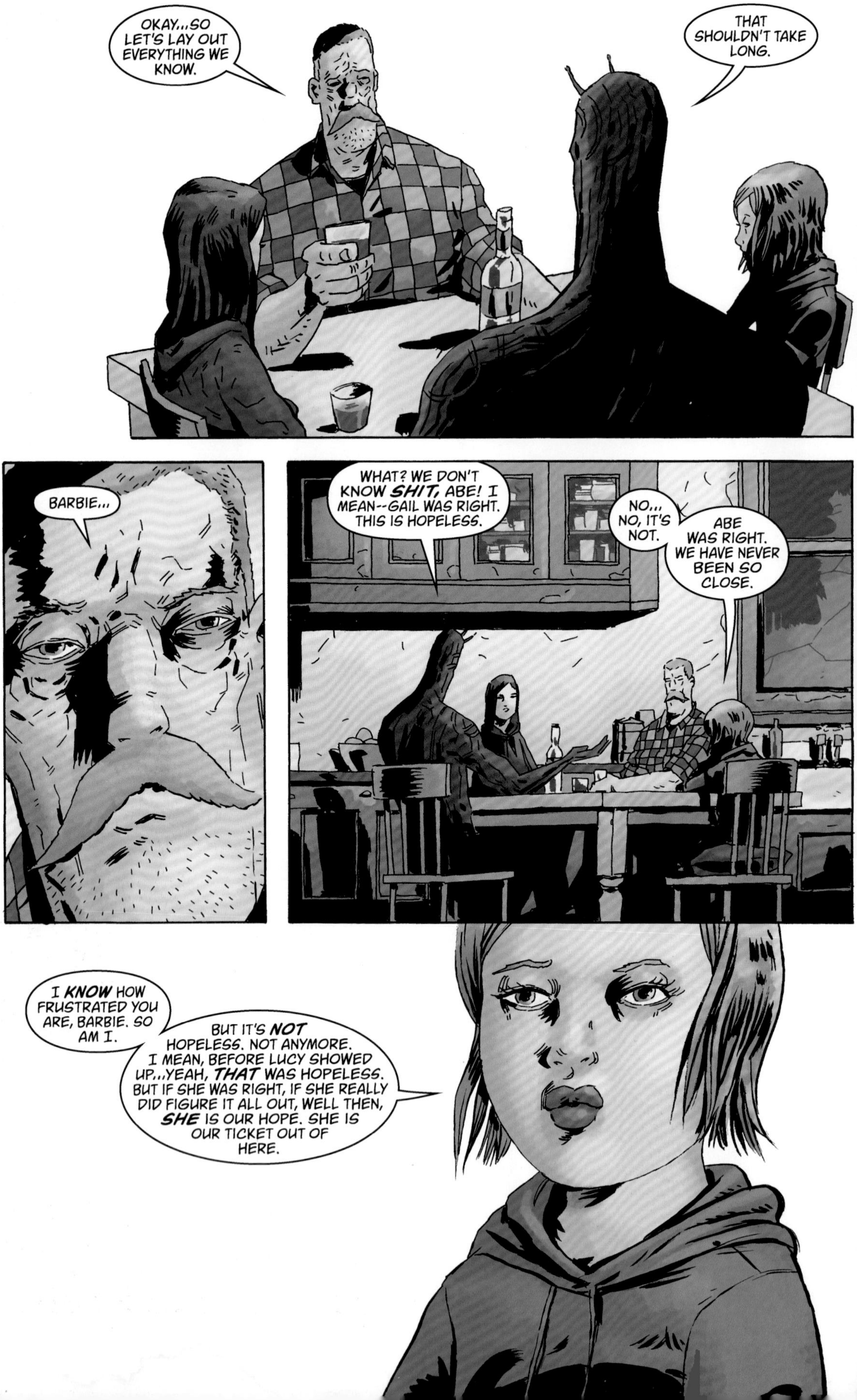
OKAY...SO LET'S LAY OUT EVERYTHING WE KNOW.
THAT SHOULDN'T TAKE LONG.
BARBIE...
WHAT? WE DON'T KNOW SHIT, ABE! I MEAN--GAIL WAS RIGHT. THIS IS HOPELESS.
NO... NO, IT'S NOT.
ABE WAS RIGHT. WE HAVE NEVER BEEN SO CLOSE.
I KNOW HOW FRUSTRATED YOU ARE, BARBIE. SO AM I.
BUT IT'S NOT HOPELESS. NOT ANYMORE. I MEAN, BEFORE LUCY SHOWED UP...YEAH, THAT WAS HOPELESS. BUT IF SHE WAS RIGHT, IF SHE REALLY DID FIGURE IT ALL OUT, WELL THEN, SHE IS OUR HOPE. SHE IS OUR TICKET OUT OF HERE.

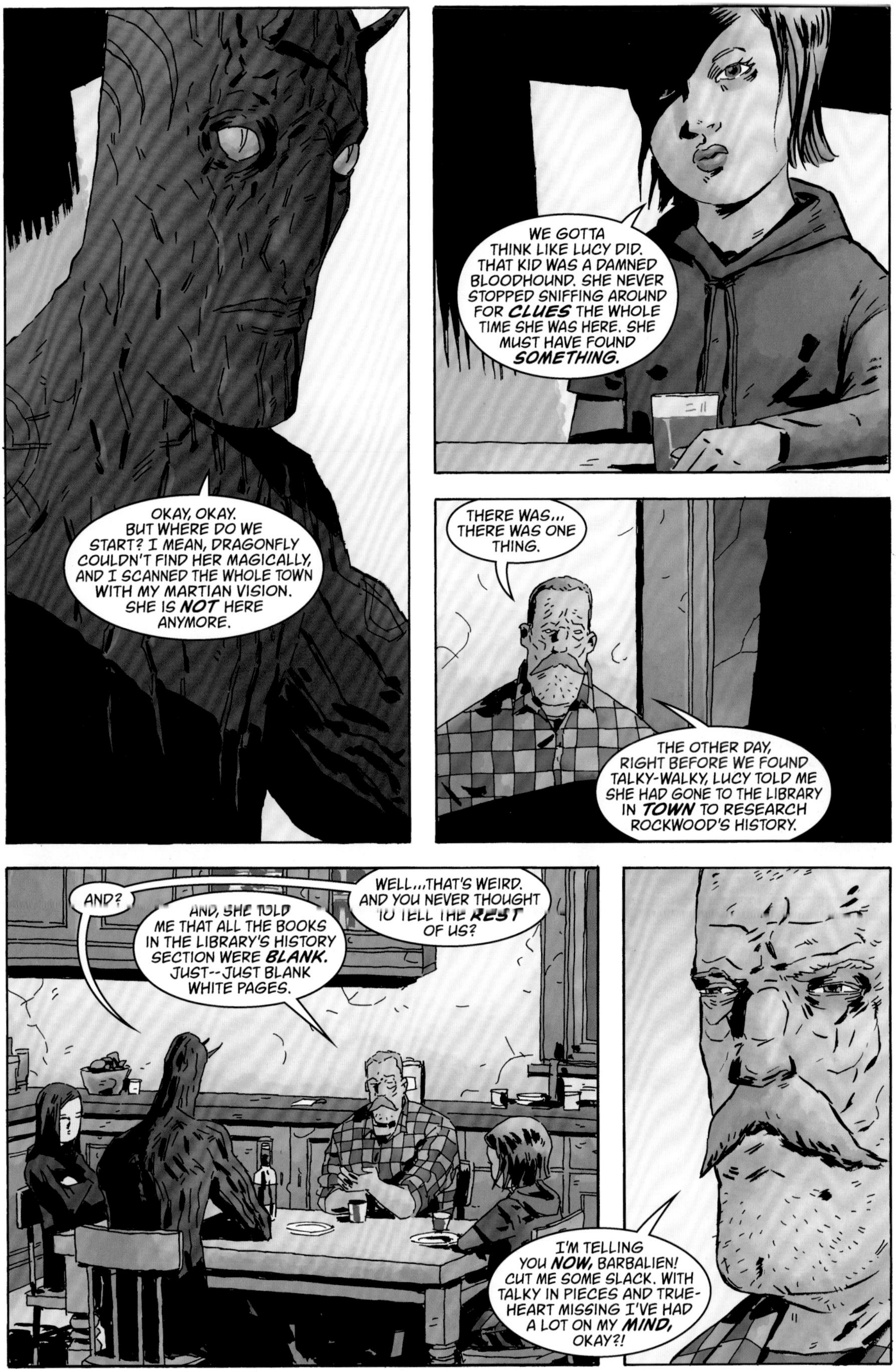
OKAY, OKAY. BUT WHERE DO WE START? I MEAN, DRAGONFLY COULDN'T FIND HER MAGICALLY, AND I SCANNED THE WHOLE TOWN WITH MY MARTIAN VISION. SHE IS NOT HERE ANYMORE.
WE GOTTA THINK LIKE LUCY DID. THAT KID WAS A DAMNED BLOODHOUND. SHE NEVER STOPPED SNIFFING AROUND FOR CLUES THE WHOLE TIME SHE WAS HERE. SHE MUST HAVE FOUND SOMETHING.
THERE WAS... THERE WAS ONE THING.
THE OTHER DAY, RIGHT BEFORE WE FOUND TALKY-WALKY, LUCY TOLD ME SHE HAD GONE TO THE LIBRARY IN TOWN TO RESEARCH ROCKWOOD'S HISTORY.
AND?
AND, SHE TOLD ME THAT ALL THE BOOKS IN THE LIBRARY'S HISTORY SECTION WERE BLANK. JUST--JUST BLANK WHITE PAGES.
WELL...THAT'S WEIRD. AND YOU NEVER THOUGHT TO TELL THE REST OF US?
I'M TELLING YOU NOW, BARBALIEN! CUT ME SOME SLACK. WITH TALKY IN PIECES AND TRUE-HEART MISSING I'VE HAD A LOT ON MY MIND, OKAY?!

BESIDES, WHERE THE HECK HAVE *YOU* BEEN LATELY? RUNNING AROUND CHASING THE TOWN *PRIEST* LIKE A SCHOOL-BOY WITH A CRUSH!

ABE!

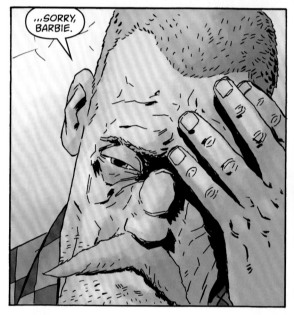

...SORRY, BARBIE.

IT'S--IT'S FINE.

LOOK, LET'S FOLLOW UP ON THE LIBRARY THING.

AND COME TO THINK OF IT, SHERIFF TRUEHEART'S DISAPPEARANCE COULD BE CONNECTED TO ALL THIS TOO. AND *TALKY.*

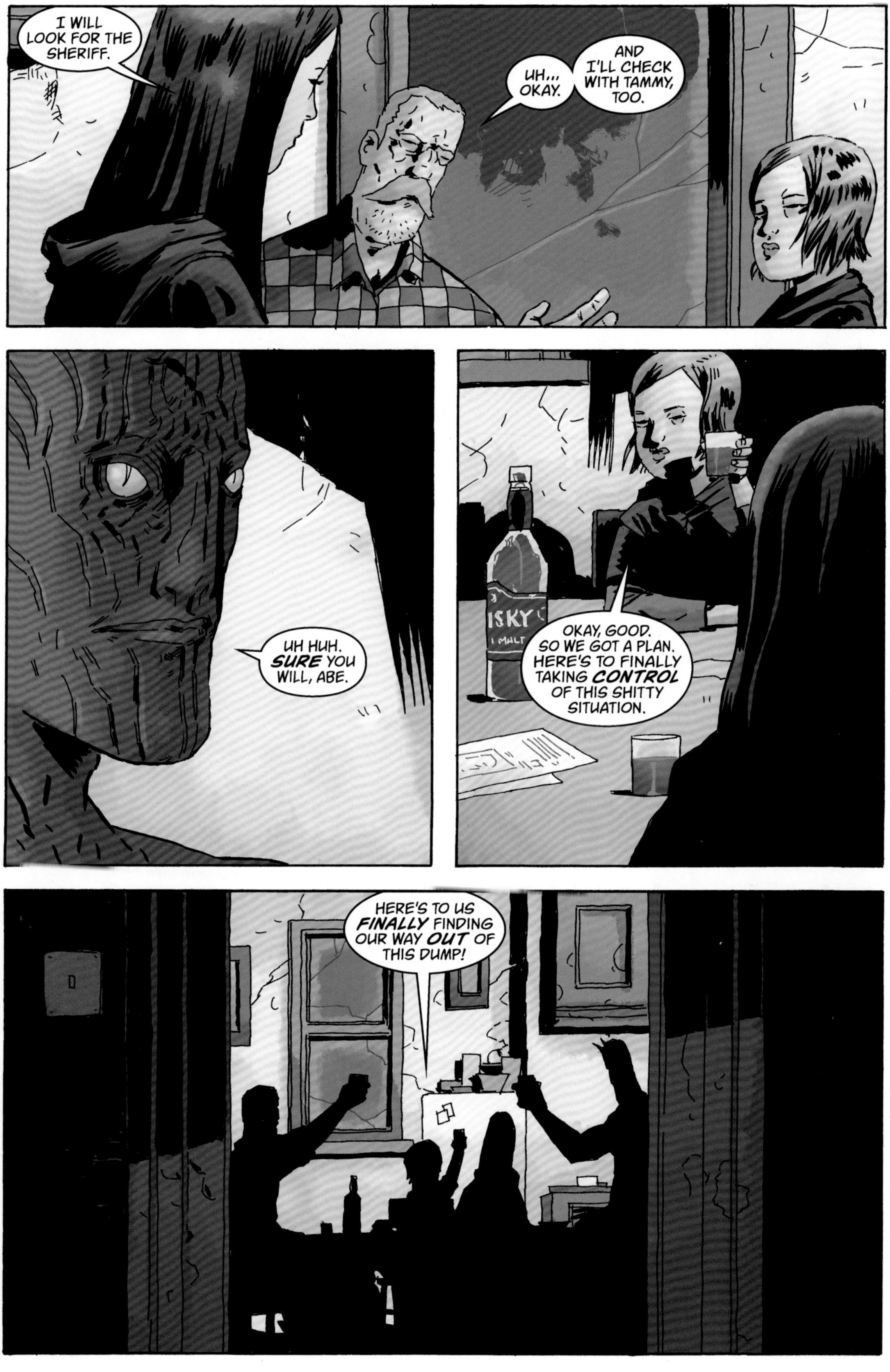

I WILL LOOK FOR THE SHERIFF.
UH... OKAY.
AND I'LL CHECK WITH TAMMY, TOO.
UH HUH. SURE YOU WILL, ABE.
OKAY, GOOD. SO WE GOT A PLAN. HERE'S TO FINALLY TAKING CONTROL OF THIS SHITTY SITUATION.
HERE'S TO US FINALLY FINDING OUR WAY OUT OF THIS DUMP!

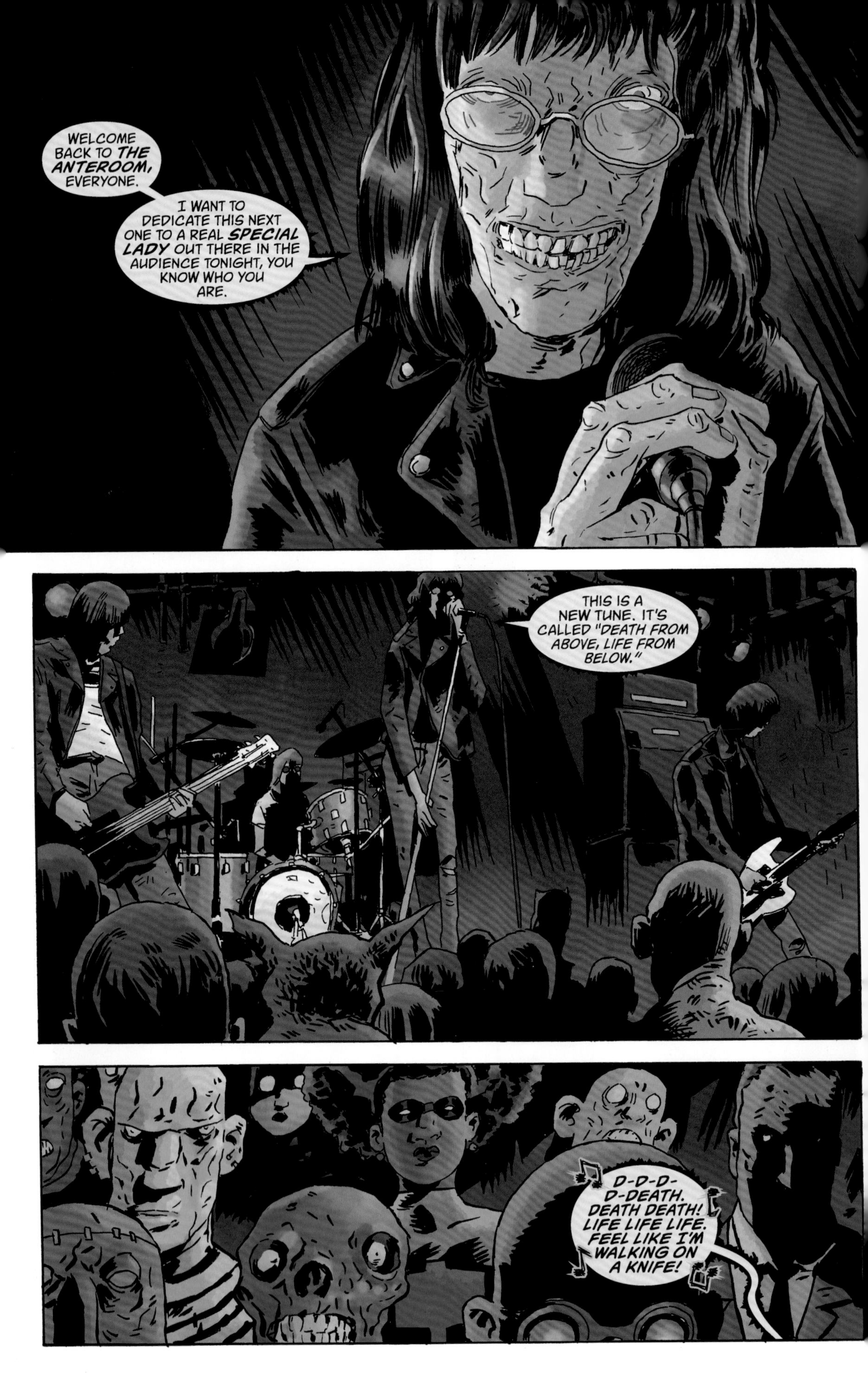
WELCOME BACK TO *THE ANTEROOM,* EVERYONE.
I WANT TO DEDICATE THIS NEXT ONE TO A REAL *SPECIAL LADY* OUT THERE IN THE AUDIENCE TONIGHT, YOU KNOW WHO YOU ARE.
THIS IS A NEW TUNE. IT'S CALLED *"DEATH FROM ABOVE, LIFE FROM BELOW."*
D-D-D-D-DEATH. DEATH DEATH! LIFE LIFE LIFE. FEEL LIKE I'M WALKING ON A KNIFE!

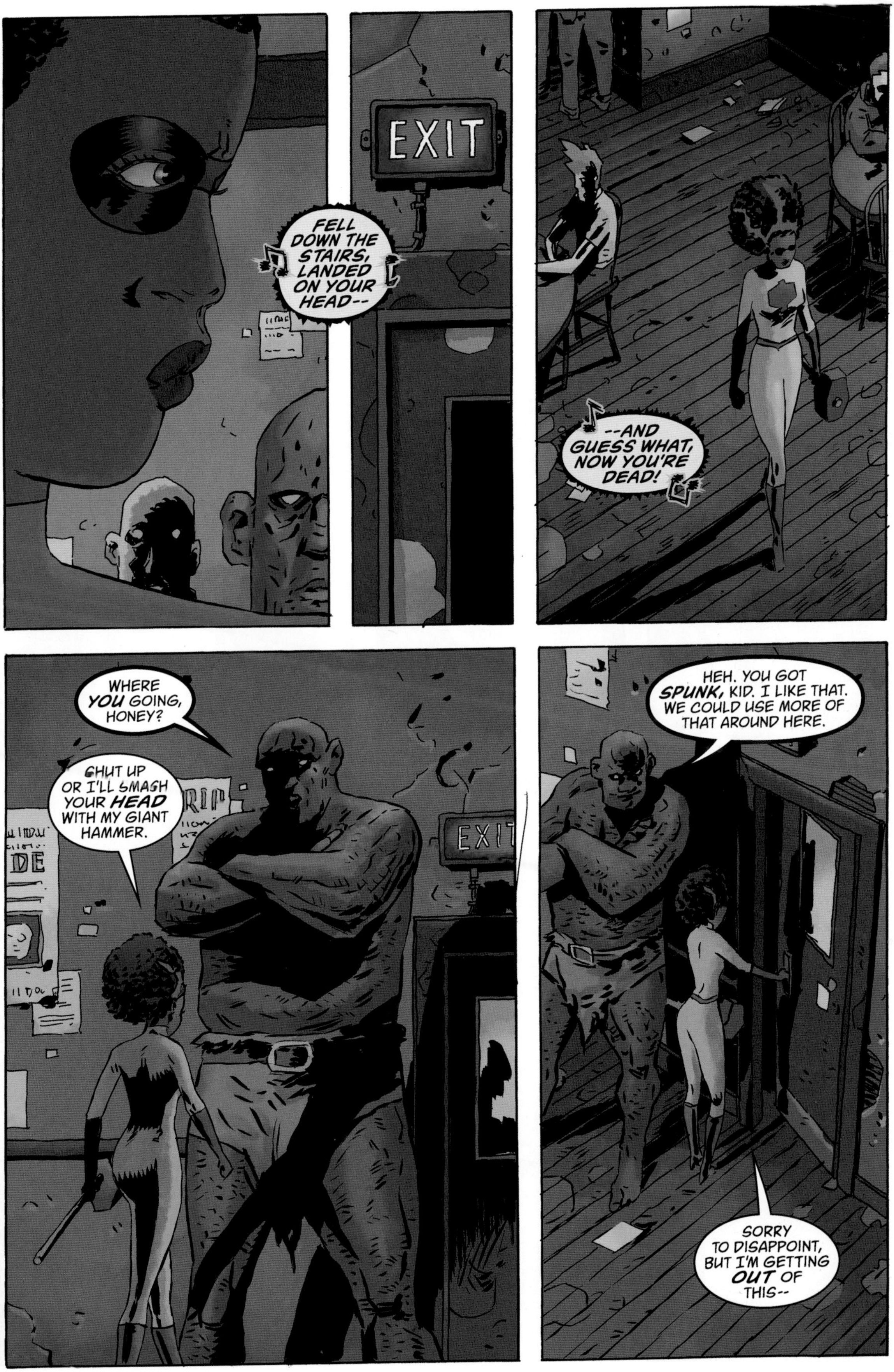
FELL DOWN THE STAIRS, LANDED ON YOUR HEAD--
EXIT
--AND GUESS WHAT, NOW YOU'RE DEAD!
WHERE YOU GOING, HONEY?
SHUT UP OR I'LL SMASH YOUR HEAD WITH MY GIANT HAMMER.
EXIT
HEH. YOU GOT SPUNK, KID. I LIKE THAT. WE COULD USE MORE OF THAT AROUND HERE.
SORRY TO DISAPPOINT, BUT I'M GETTING OUT OF THIS--

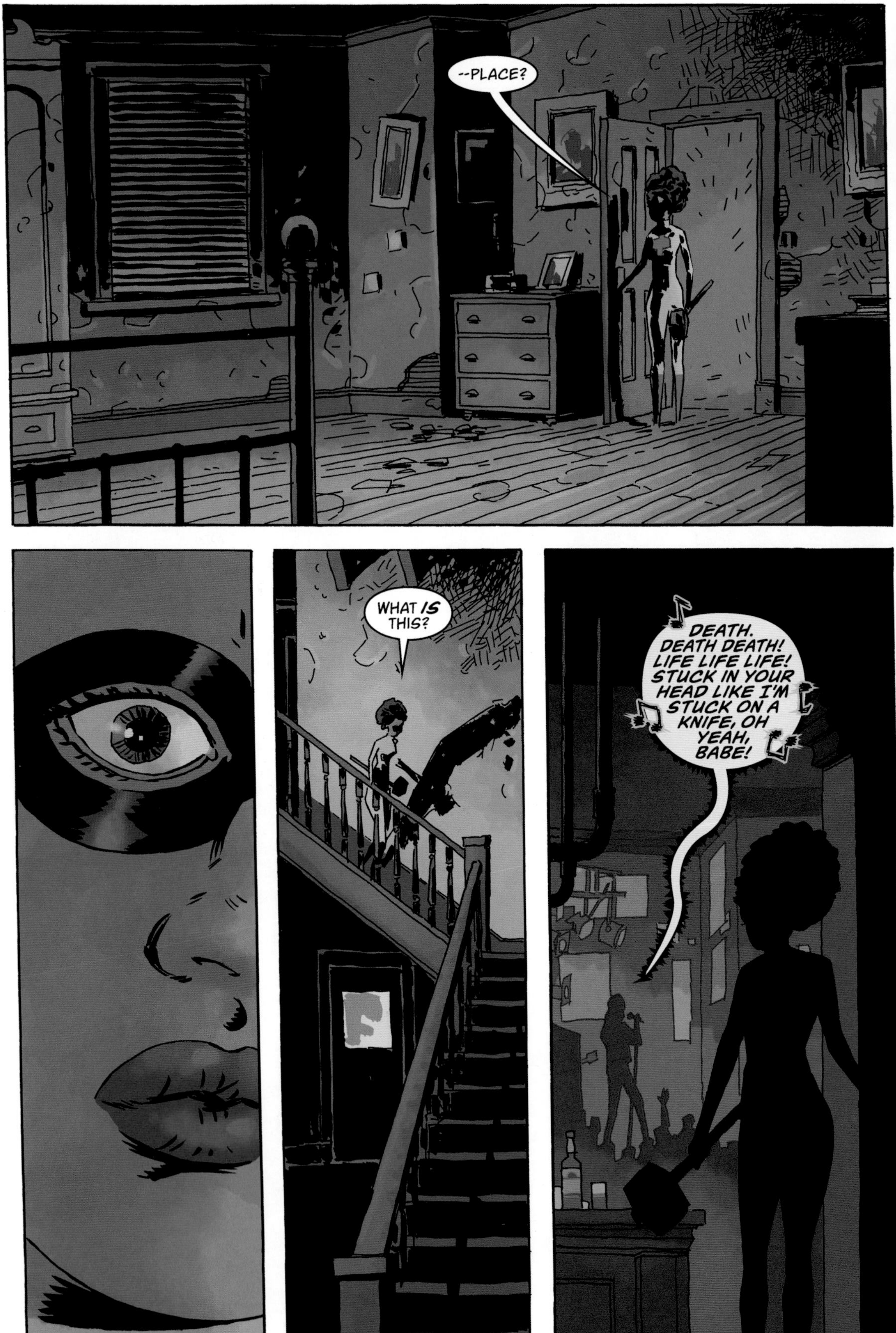
--PLACE?
WHAT *IS* THIS?
DEATH. DEATH DEATH! LIFE LIFE LIFE! STUCK IN YOUR HEAD LIKE I'M STUCK ON A KNIFE, OH YEAH, BABE!

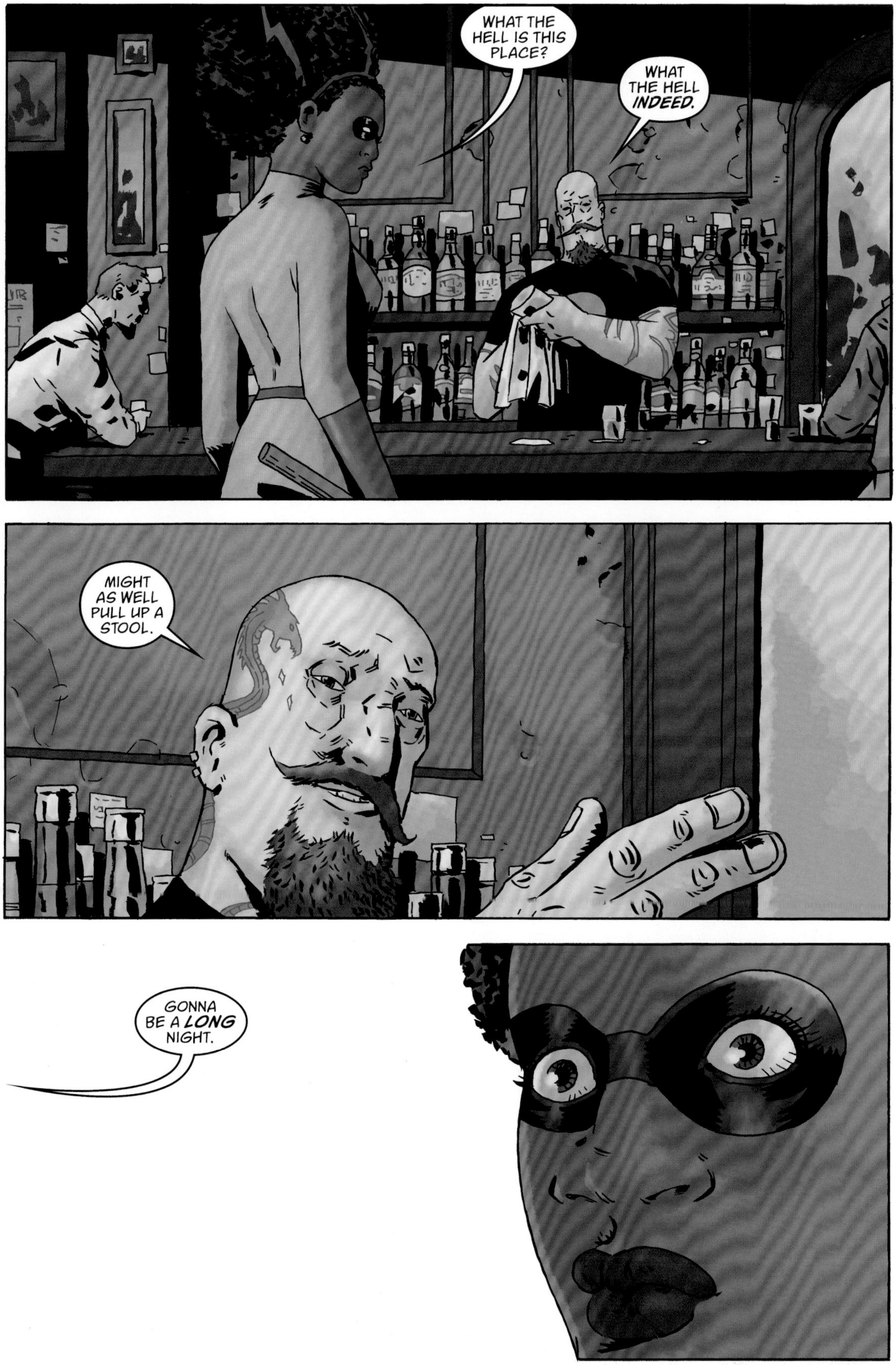
WHAT THE HELL IS THIS PLACE?
WHAT THE HELL *INDEED.*
MIGHT AS WELL PULL UP A STOOL.
GONNA BE A *LONG* NIGHT.

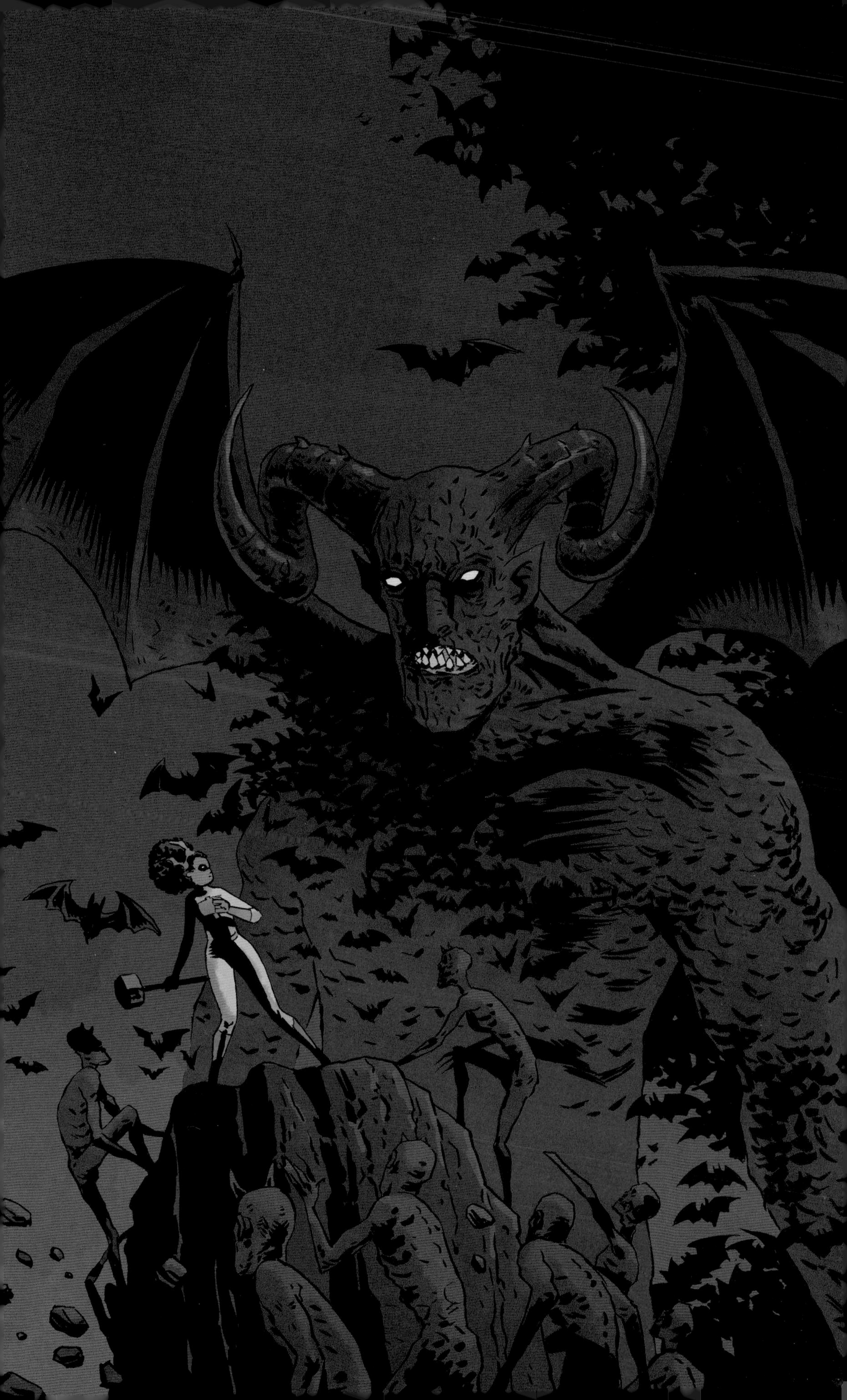

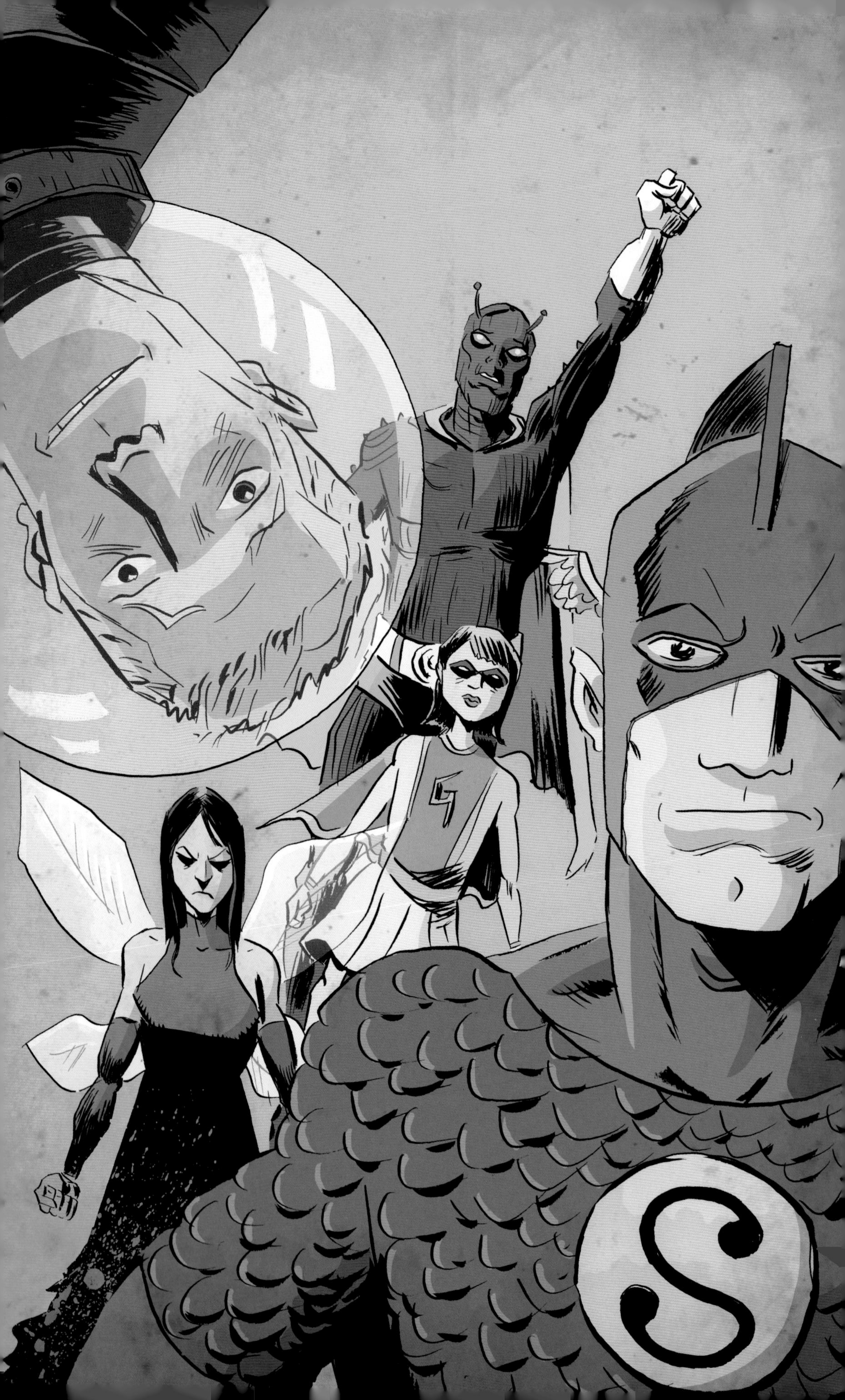

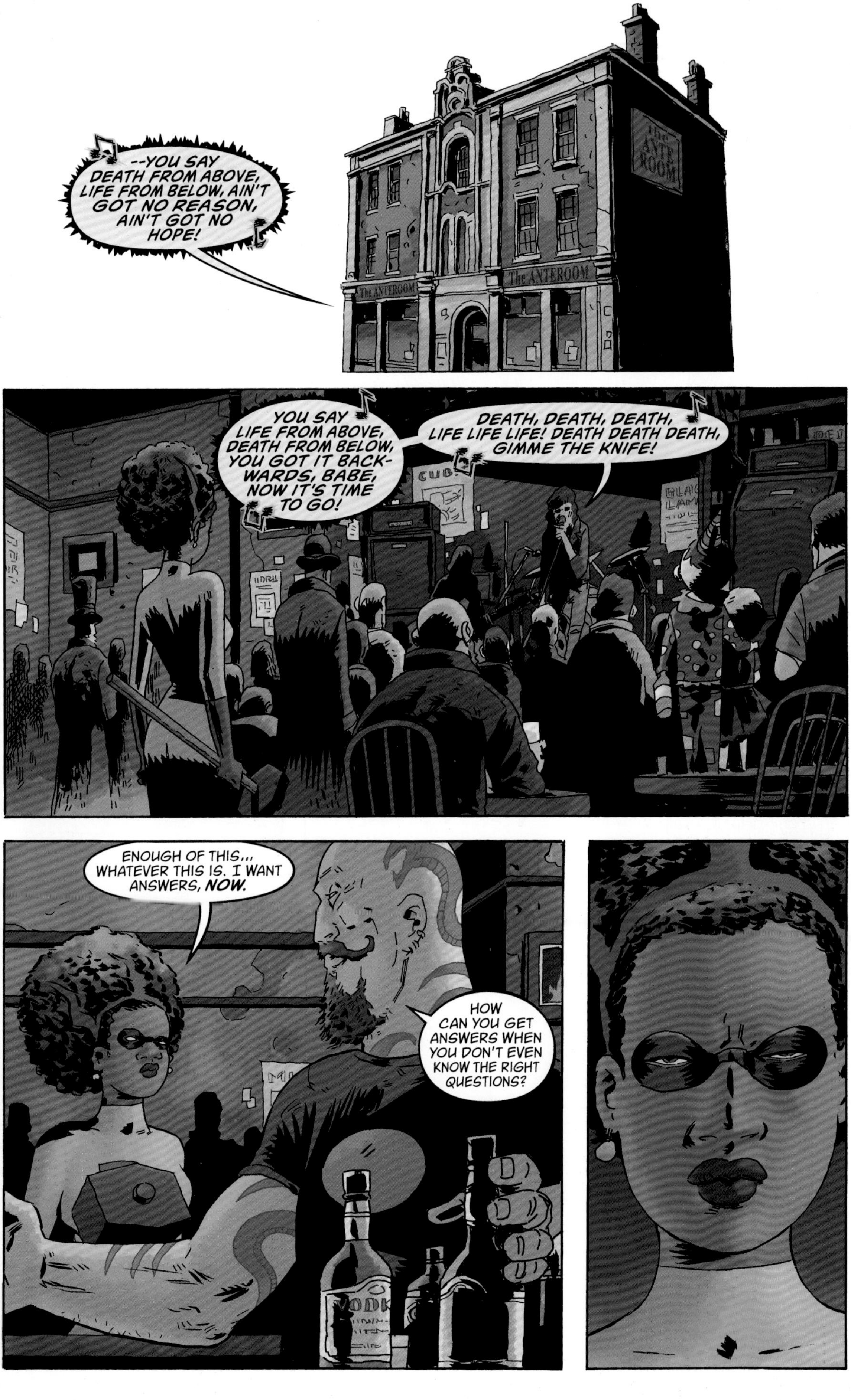
the ANTE ROOM
The ANTEROOM
The ANTEROOM
--YOU SAY DEATH FROM ABOVE, LIFE FROM BELOW, AIN'T GOT NO REASON, AIN'T GOT NO HOPE!
YOU SAY LIFE FROM ABOVE, DEATH FROM BELOW, YOU GOT IT BACK-WARDS, BABE, NOW IT'S TIME TO GO!
DEATH, DEATH, DEATH, LIFE LIFE LIFE! DEATH DEATH DEATH, GIMME THE KNIFE!
ENOUGH OF THIS... WHATEVER THIS IS. I WANT ANSWERS, NOW.
HOW CAN YOU GET ANSWERS WHEN YOU DON'T EVEN KNOW THE RIGHT QUESTIONS?

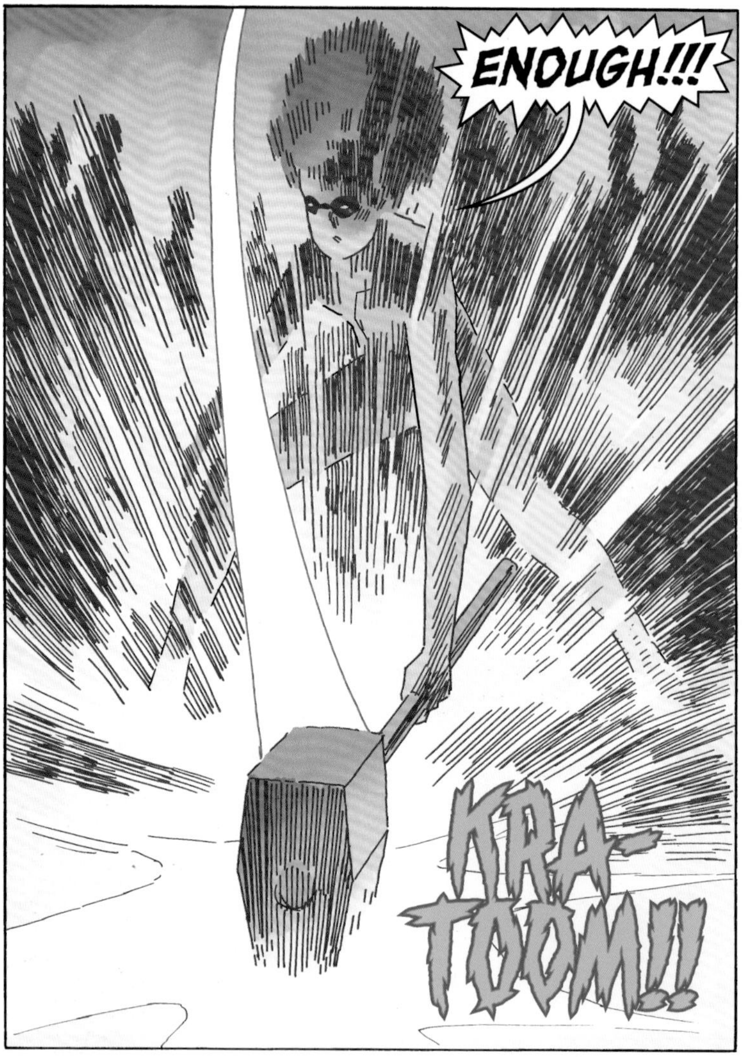
ENOUGH!!!
KRA-TOOM!!

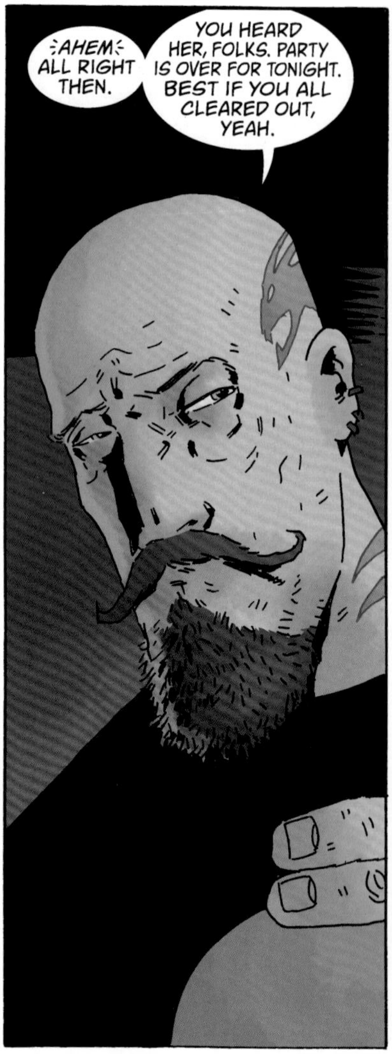
AHEM ALL RIGHT THEN.
YOU HEARD HER, FOLKS. PARTY IS OVER FOR TONIGHT. BEST IF YOU ALL CLEARED OUT, YEAH.

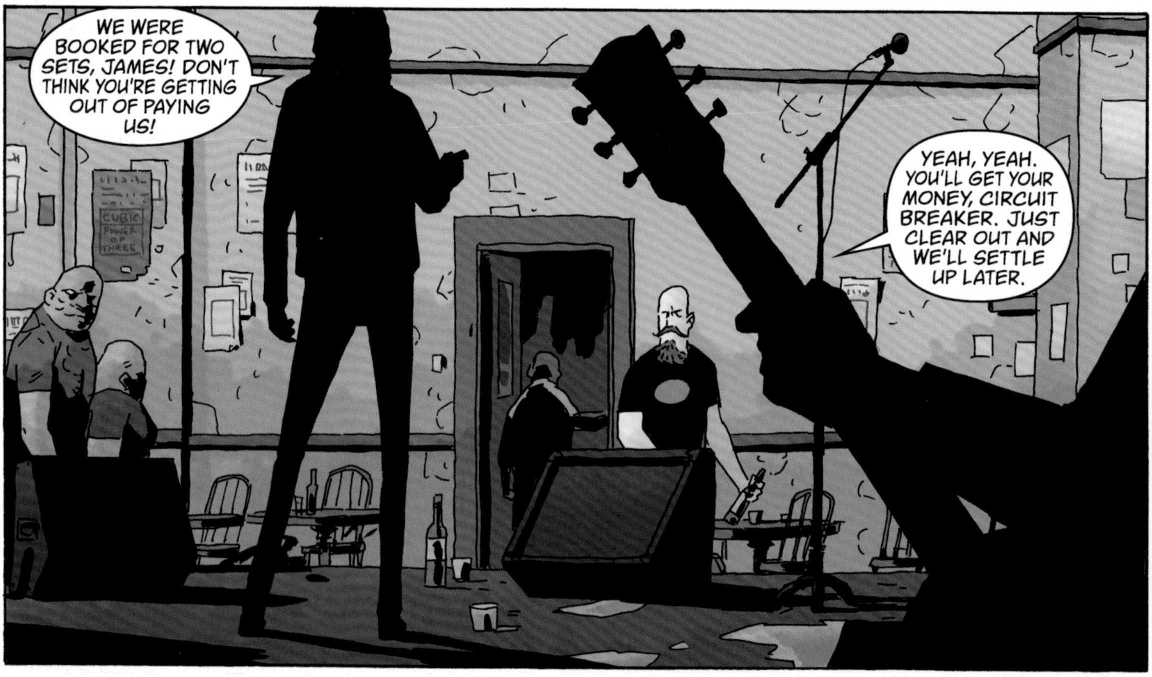
WE WERE BOOKED FOR TWO SETS, JAMES! DON'T THINK YOU'RE GETTING OUT OF PAYING US!
CUBIC POWER OF THREE
YEAH, YEAH. YOU'LL GET YOUR MONEY, CIRCUIT BREAKER. JUST CLEAR OUT AND WE'LL SETTLE UP LATER.

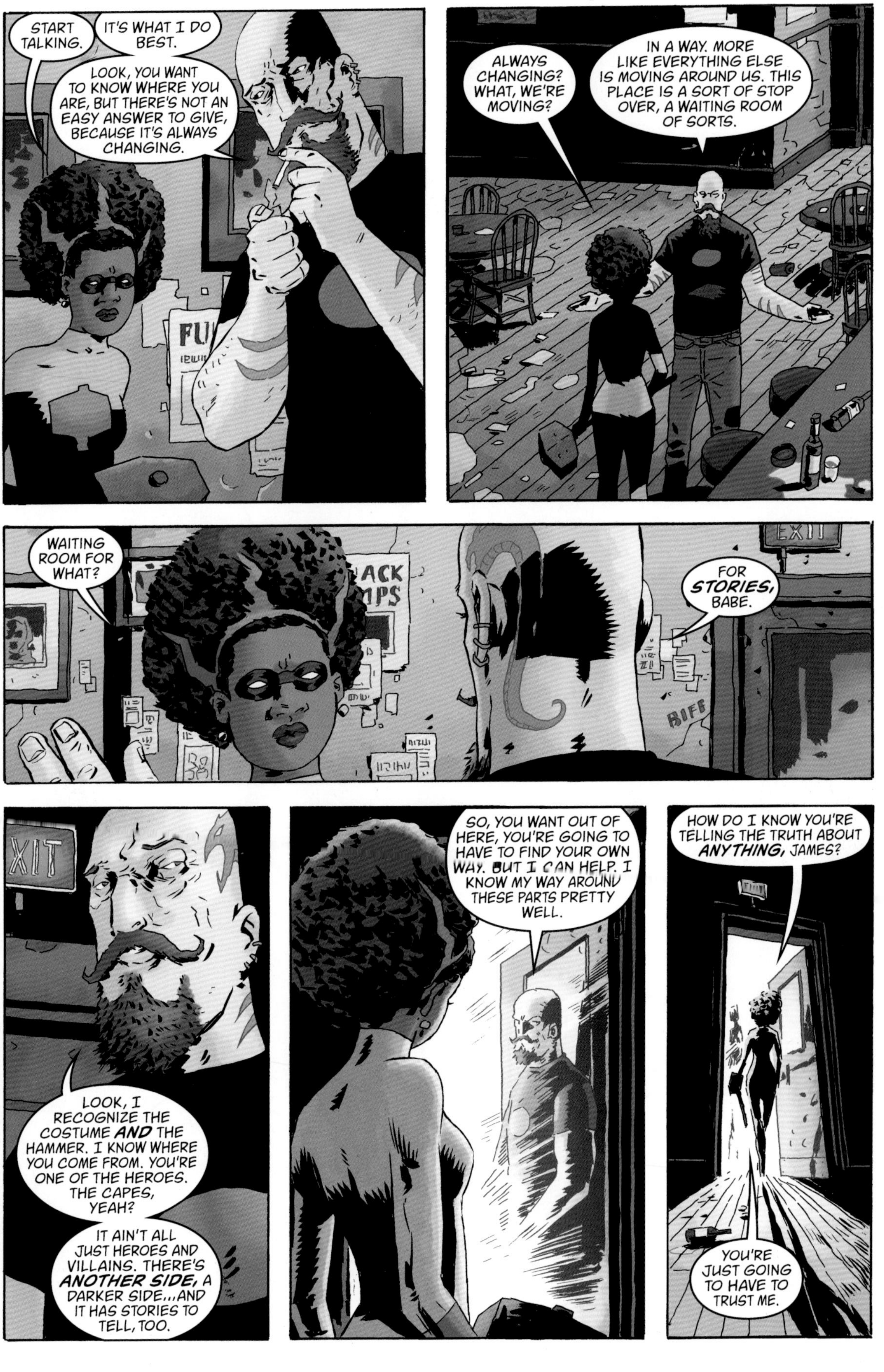
START TALKING.
IT'S WHAT I DO BEST.
LOOK, YOU WANT TO KNOW WHERE YOU ARE, BUT THERE'S NOT AN EASY ANSWER TO GIVE, BECAUSE IT'S ALWAYS CHANGING.
ALWAYS CHANGING? WHAT, WE'RE MOVING?
IN A WAY. MORE LIKE EVERYTHING ELSE IS MOVING AROUND US. THIS PLACE IS A SORT OF STOP OVER, A WAITING ROOM OF SORTS.
WAITING ROOM FOR WHAT?
FOR *STORIES,* BABE.
BIFF
LOOK, I RECOGNIZE THE COSTUME *AND* THE HAMMER. I KNOW WHERE YOU COME FROM. YOU'RE ONE OF THE HEROES. THE CAPES, YEAH?
IT AIN'T ALL JUST HEROES AND VILLAINS. THERE'S *ANOTHER SIDE,* A DARKER SIDE...AND IT HAS STORIES TO TELL, TOO.
SO, YOU WANT OUT OF HERE, YOU'RE GOING TO HAVE TO FIND YOUR OWN WAY. BUT I CAN HELP. I KNOW MY WAY AROUND THESE PARTS PRETTY WELL.
HOW DO I KNOW YOU'RE TELLING THE TRUTH ABOUT *ANYTHING,* JAMES?
YOU'RE JUST GOING TO HAVE TO TRUST ME.

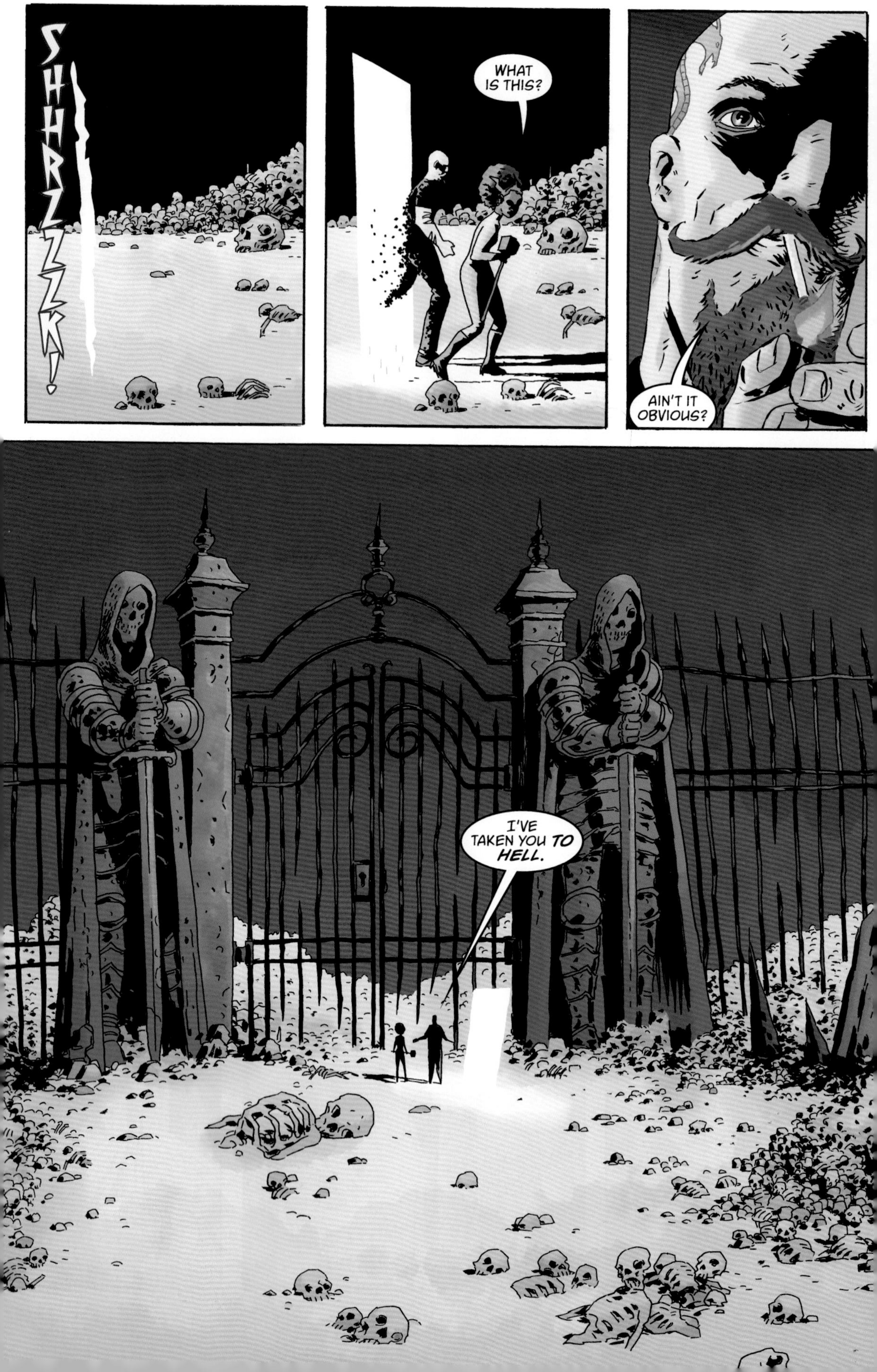
SHHRZZZK!
WHAT IS THIS?
AIN'T IT OBVIOUS?
I'VE TAKEN YOU TO HELL.

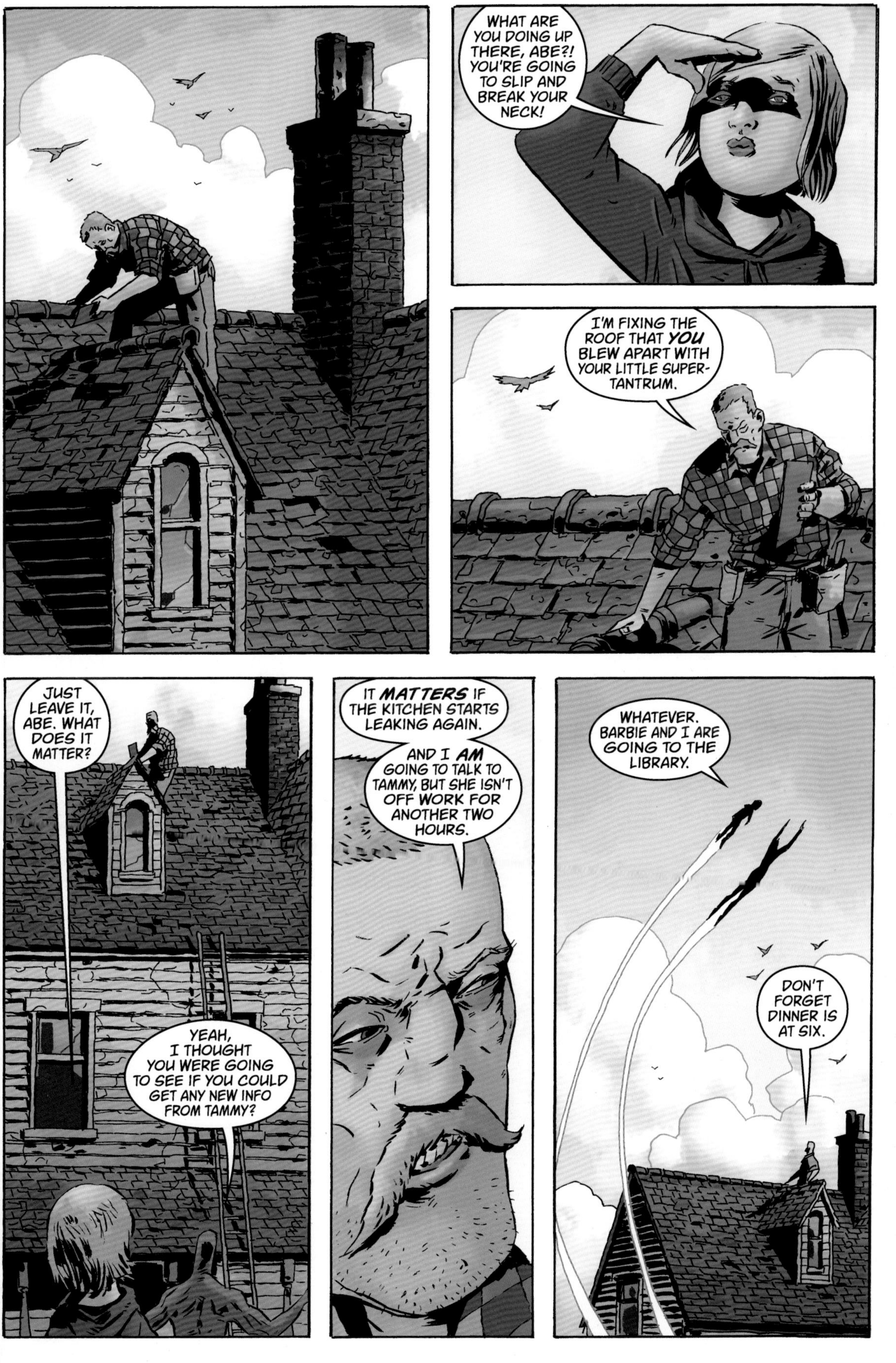
WHAT ARE YOU DOING UP THERE, ABE?! YOU'RE GOING TO SLIP AND BREAK YOUR NECK!
I'M FIXING THE ROOF THAT YOU BLEW APART WITH YOUR LITTLE SUPER-TANTRUM.
JUST LEAVE IT, ABE. WHAT DOES IT MATTER?
YEAH, I THOUGHT YOU WERE GOING TO SEE IF YOU COULD GET ANY NEW INFO FROM TAMMY?
IT MATTERS IF THE KITCHEN STARTS LEAKING AGAIN.
AND I AM GOING TO TALK TO TAMMY, BUT SHE ISN'T OFF WORK FOR ANOTHER TWO HOURS.
WHATEVER. BARBIE AND I ARE GOING TO THE LIBRARY.
DON'T FORGET DINNER IS AT SIX.

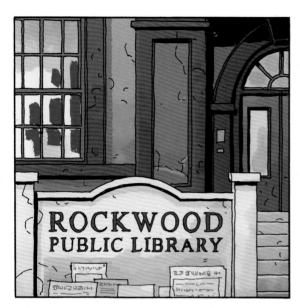

ROCKWOOD
PUBLIC LIBRARY

EXCUSE ME.

YES? HOW CAN I HELP YOU, YOUNG LADY?

CAN YOU TELL US WHERE WE CAN FIND BOOKS ABOUT THE TOWN'S HISTORY?

WELL, OUR **CHILDREN'S SECTION** IS IN THE BACK, DEAR.

DID I **SAY** I WANTED A KIDS' BOOK?

≔AHEM≔ NOW, NOW, GAIL. THE NICE LADY IS JUST TRYING TO HELP.

MY NIECE IS ACTUALLY HELPING **ME** WITH A LITTLE PROJECT. SO WE ARE INDEED LOOKING FOR ANYTHING YOU HAVE ON LOCAL HISTORY.

I SEE. WELL, ANYTHING WE HAVE WILL BE IN AISLES C AND D.

UNFORTUNATELY WE DON'T HAVE ANY BOOKS ON **PROPER MANNERS FOR CHILDREN** THERE.

I GOT YOUR MANNERS RIGHT HERE YOU OL--

OKAY, GAIL! HOW ABOUT WE GET TO WORK, HUH?

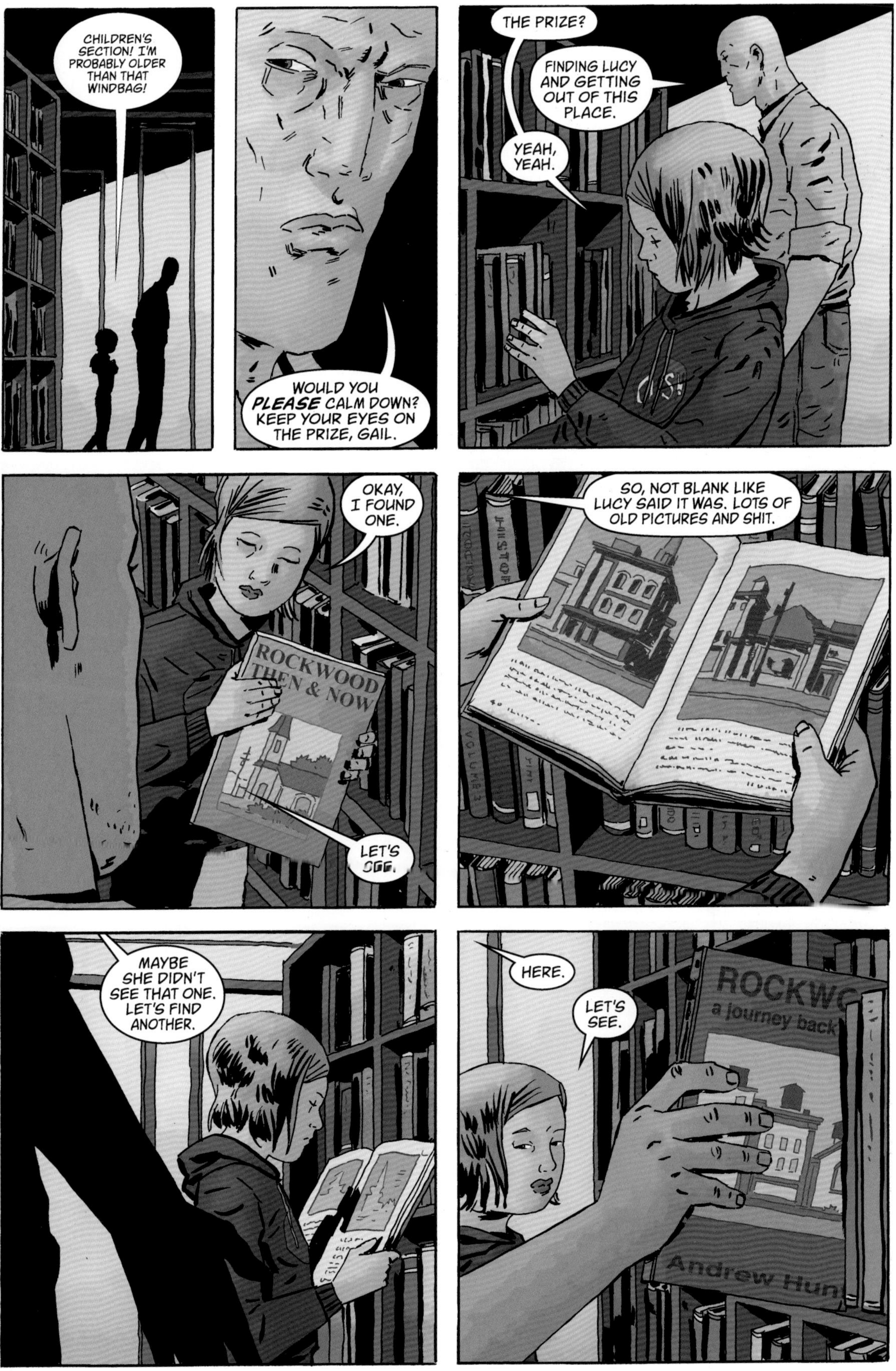
CHILDREN'S SECTION! I'M PROBABLY OLDER THAN THAT WINDBAG!
WOULD YOU *PLEASE* CALM DOWN? KEEP YOUR EYES ON THE PRIZE, GAIL.
THE PRIZE?
FINDING LUCY AND GETTING OUT OF THIS PLACE.
YEAH, YEAH.
OKAY, I FOUND ONE.
ROCKWOOD THEN & NOW
LET'S SEE.
SO, NOT BLANK LIKE LUCY SAID IT WAS. LOTS OF OLD PICTURES AND SHIT.
MAYBE SHE DIDN'T SEE THAT ONE. LET'S FIND ANOTHER.
HERE.
LET'S SEE.
ROCKWO
a journey back
Andrew Hun

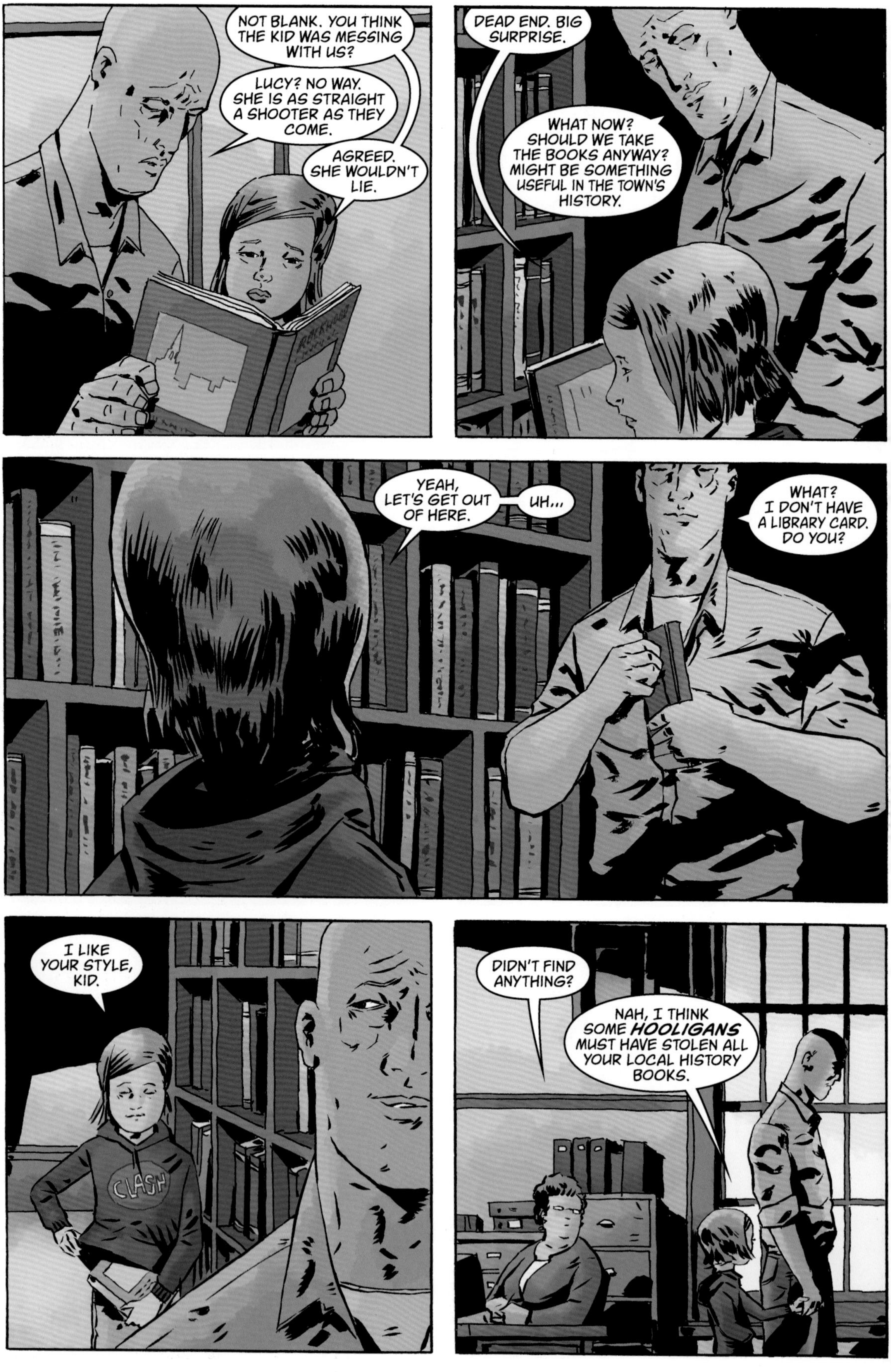
NOT BLANK. YOU THINK THE KID WAS MESSING WITH US?
LUCY? NO WAY. SHE IS AS STRAIGHT A SHOOTER AS THEY COME.
AGREED. SHE WOULDN'T LIE.
DEAD END. BIG SURPRISE.
WHAT NOW? SHOULD WE TAKE THE BOOKS ANYWAY? MIGHT BE SOMETHING USEFUL IN THE TOWN'S HISTORY.
YEAH, LET'S GET OUT OF HERE.
UH...
WHAT? I DON'T HAVE A LIBRARY CARD. DO YOU?
I LIKE YOUR STYLE, KID.
CLASH
DIDN'T FIND ANYTHING?
NAH, I THINK SOME ***HOOLIGANS*** MUST HAVE STOLEN ALL YOUR LOCAL HISTORY BOOKS.

ELSEWHERE.

HELL?! I THOUGHT YOU WERE SHOWING ME THE WAY OUT!

I NEVER SAID THAT.

THAT'S WHAT YOU GET FOR BELIEVING ME. I'M A *CONNIVING BASTARD.* ASK ANYONE.

SHHRZZZK!

TA.

HEY!

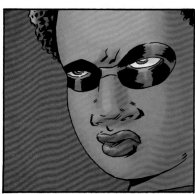

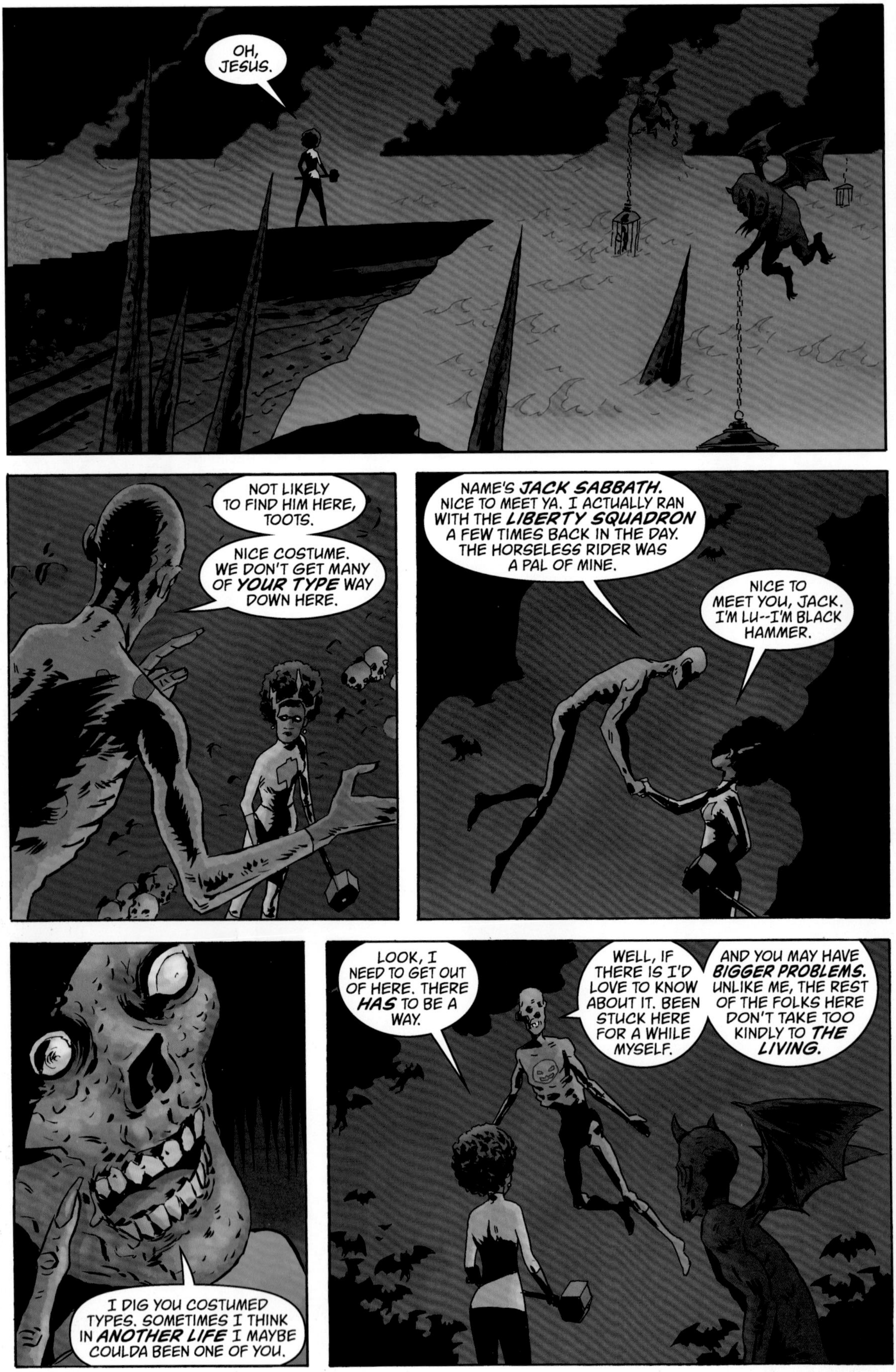
OH, JESUS.
NOT LIKELY TO FIND HIM HERE, TOOTS.
NICE COSTUME. WE DON'T GET MANY OF YOUR TYPE WAY DOWN HERE.
NAME'S JACK SABBATH. NICE TO MEET YA. I ACTUALLY RAN WITH THE LIBERTY SQUADRON A FEW TIMES BACK IN THE DAY. THE HORSELESS RIDER WAS A PAL OF MINE.
NICE TO MEET YOU, JACK. I'M LU--I'M BLACK HAMMER.
I DIG YOU COSTUMED TYPES. SOMETIMES I THINK IN ANOTHER LIFE I MAYBE COULDA BEEN ONE OF YOU.
LOOK, I NEED TO GET OUT OF HERE. THERE HAS TO BE A WAY.
WELL, IF THERE IS I'D LOVE TO KNOW ABOUT IT. BEEN STUCK HERE FOR A WHILE MYSELF.
AND YOU MAY HAVE BIGGER PROBLEMS. UNLIKE ME, THE REST OF THE FOLKS HERE DON'T TAKE TOO KINDLY TO THE LIVING.

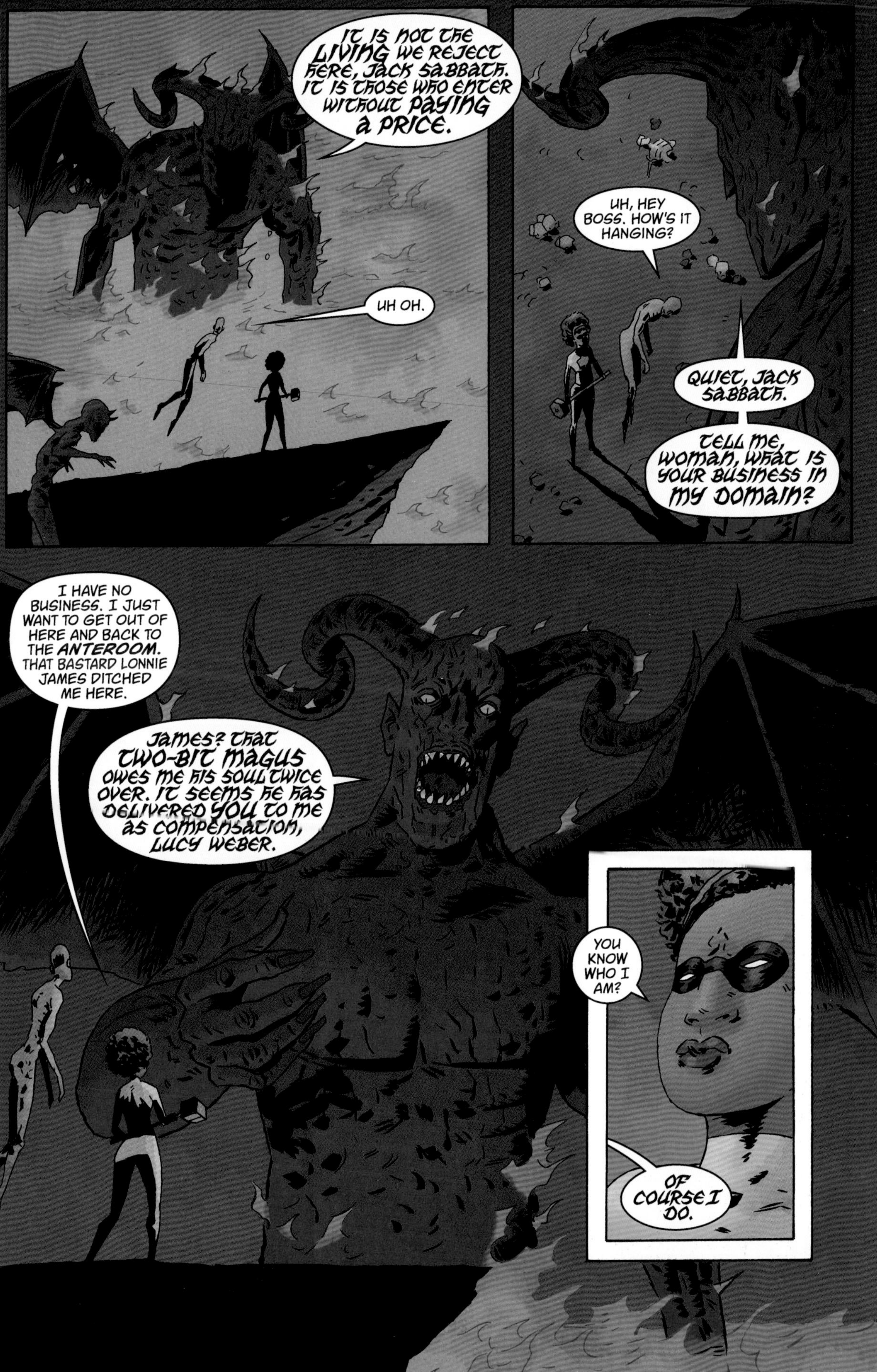
IT IS NOT THE LIVING WE REJECT HERE, JACK SABBATH. IT IS THOSE WHO ENTER WITHOUT PAYING A PRICE.
UH OH.
UH, HEY BOSS. HOW'S IT HANGING?
QUIET, JACK SABBATH.
TELL ME, WOMAN, WHAT IS YOUR BUSINESS IN MY DOMAIN?
I HAVE NO BUSINESS. I JUST WANT TO GET OUT OF HERE AND BACK TO THE ANTEROOM. THAT BASTARD LONNIE JAMES DITCHED ME HERE.
JAMES? THAT TWO-BIT MAGUS OWES ME HIS SOUL TWICE OVER. IT SEEMS HE HAS DELIVERED YOU TO ME AS COMPENSATION, LUCY WEBER.
YOU KNOW WHO I AM?
OF COURSE I DO.

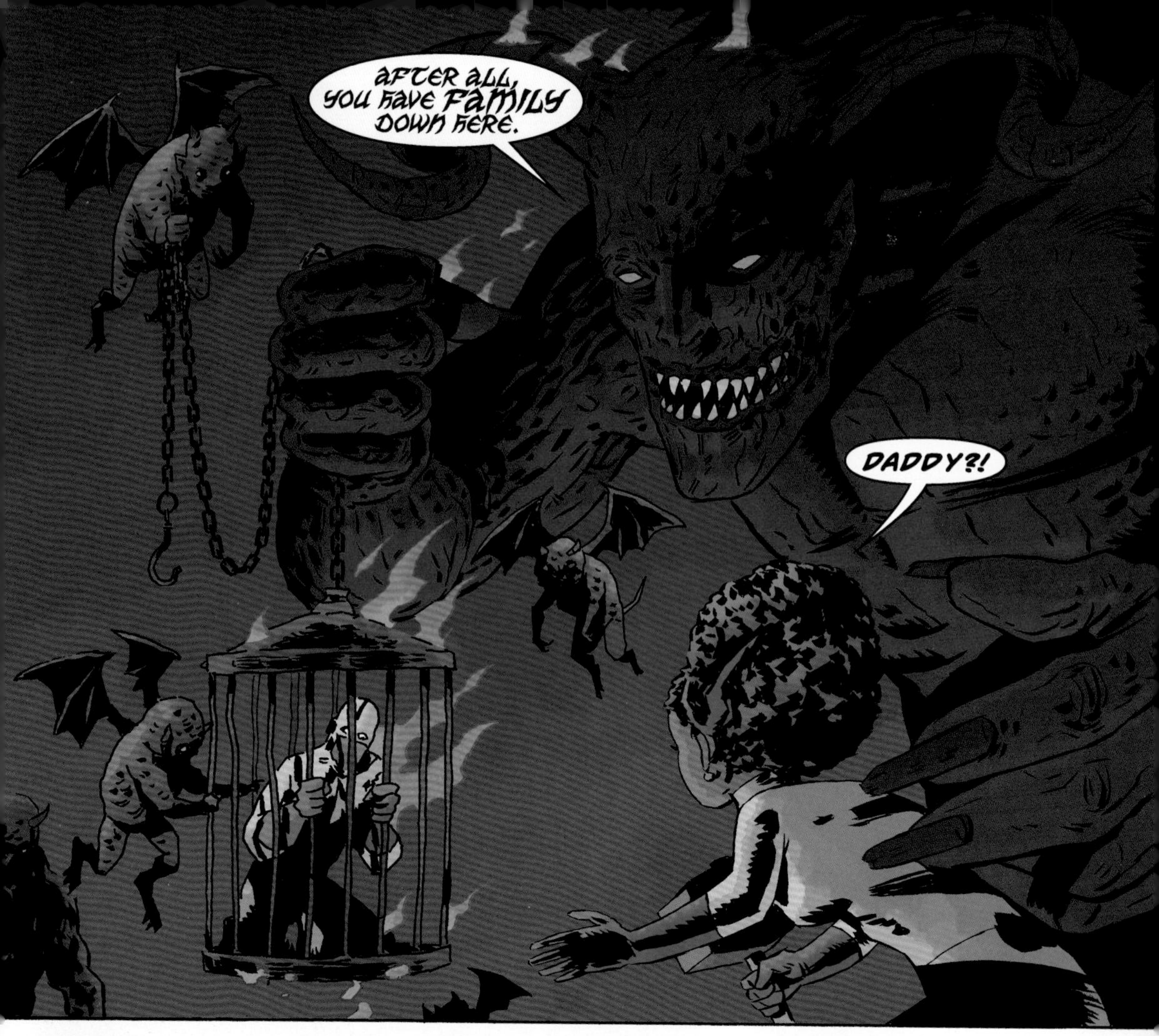
AFTER ALL, YOU HAVE FAMILY DOWN HERE.
DADDY?!

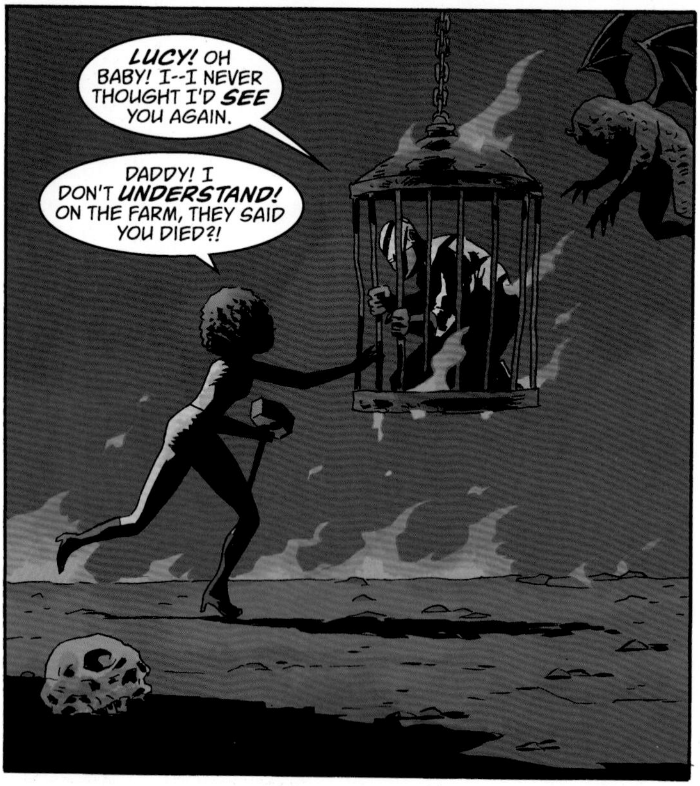
LUCY! OH BABY! I--I NEVER THOUGHT I'D SEE YOU AGAIN.
DADDY! I DON'T UNDERSTAND! ON THE FARM, THEY SAID YOU DIED?!

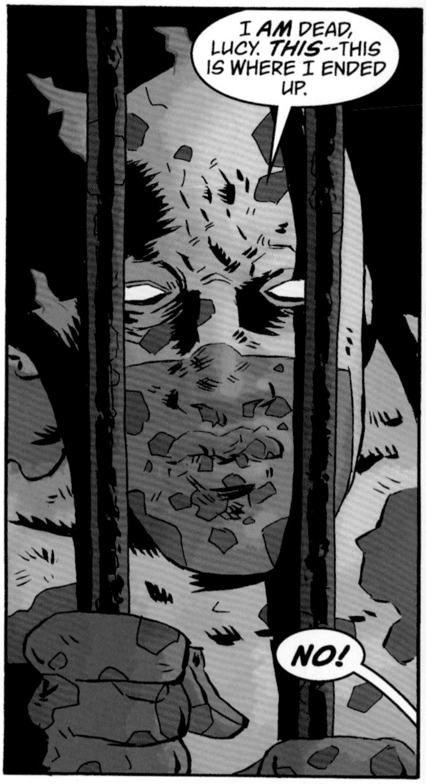
I AM DEAD, LUCY. THIS--THIS IS WHERE I ENDED UP.
NO!

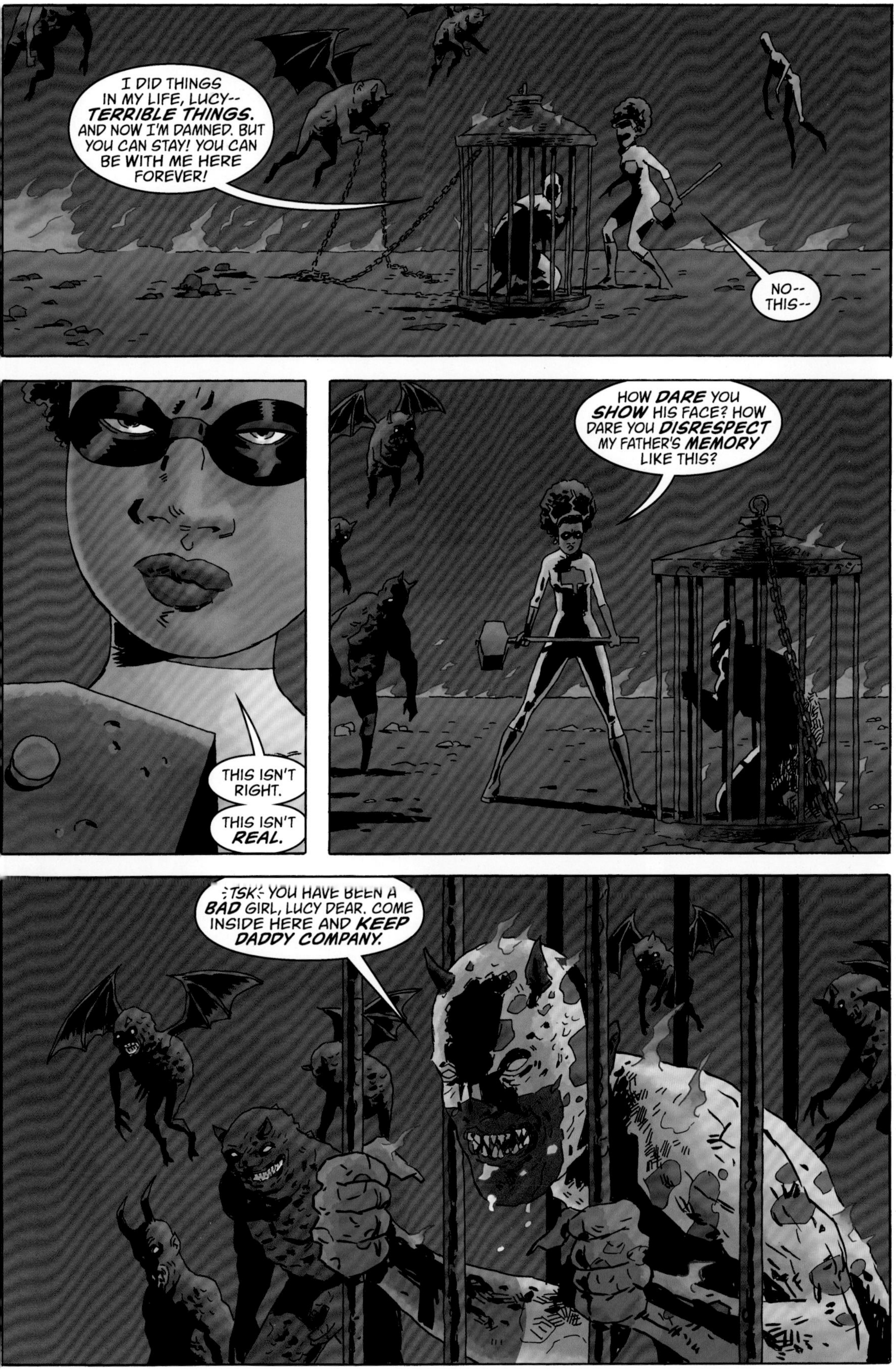

I DID THINGS IN MY LIFE, LUCY-- TERRIBLE THINGS. AND NOW I'M DAMNED. BUT YOU CAN STAY! YOU CAN BE WITH ME HERE FOREVER!
NO-- THIS--
THIS ISN'T RIGHT.
THIS ISN'T REAL.
HOW DARE YOU SHOW HIS FACE? HOW DARE YOU DISRESPECT MY FATHER'S MEMORY LIKE THIS?
TSK YOU HAVE BEEN A BAD GIRL, LUCY DEAR. COME INSIDE HERE AND KEEP DADDY COMPANY.

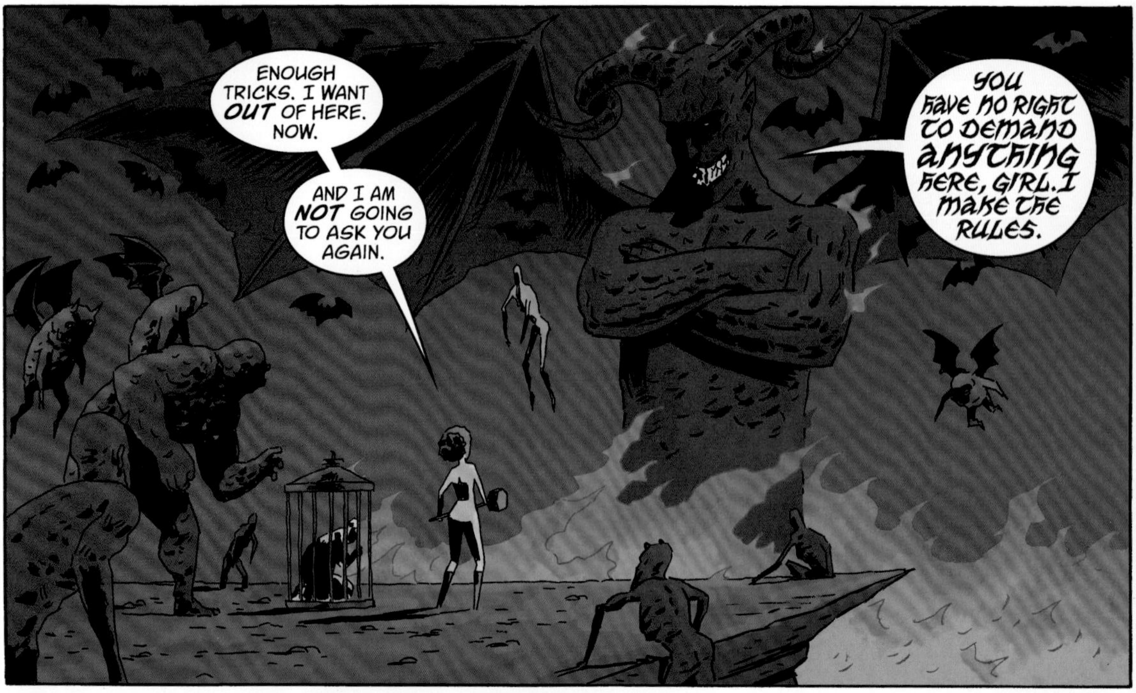
ENOUGH TRICKS. I WANT OUT OF HERE. NOW.
AND I AM NOT GOING TO ASK YOU AGAIN.
YOU HAVE NO RIGHT TO DEMAND ANYTHING HERE, GIRL. I MAKE THE RULES.

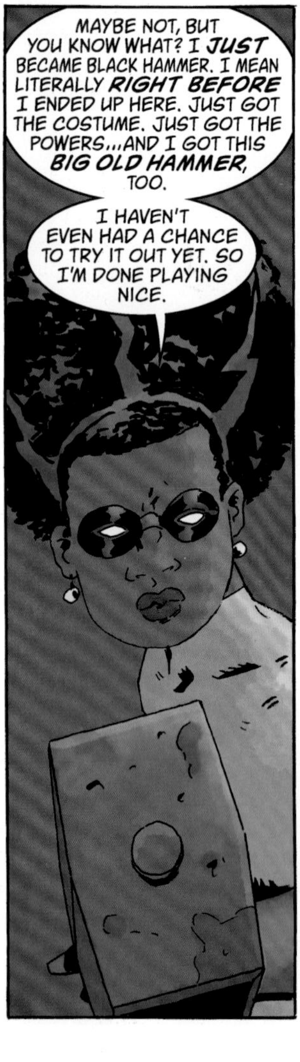
MAYBE NOT, BUT YOU KNOW WHAT? I JUST BECAME BLACK HAMMER. I MEAN LITERALLY RIGHT BEFORE I ENDED UP HERE. JUST GOT THE COSTUME. JUST GOT THE POWERS...AND I GOT THIS BIG OLD HAMMER, TOO.
I HAVEN'T EVEN HAD A CHANCE TO TRY IT OUT YET. SO I'M DONE PLAYING NICE.

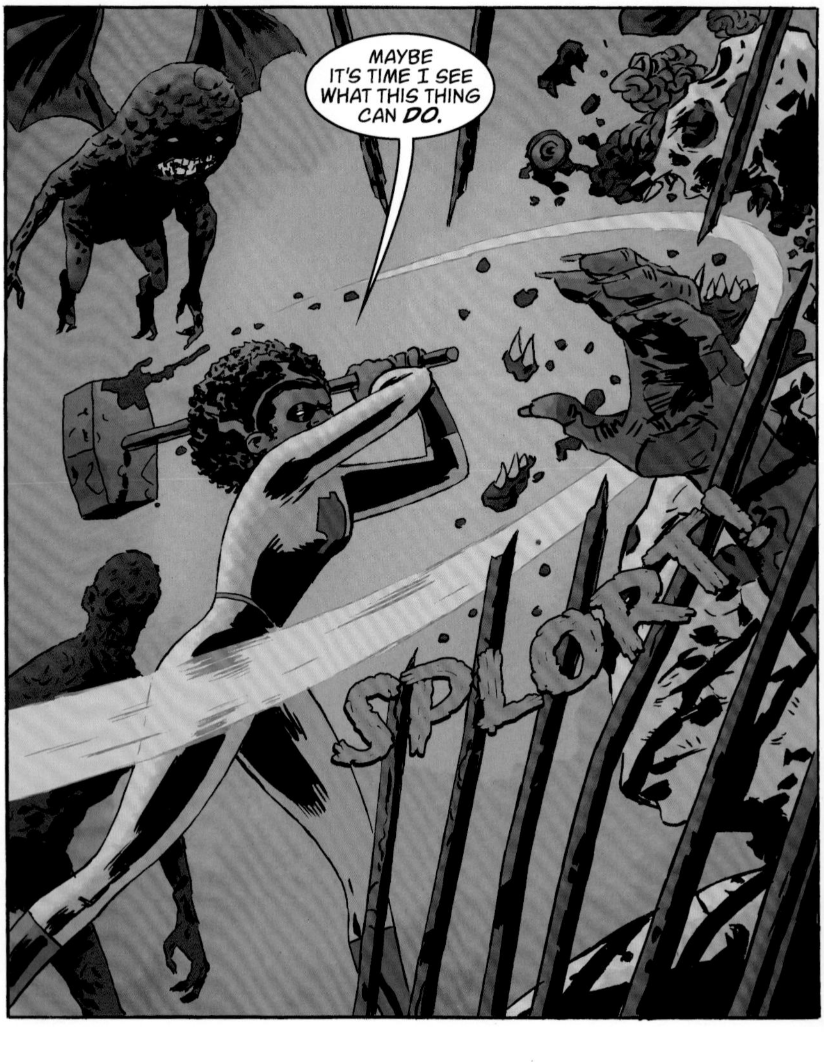
MAYBE IT'S TIME I SEE WHAT THIS THING CAN DO.
SPLORT

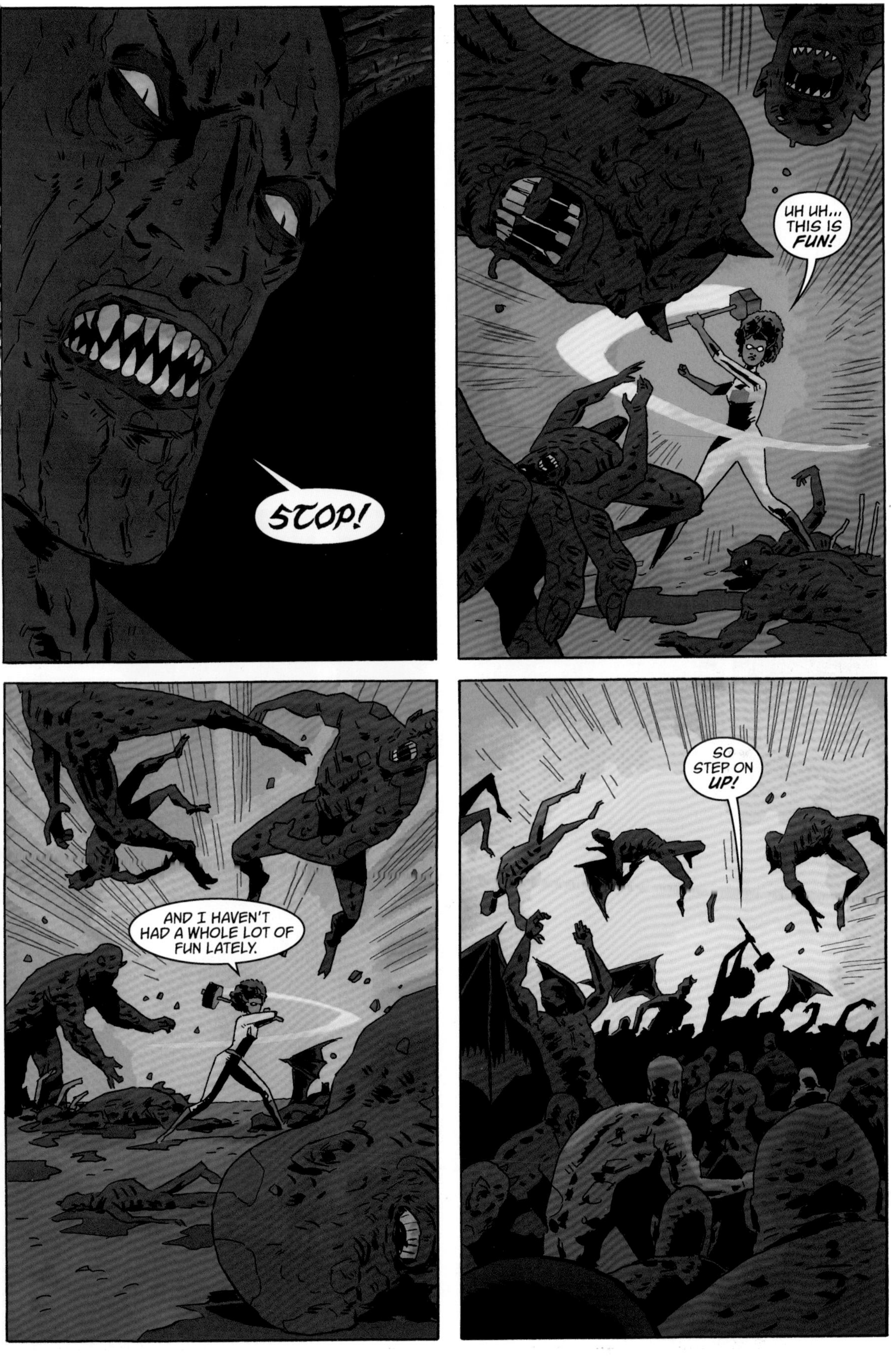
STOP!
UH UH... THIS IS FUN!
AND I HAVEN'T HAD A WHOLE LOT OF FUN LATELY.
SO STEP ON UP!

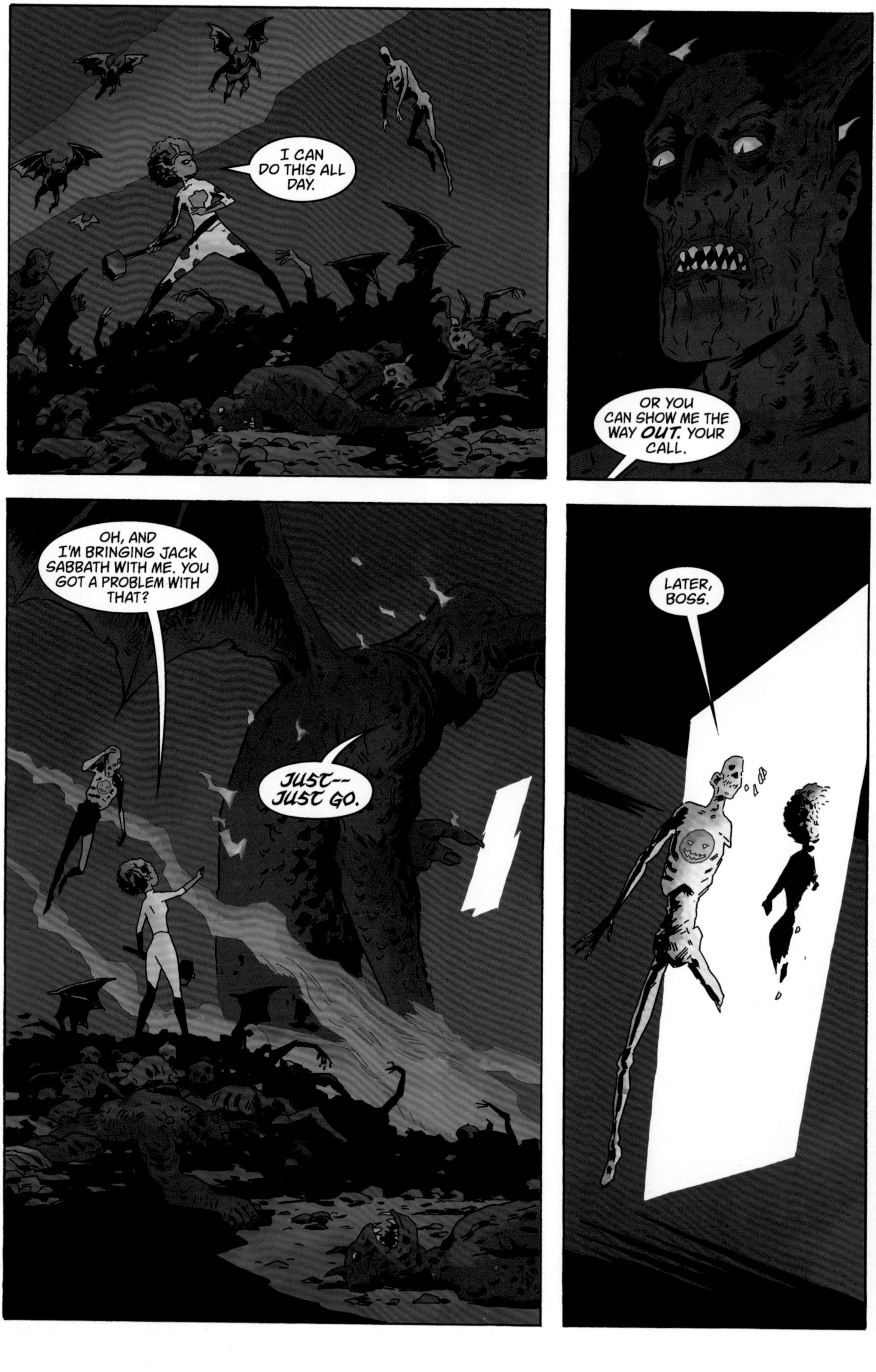
I CAN DO THIS ALL DAY.
OR YOU CAN SHOW ME THE WAY OUT. YOUR CALL.
OH, AND I'M BRINGING JACK SABBATH WITH ME. YOU GOT A PROBLEM WITH THAT?
JUST-- JUST GO.
LATER, BOSS.

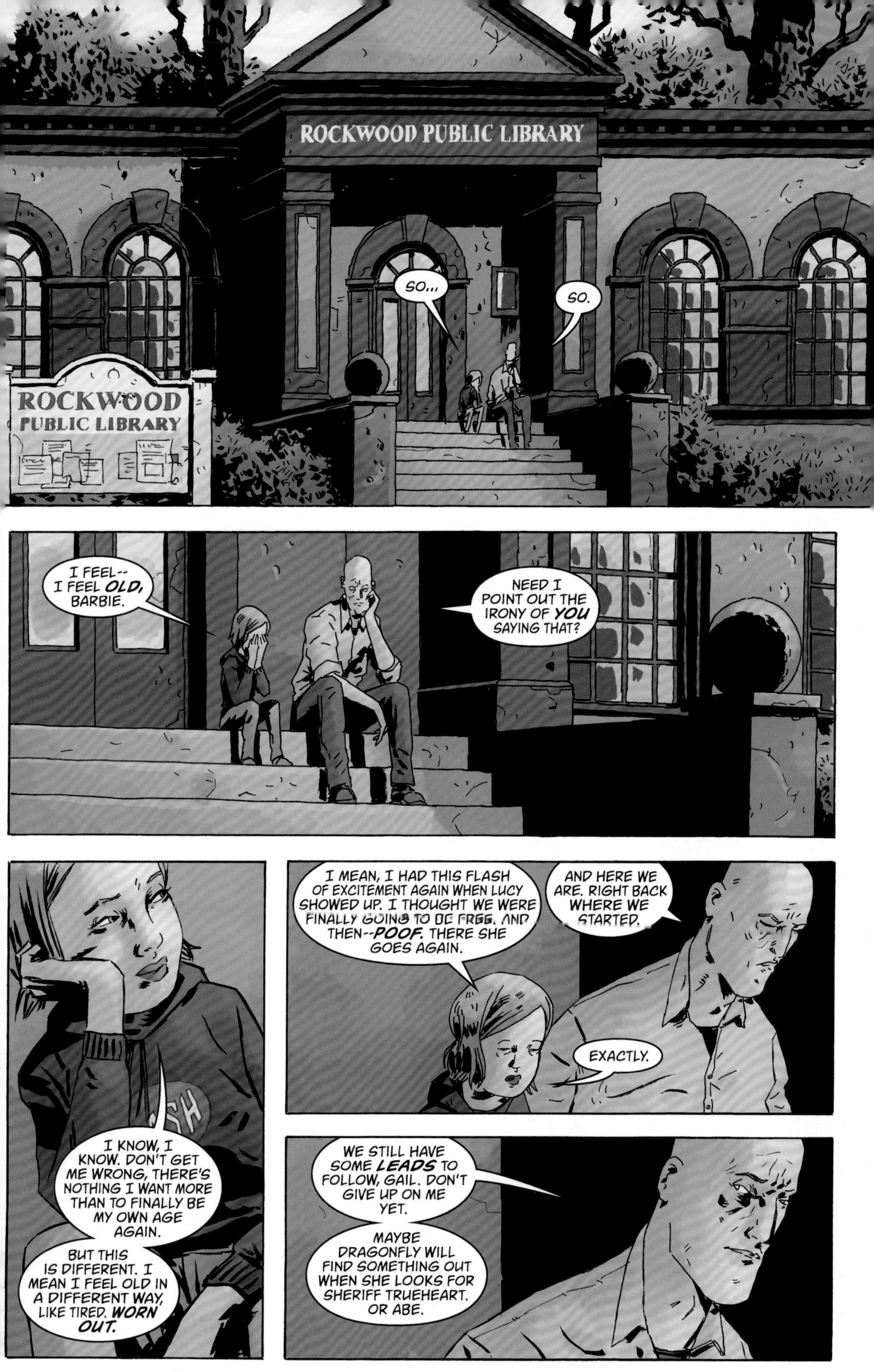
ROCKWOOD PUBLIC LIBRARY
ROCKWOOD PUBLIC LIBRARY
SO...
SO.
I FEEL-- I FEEL OLD, BARBIE.
NEED I POINT OUT THE IRONY OF YOU SAYING THAT?
I KNOW, I KNOW. DON'T GET ME WRONG, THERE'S NOTHING I WANT MORE THAN TO FINALLY BE MY OWN AGE AGAIN.
BUT THIS IS DIFFERENT. I MEAN I FEEL OLD IN A DIFFERENT WAY, LIKE TIRED. WORN OUT.
I MEAN, I HAD THIS FLASH OF EXCITEMENT AGAIN WHEN LUCY SHOWED UP. I THOUGHT WE WERE FINALLY GOING TO BE FREE. AND THEN--POOF. THERE SHE GOES AGAIN.
AND HERE WE ARE. RIGHT BACK WHERE WE STARTED.
EXACTLY.
WE STILL HAVE SOME LEADS TO FOLLOW, GAIL. DON'T GIVE UP ON ME YET.
MAYBE DRAGONFLY WILL FIND SOMETHING OUT WHEN SHE LOOKS FOR SHERIFF TRUEHEART. OR ABE.

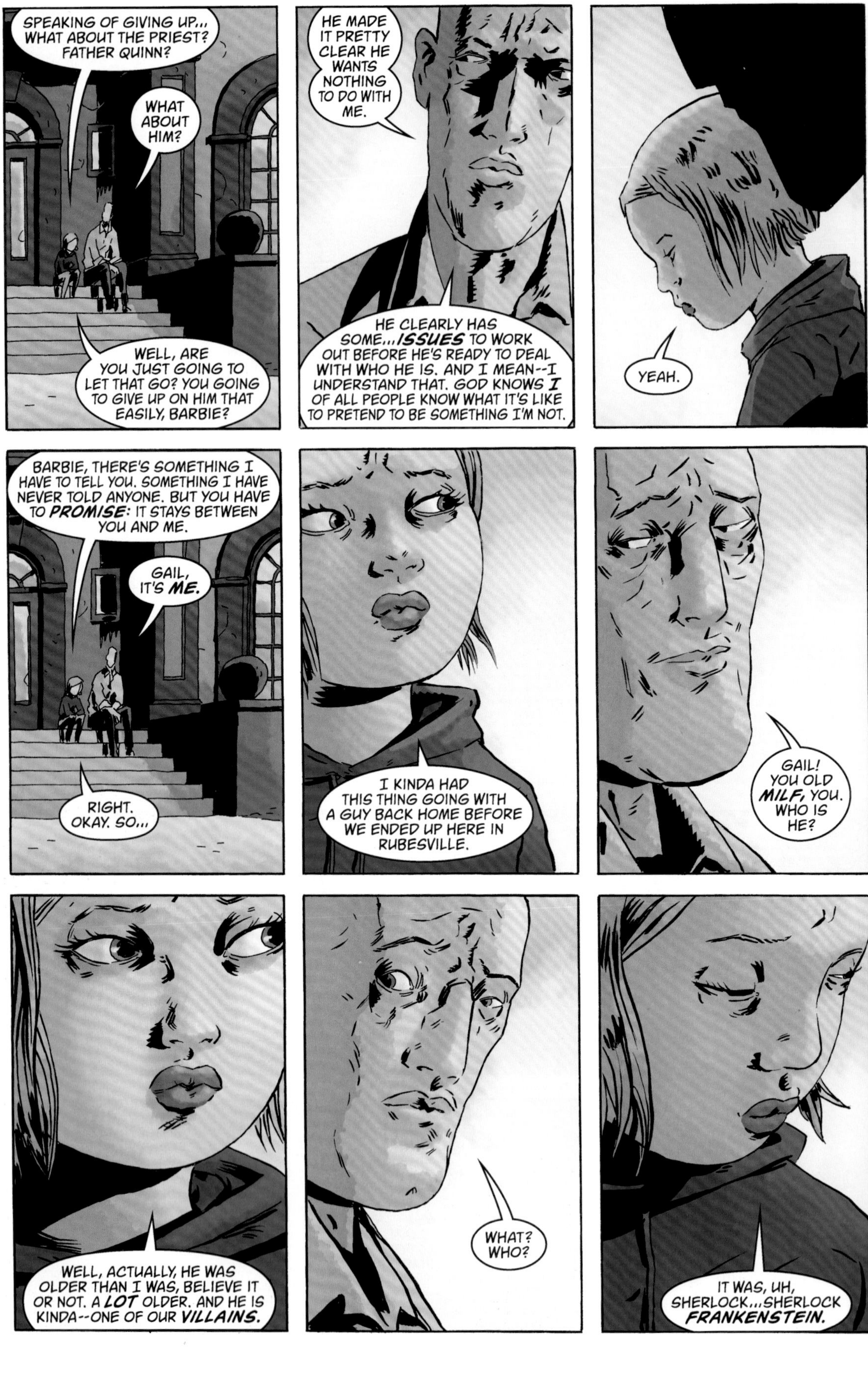
SPEAKING OF GIVING UP... WHAT ABOUT THE PRIEST? FATHER QUINN?
WHAT ABOUT HIM?
WELL, ARE YOU JUST GOING TO LET THAT GO? YOU GOING TO GIVE UP ON HIM THAT EASILY, BARBIE?
HE MADE IT PRETTY CLEAR HE WANTS NOTHING TO DO WITH ME.
HE CLEARLY HAS SOME... ISSUES TO WORK OUT BEFORE HE'S READY TO DEAL WITH WHO HE IS. AND I MEAN--I UNDERSTAND THAT. GOD KNOWS I OF ALL PEOPLE KNOW WHAT IT'S LIKE TO PRETEND TO BE SOMETHING I'M NOT.
YEAH.
BARBIE, THERE'S SOMETHING I HAVE TO TELL YOU. SOMETHING I HAVE NEVER TOLD ANYONE. BUT YOU HAVE TO PROMISE: IT STAYS BETWEEN YOU AND ME.
GAIL, IT'S ME.
RIGHT. OKAY. SO...
I KINDA HAD THIS THING GOING WITH A GUY BACK HOME BEFORE WE ENDED UP HERE IN RUBESVILLE.
GAIL! YOU OLD MILF, YOU. WHO IS HE?
WELL, ACTUALLY, HE WAS OLDER THAN I WAS, BELIEVE IT OR NOT. A LOT OLDER. AND HE IS KINDA--ONE OF OUR VILLAINS.
WHAT? WHO?
IT WAS, UH, SHERLOCK... SHERLOCK FRANKENSTEIN.

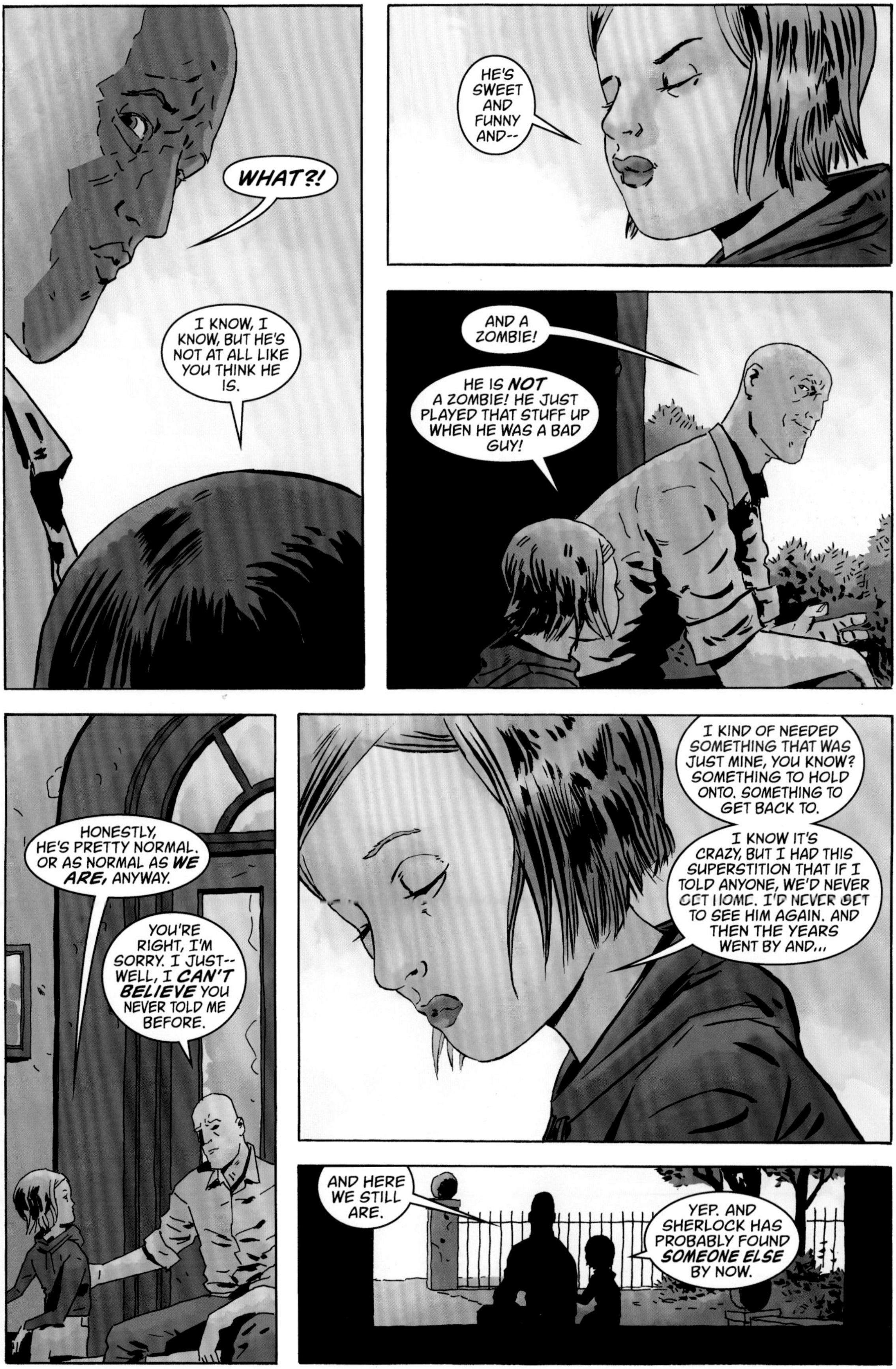
WHAT?!
I KNOW, I KNOW, BUT HE'S NOT AT ALL LIKE YOU THINK HE IS.
HE'S SWEET AND FUNNY AND--
AND A ZOMBIE!
HE IS NOT A ZOMBIE! HE JUST PLAYED THAT STUFF UP WHEN HE WAS A BAD GUY!
HONESTLY, HE'S PRETTY NORMAL. OR AS NORMAL AS WE ARE, ANYWAY.
YOU'RE RIGHT, I'M SORRY. I JUST-- WELL, I CAN'T BELIEVE YOU NEVER TOLD ME BEFORE.
I KIND OF NEEDED SOMETHING THAT WAS JUST MINE, YOU KNOW? SOMETHING TO HOLD ONTO. SOMETHING TO GET BACK TO.
I KNOW IT'S CRAZY, BUT I HAD THIS SUPERSTITION THAT IF I TOLD ANYONE, WE'D NEVER GET HOME. I'D NEVER GET TO SEE HIM AGAIN. AND THEN THE YEARS WENT BY AND...
AND HERE WE STILL ARE.
YEP. AND SHERLOCK HAS PROBABLY FOUND SOMEONE ELSE BY NOW.

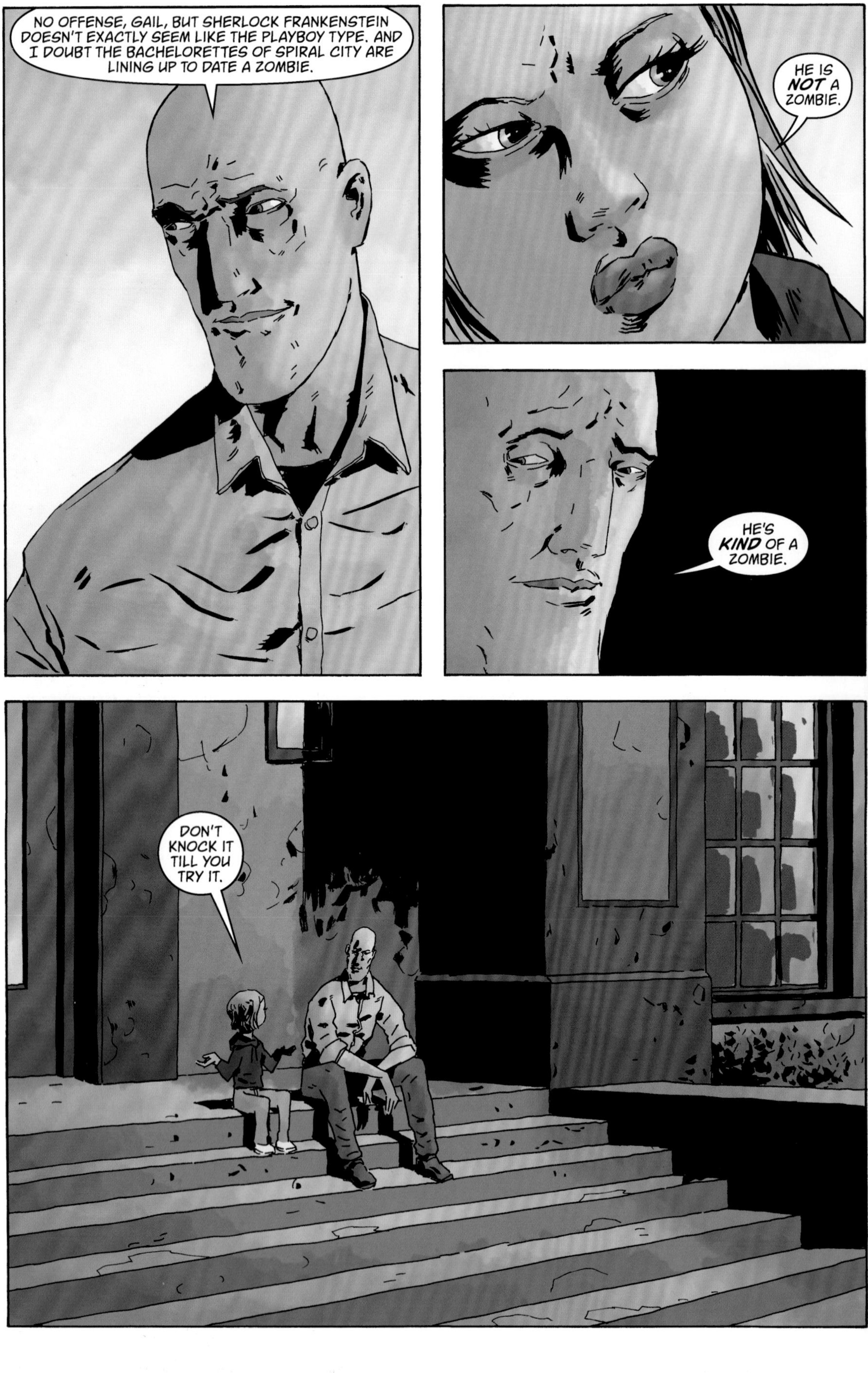
NO OFFENSE, GAIL, BUT SHERLOCK FRANKENSTEIN DOESN'T EXACTLY SEEM LIKE THE PLAYBOY TYPE. AND I DOUBT THE BACHELORETTES OF SPIRAL CITY ARE LINING UP TO DATE A ZOMBIE.
HE IS NOT A ZOMBIE.
HE'S KIND OF A ZOMBIE.
DON'T KNOCK IT TILL YOU TRY IT.

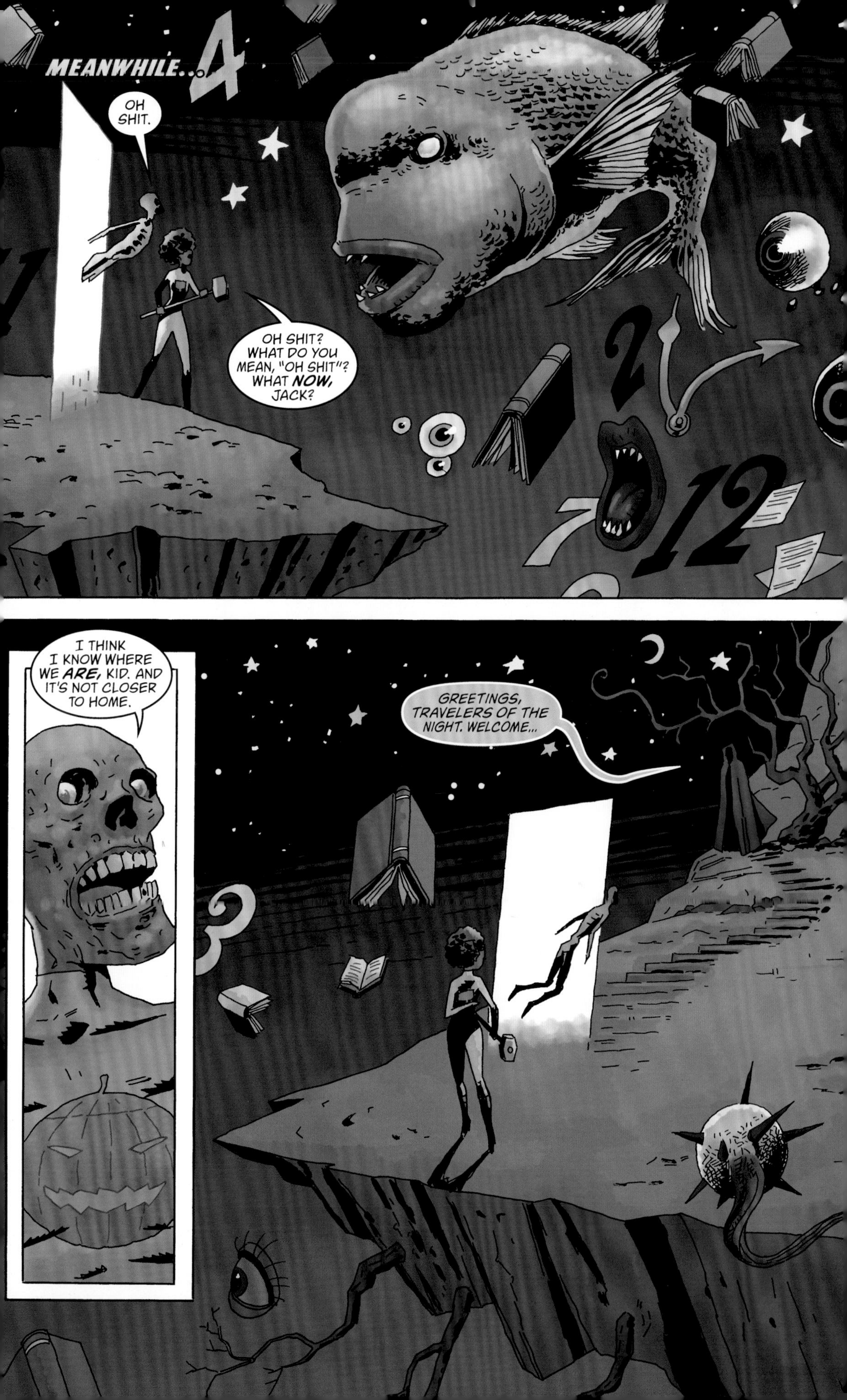
MEANWHILE...
OH SHIT.
OH SHIT? WHAT DO YOU MEAN, "OH SHIT"? WHAT NOW, JACK?
I THINK I KNOW WHERE WE ARE, KID. AND IT'S NOT CLOSER TO HOME.
GREETINGS, TRAVELERS OF THE NIGHT. WELCOME...

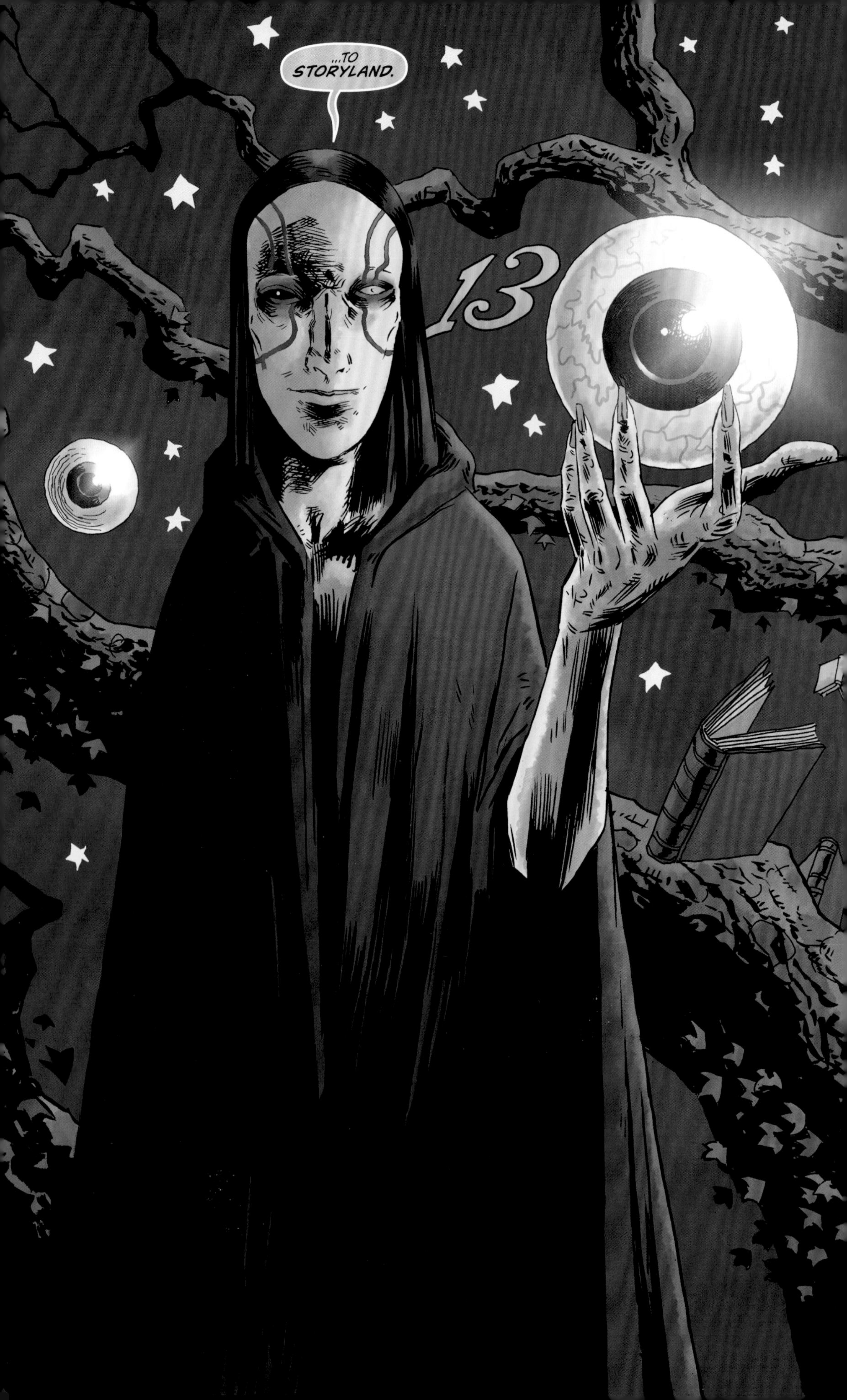
...TO STORYLAND.
13

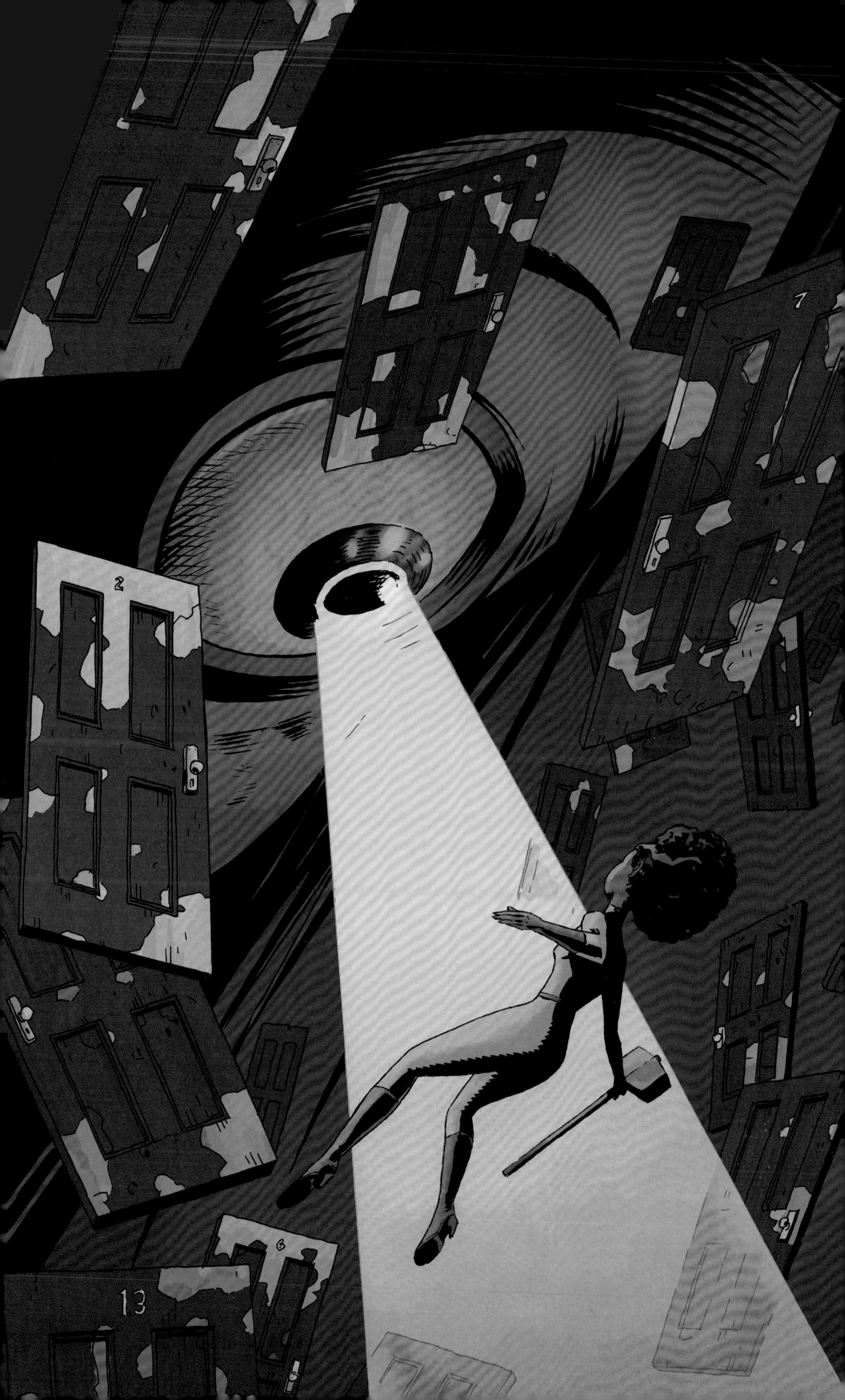
13

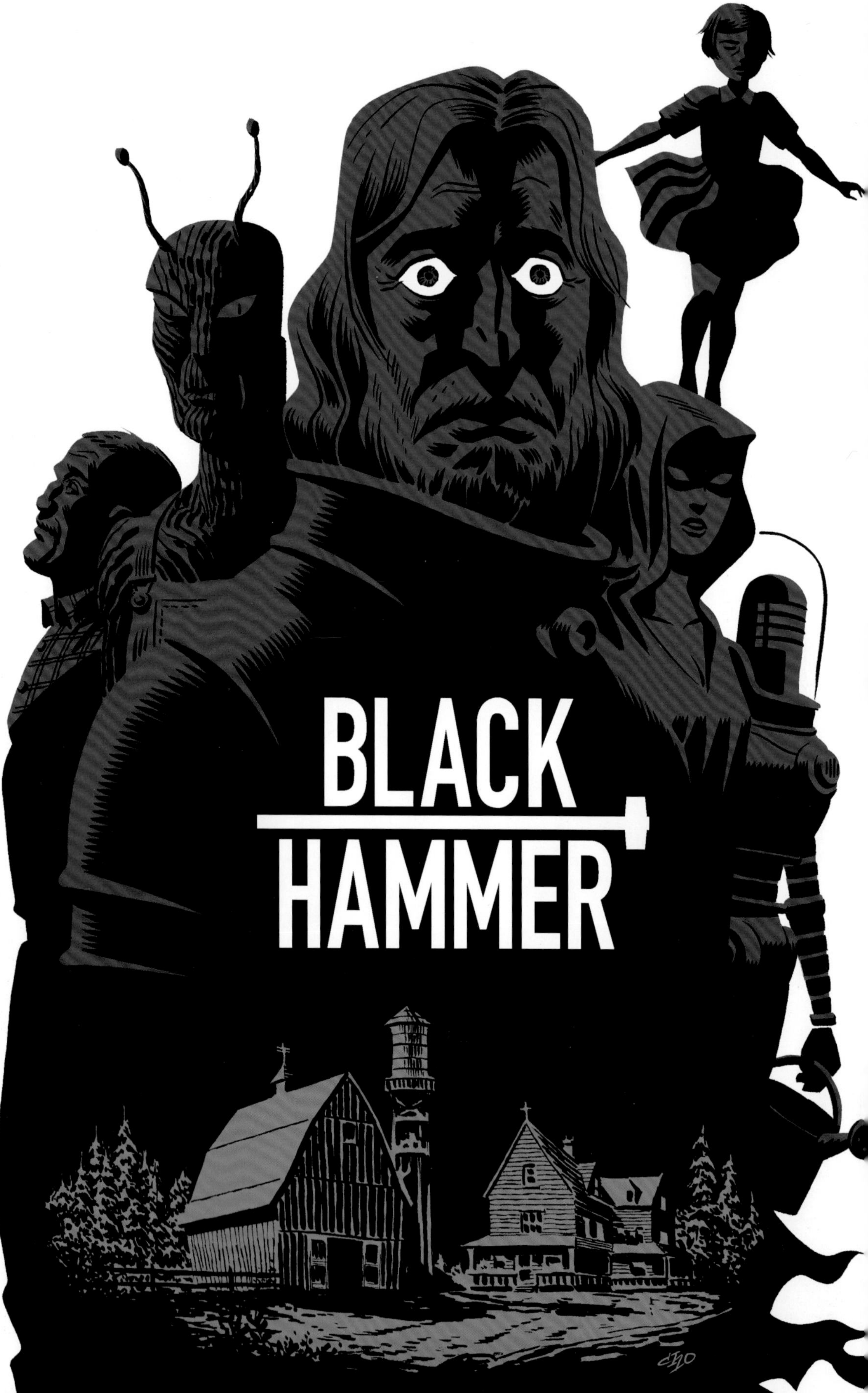
BLACK
HAMMER

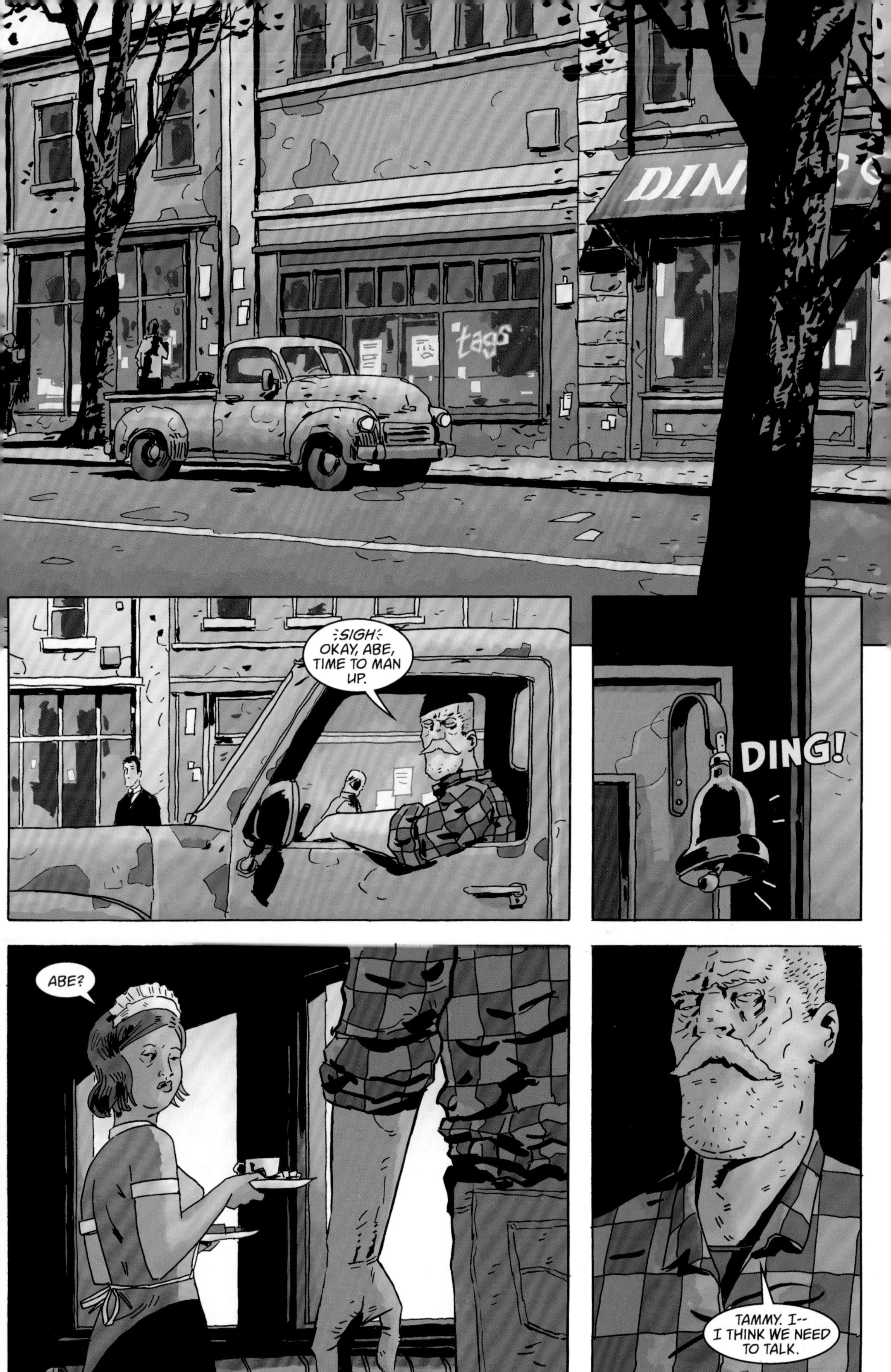
DIN
tags
SIGH
OKAY, ABE, TIME TO MAN UP.
DING!
ABE?
TAMMY. I-- I THINK WE NEED TO TALK.

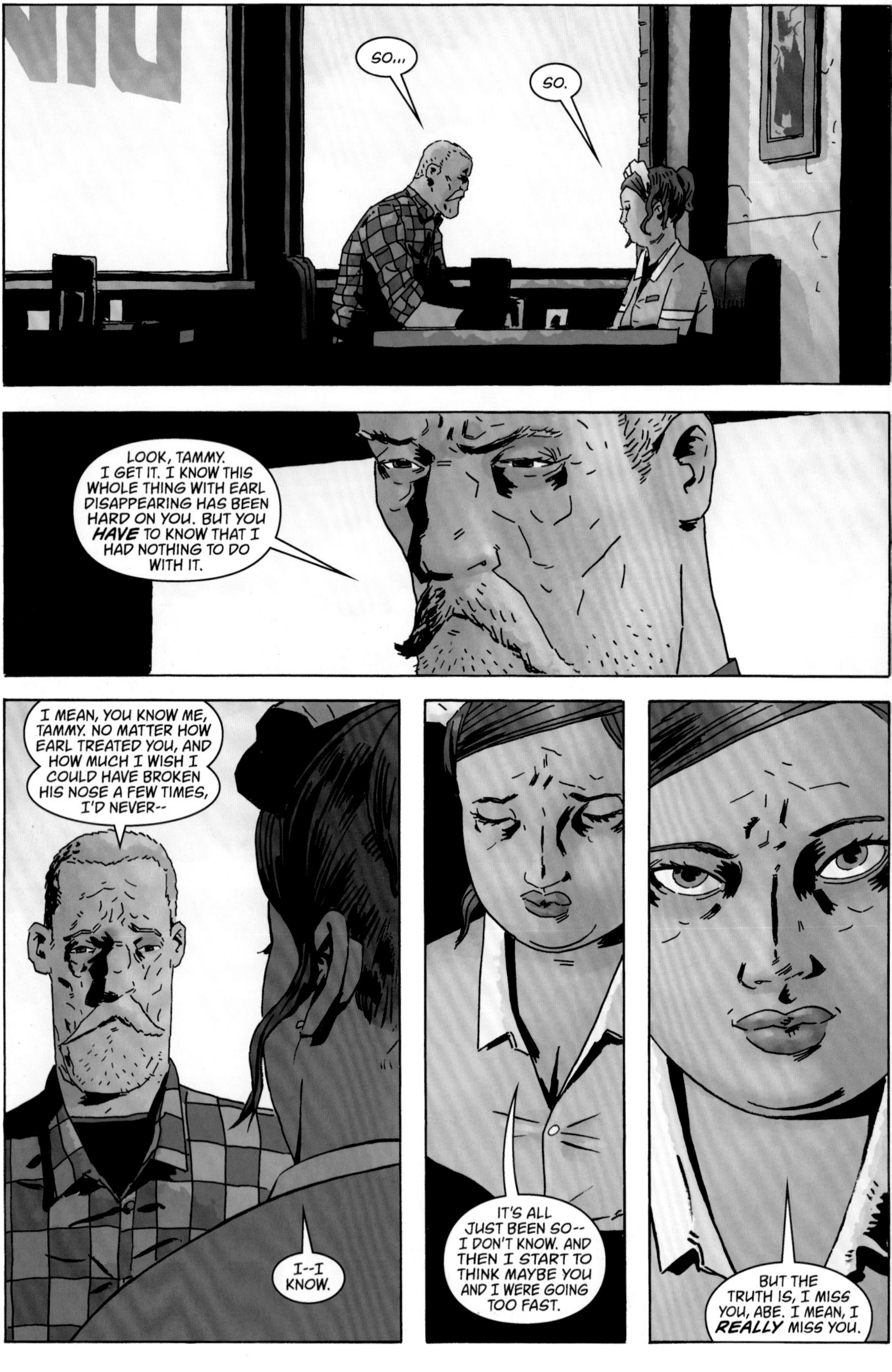
SO...
SO.
LOOK, TAMMY. I GET IT. I KNOW THIS WHOLE THING WITH EARL DISAPPEARING HAS BEEN HARD ON YOU. BUT YOU HAVE TO KNOW THAT I HAD NOTHING TO DO WITH IT.
I MEAN, YOU KNOW ME, TAMMY. NO MATTER HOW EARL TREATED YOU, AND HOW MUCH I WISH I COULD HAVE BROKEN HIS NOSE A FEW TIMES, I'D NEVER--
I--I KNOW.
IT'S ALL JUST BEEN SO-- I DON'T KNOW. AND THEN I START TO THINK MAYBE YOU AND I WERE GOING TOO FAST.
BUT THE TRUTH IS, I MISS YOU, ABE. I MEAN, I REALLY MISS YOU.

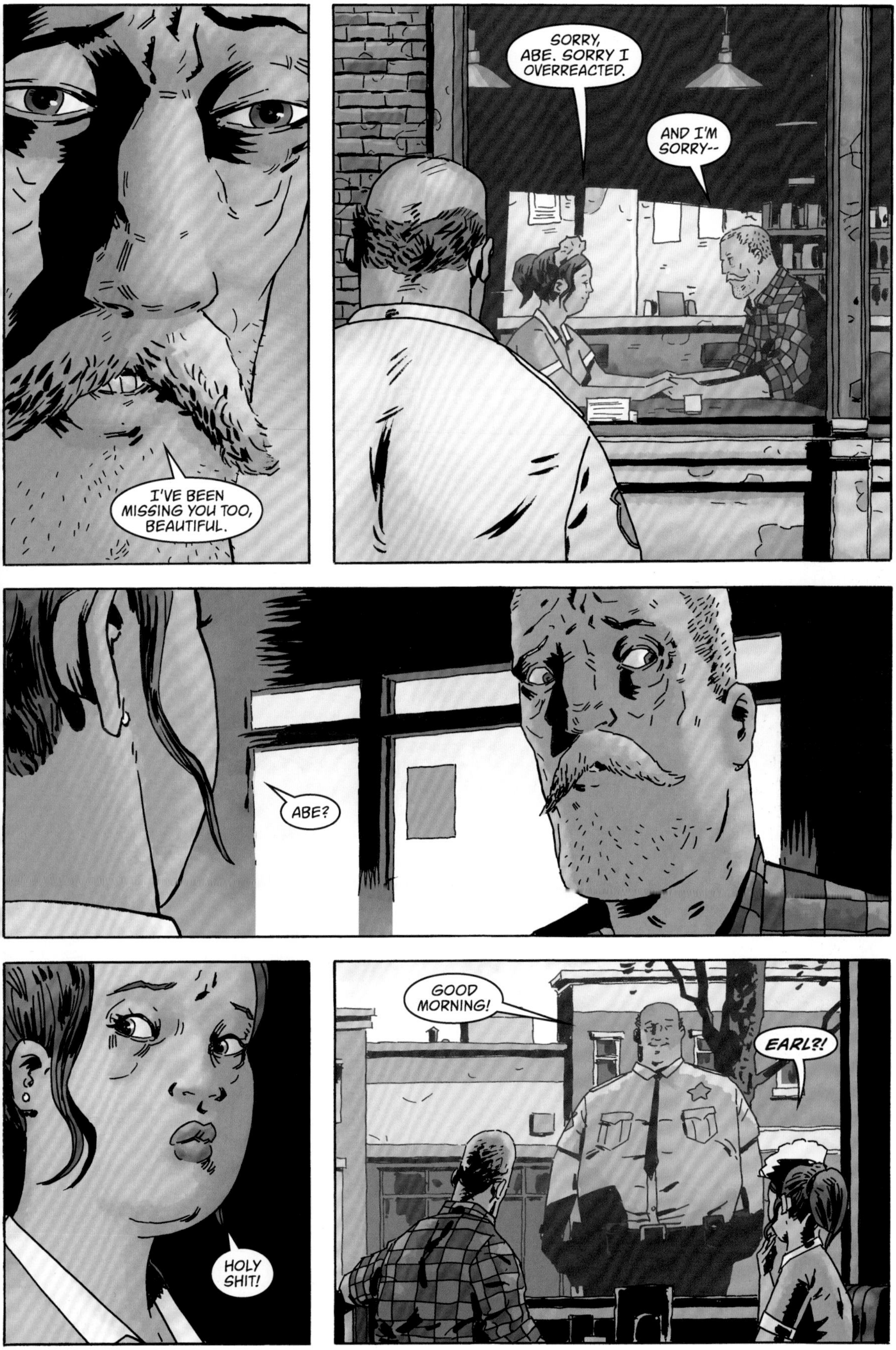
I'VE BEEN MISSING YOU TOO, BEAUTIFUL.
SORRY, ABE. SORRY I OVERREACTED.
AND I'M SORRY--
ABE?
HOLY SHIT!
GOOD MORNING!
EARL?!

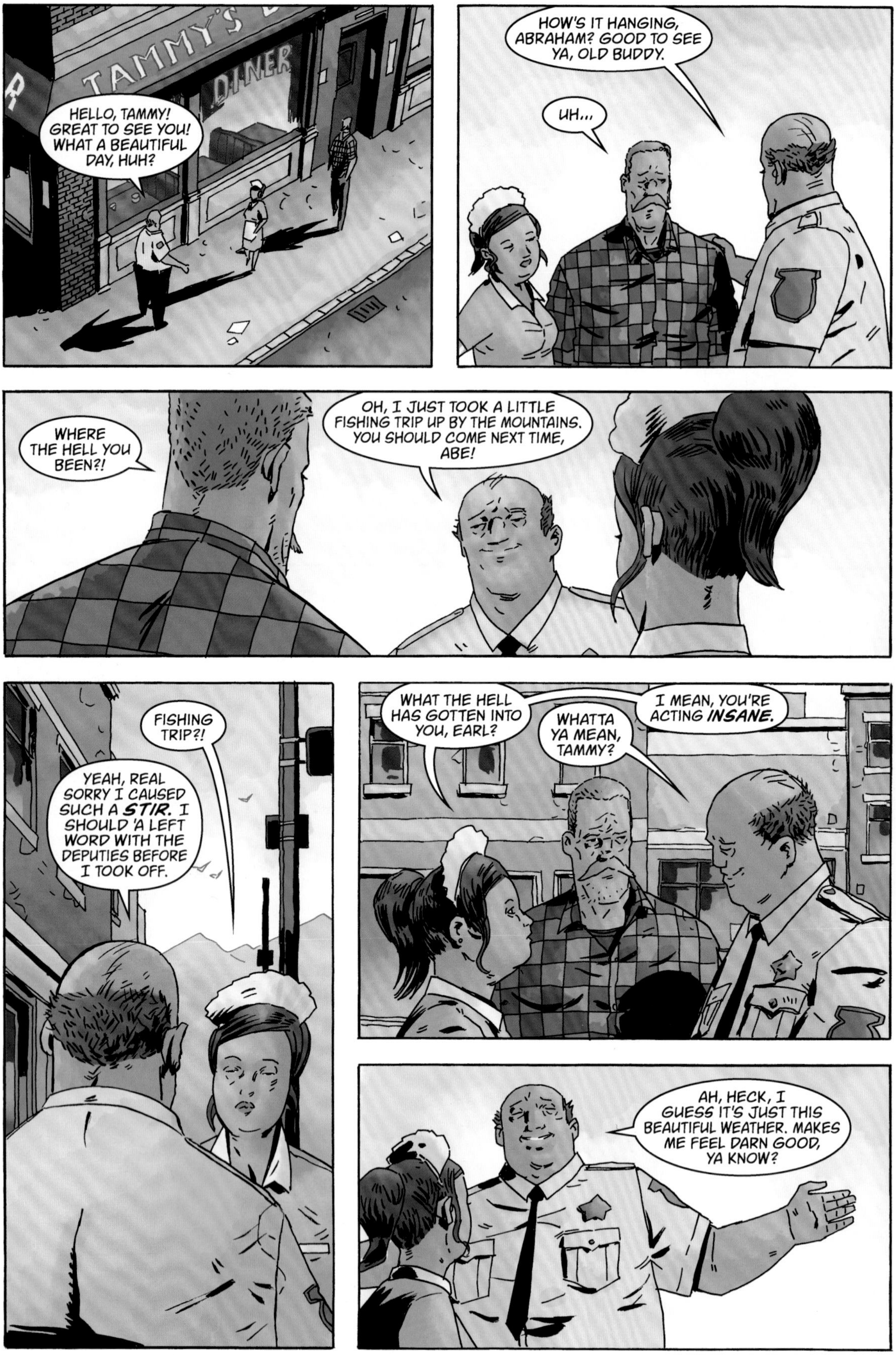
TAMMY'S
DINER
HELLO, TAMMY! GREAT TO SEE YOU! WHAT A BEAUTIFUL DAY, HUH?
HOW'S IT HANGING, ABRAHAM? GOOD TO SEE YA, OLD BUDDY.
UH...
WHERE THE HELL YOU BEEN?!
OH, I JUST TOOK A LITTLE FISHING TRIP UP BY THE MOUNTAINS. YOU SHOULD COME NEXT TIME, ABE!
FISHING TRIP?!
YEAH, REAL SORRY I CAUSED SUCH A STIR. I SHOULD 'A LEFT WORD WITH THE DEPUTIES BEFORE I TOOK OFF.
WHAT THE HELL HAS GOTTEN INTO YOU, EARL?
I MEAN, YOU'RE ACTING INSANE.
WHATTA YA MEAN, TAMMY?
AH, HECK, I GUESS IT'S JUST THIS BEAUTIFUL WEATHER. MAKES ME FEEL DARN GOOD, YA KNOW?

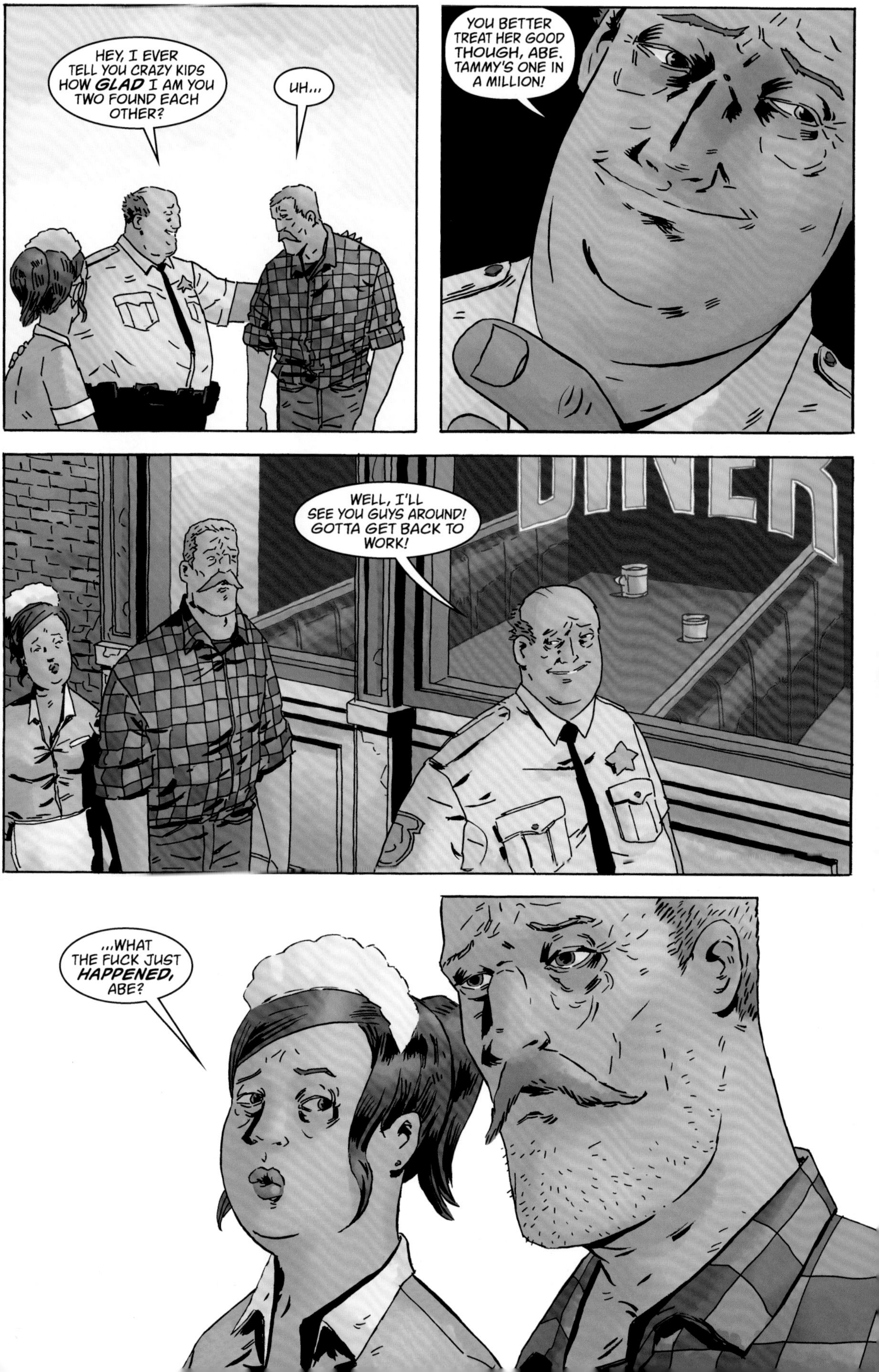
HEY, I EVER TELL YOU CRAZY KIDS HOW GLAD I AM YOU TWO FOUND EACH OTHER?
UH...
YOU BETTER TREAT HER GOOD THOUGH, ABE. TAMMY'S ONE IN A MILLION!
DINER
WELL, I'LL SEE YOU GUYS AROUND! GOTTA GET BACK TO WORK!
...WHAT THE FUCK JUST HAPPENED, ABE?

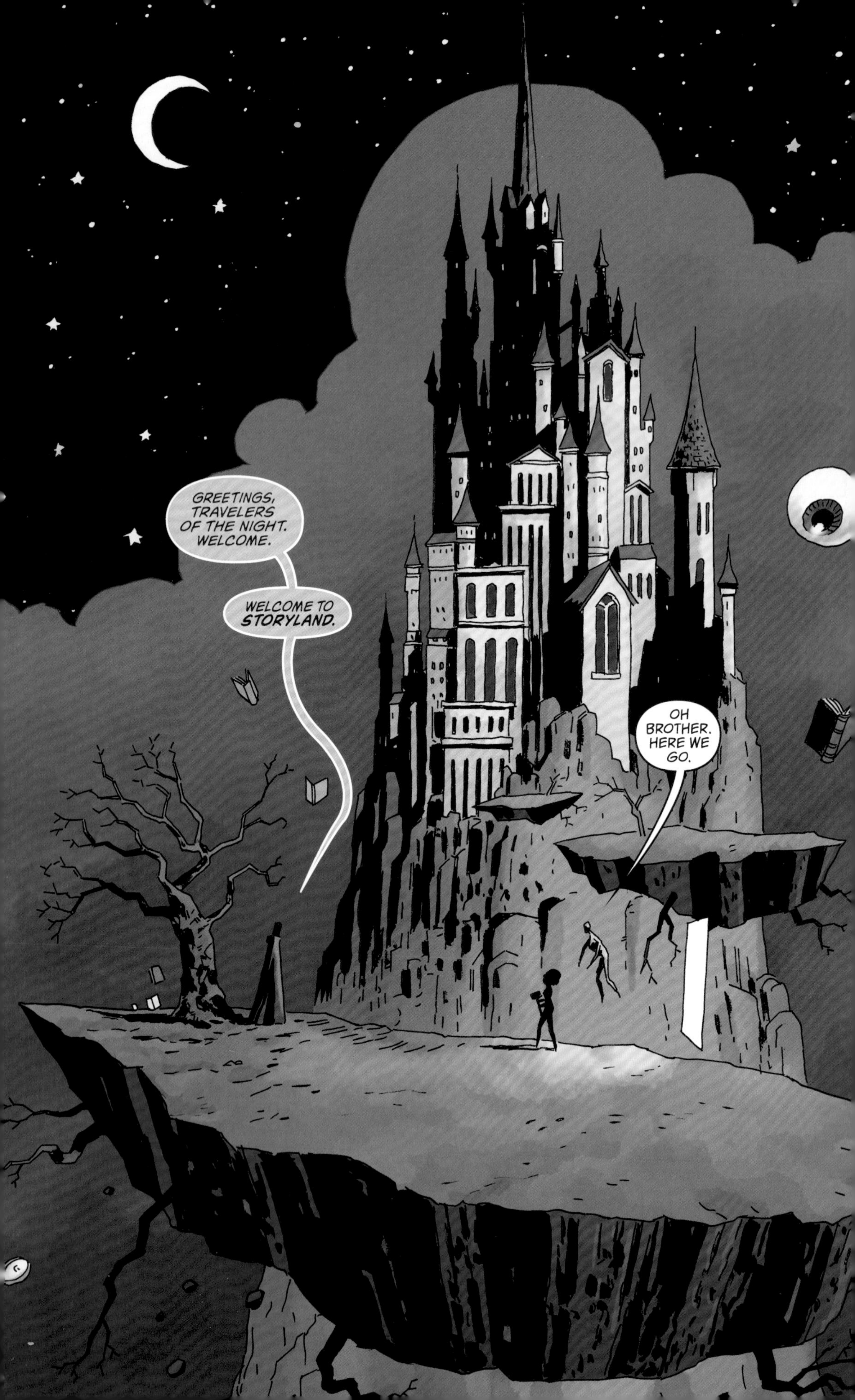
GREETINGS, TRAVELERS OF THE NIGHT. WELCOME.
WELCOME TO STORYLAND.
OH BROTHER. HERE WE GO.

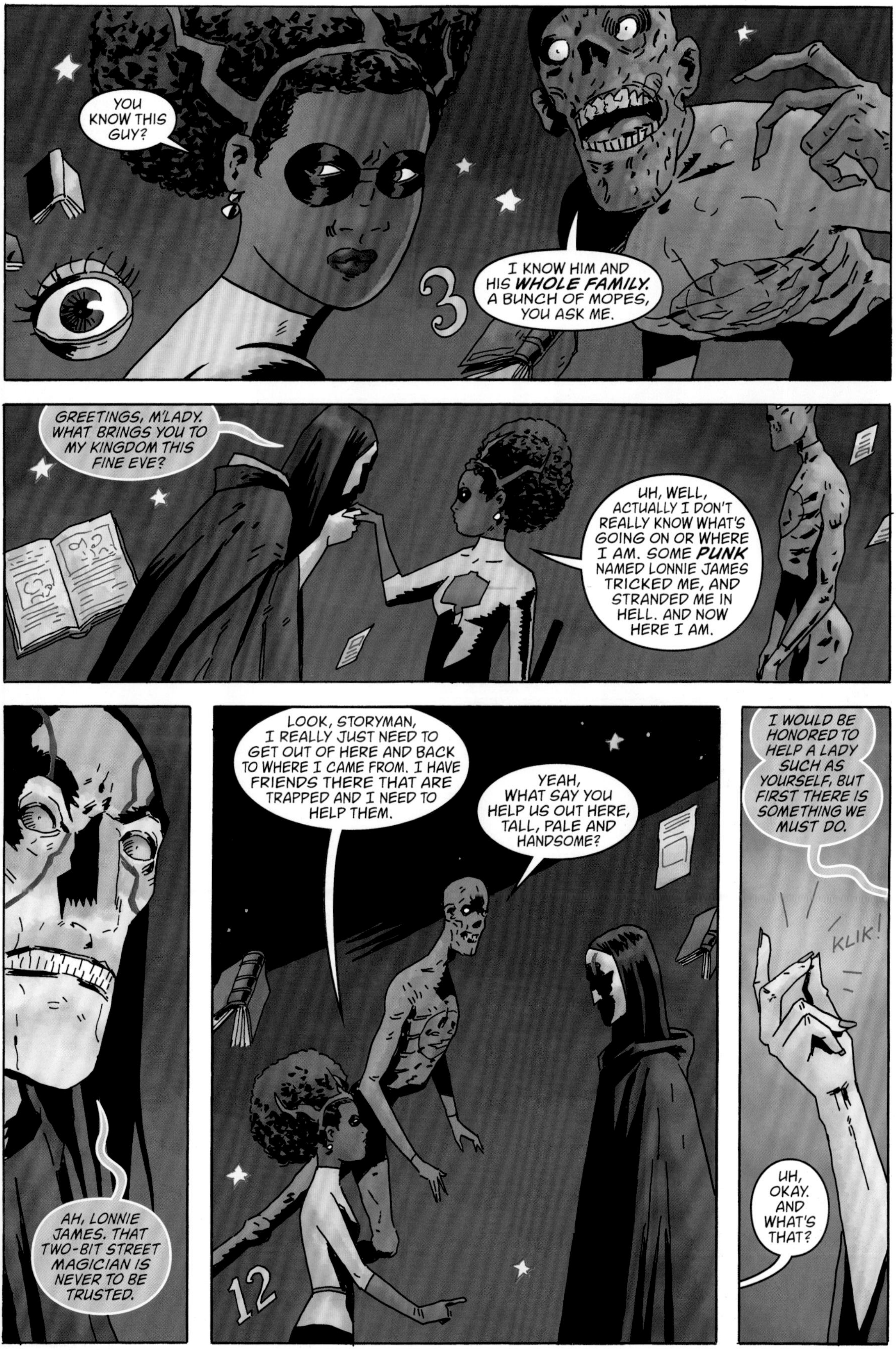
YOU KNOW THIS GUY?
I KNOW HIM AND HIS WHOLE FAMILY. A BUNCH OF MOPES, YOU ASK ME.
GREETINGS, M'LADY. WHAT BRINGS YOU TO MY KINGDOM THIS FINE EVE?
UH, WELL, ACTUALLY I DON'T REALLY KNOW WHAT'S GOING ON OR WHERE I AM. SOME PUNK NAMED LONNIE JAMES TRICKED ME, AND STRANDED ME IN HELL. AND NOW HERE I AM.
AH, LONNIE JAMES. THAT TWO-BIT STREET MAGICIAN IS NEVER TO BE TRUSTED.
LOOK, STORYMAN, I REALLY JUST NEED TO GET OUT OF HERE AND BACK TO WHERE I CAME FROM. I HAVE FRIENDS THERE THAT ARE TRAPPED AND I NEED TO HELP THEM.
YEAH, WHAT SAY YOU HELP US OUT HERE, TALL, PALE AND HANDSOME?
I WOULD BE HONORED TO HELP A LADY SUCH AS YOURSELF, BUT FIRST THERE IS SOMETHING WE MUST DO.
KLIK!
UH, OKAY. AND WHAT'S THAT?

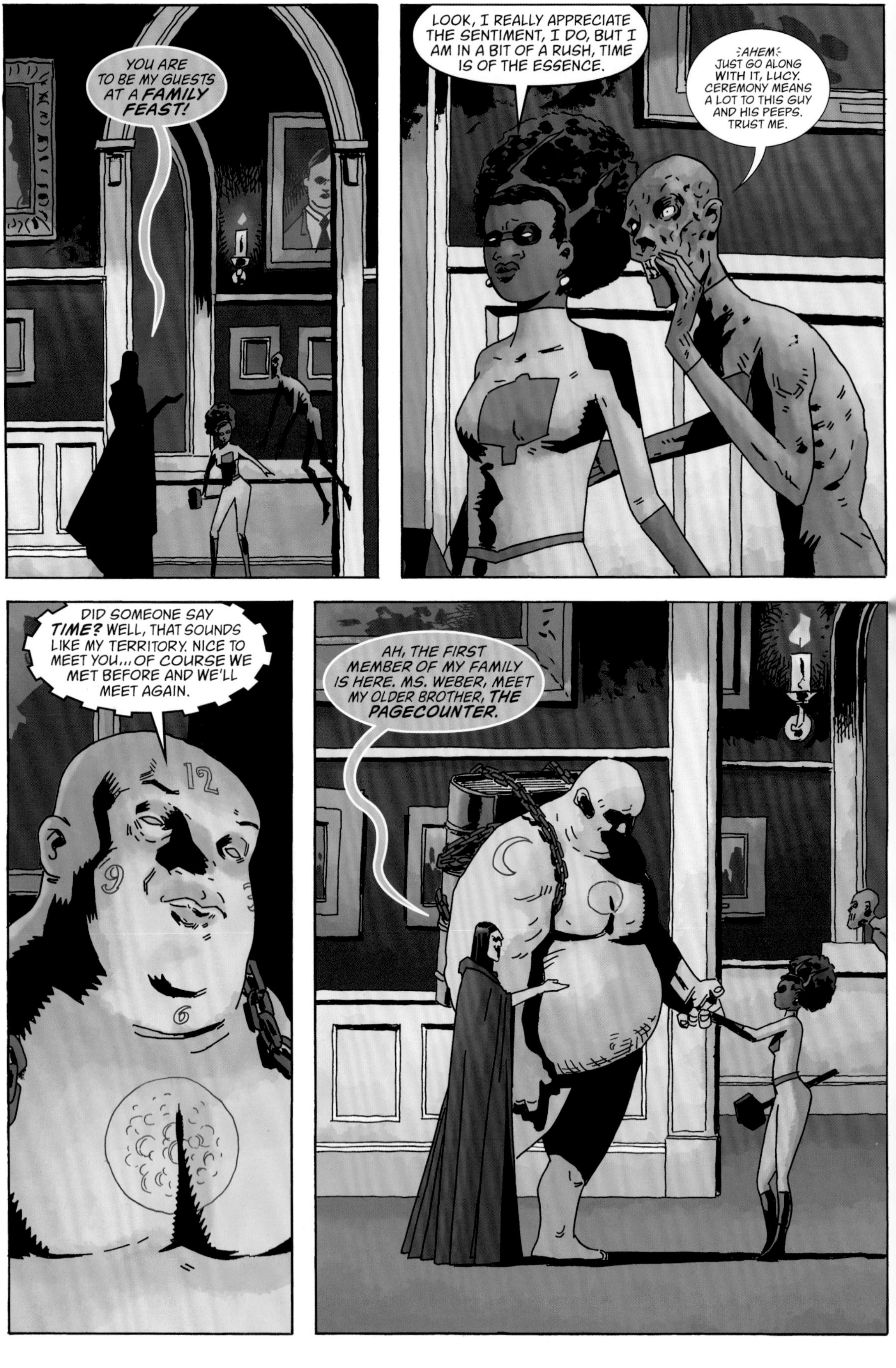
YOU ARE TO BE MY GUESTS AT A FAMILY FEAST!
LOOK, I REALLY APPRECIATE THE SENTIMENT, I DO, BUT I AM IN A BIT OF A RUSH, TIME IS OF THE ESSENCE.
AHEM JUST GO ALONG WITH IT, LUCY. CEREMONY MEANS A LOT TO THIS GUY AND HIS PEEPS. TRUST ME.
DID SOMEONE SAY TIME? WELL, THAT SOUNDS LIKE MY TERRITORY. NICE TO MEET YOU... OF COURSE WE MET BEFORE AND WE'LL MEET AGAIN.
AH, THE FIRST MEMBER OF MY FAMILY IS HERE. MS. WEBER, MEET MY OLDER BROTHER, THE PAGECOUNTER.

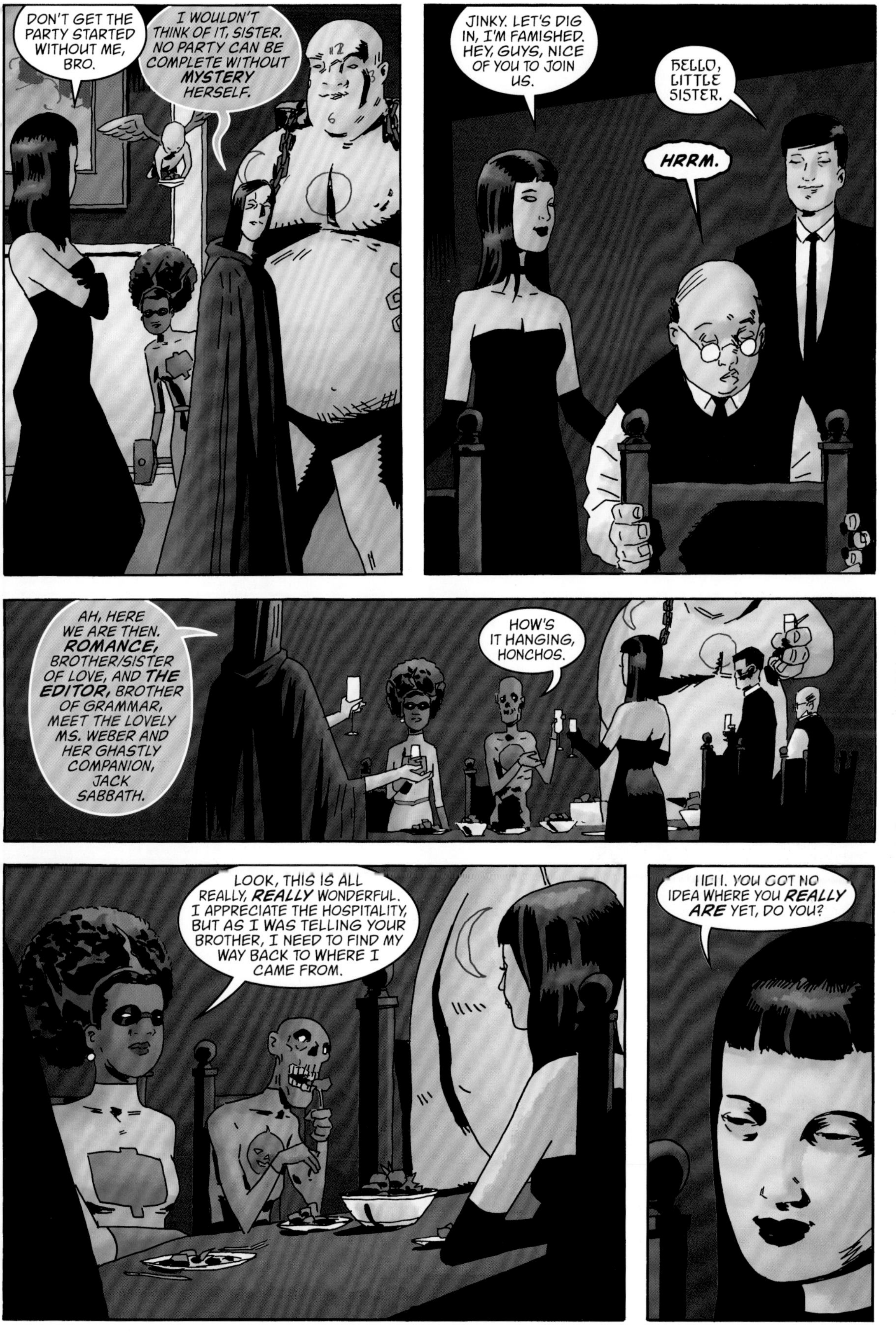
DON'T GET THE PARTY STARTED WITHOUT ME, BRO.
I WOULDN'T THINK OF IT, SISTER. NO PARTY CAN BE COMPLETE WITHOUT MYSTERY HERSELF.
JINKY. LET'S DIG IN, I'M FAMISHED. HEY, GUYS, NICE OF YOU TO JOIN US.
HELLO, LITTLE SISTER.
HRRM.
AH, HERE WE ARE THEN. ROMANCE, BROTHER/SISTER OF LOVE, AND THE EDITOR, BROTHER OF GRAMMAR, MEET THE LOVELY MS. WEBER AND HER GHASTLY COMPANION, JACK SABBATH.
HOW'S IT HANGING, HONCHOS.
LOOK, THIS IS ALL REALLY, REALLY WONDERFUL. I APPRECIATE THE HOSPITALITY, BUT AS I WAS TELLING YOUR BROTHER, I NEED TO FIND MY WAY BACK TO WHERE I CAME FROM.
HEH. YOU GOT NO IDEA WHERE YOU REALLY ARE YET, DO YOU?

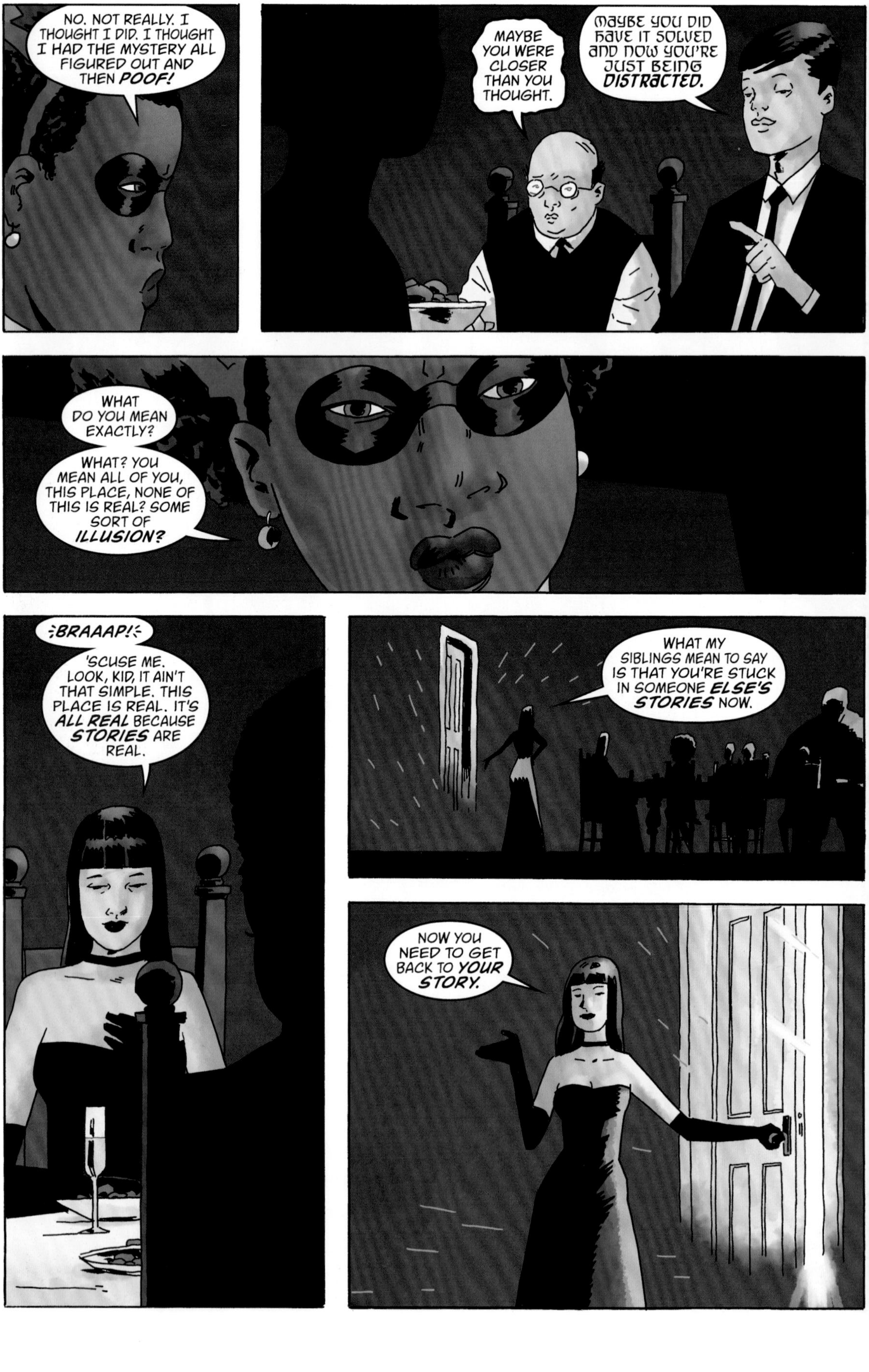
NO. NOT REALLY. I THOUGHT I DID. I THOUGHT I HAD THE MYSTERY ALL FIGURED OUT AND THEN *POOF!*
MAYBE YOU WERE CLOSER THAN YOU THOUGHT.
MAYBE YOU DID HAVE IT SOLVED AND NOW YOU'RE JUST BEING *DISTRACTED.*
WHAT DO YOU MEAN EXACTLY?
WHAT? YOU MEAN ALL OF YOU, THIS PLACE, NONE OF THIS IS REAL? SOME SORT OF *ILLUSION?*
BRAAAP!
'SCUSE ME. LOOK, KID, IT AIN'T THAT SIMPLE. THIS PLACE IS REAL. IT'S *ALL REAL* BECAUSE *STORIES* ARE REAL.
WHAT MY SIBLINGS MEAN TO SAY IS THAT YOU'RE STUCK IN SOMEONE *ELSE'S STORIES* NOW.
NOW YOU NEED TO GET BACK TO *YOUR STORY.*

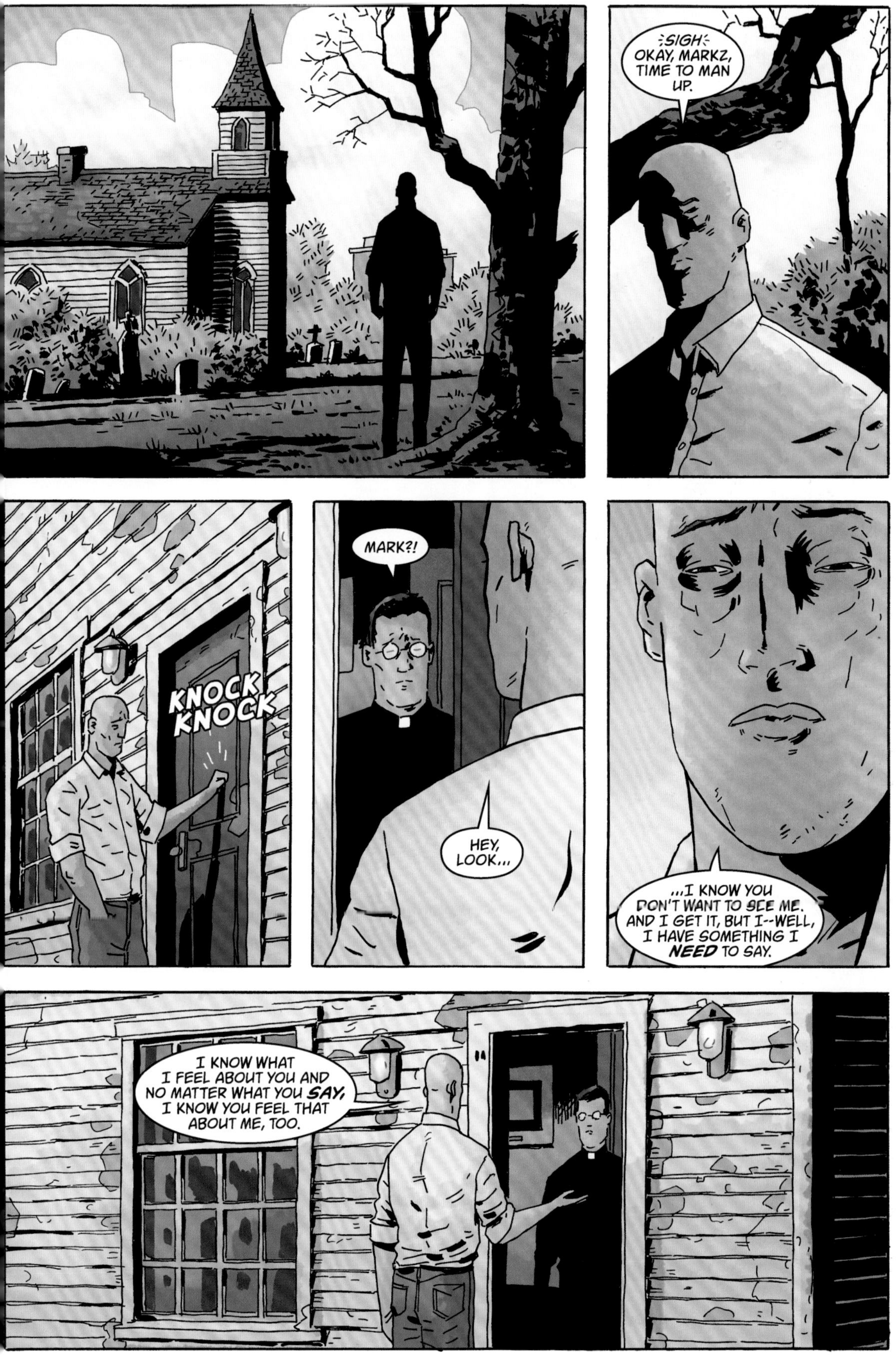
SIGH
OKAY, MARKZ, TIME TO MAN UP.
KNOCK KNOCK
MARK?!
HEY, LOOK...
...I KNOW YOU DON'T WANT TO SEE ME. AND I GET IT, BUT I--WELL, I HAVE SOMETHING I NEED TO SAY.
I KNOW WHAT I FEEL ABOUT YOU AND NO MATTER WHAT YOU SAY, I KNOW YOU FEEL THAT ABOUT ME, TOO.

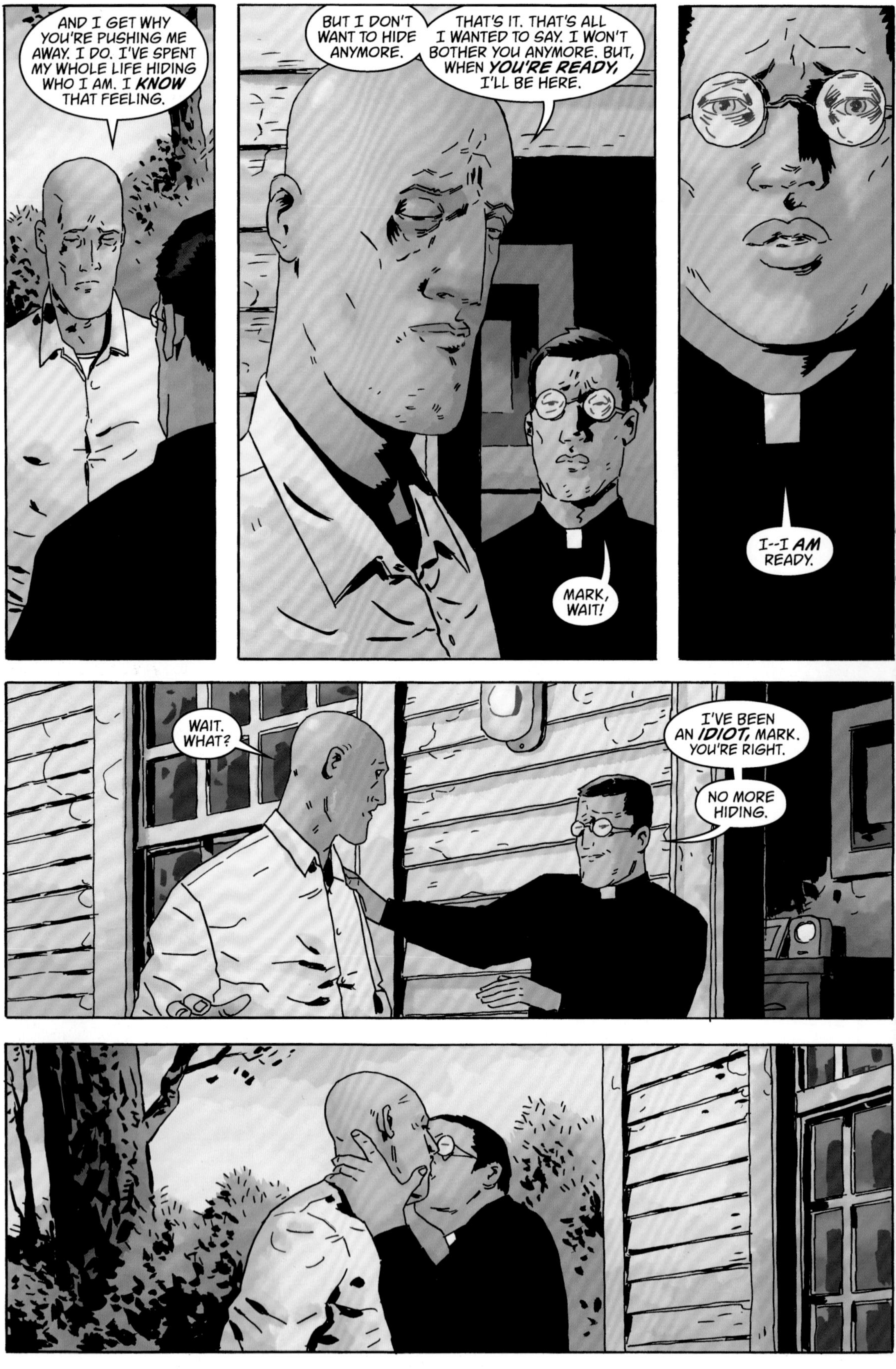
AND I GET WHY YOU'RE PUSHING ME AWAY. I DO. I'VE SPENT MY WHOLE LIFE HIDING WHO I AM. I **KNOW** THAT FEELING.
BUT I DON'T WANT TO HIDE ANYMORE.
THAT'S IT. THAT'S ALL I WANTED TO SAY. I WON'T BOTHER YOU ANYMORE. BUT, WHEN ***YOU'RE READY,*** I'LL BE HERE.
MARK, WAIT!
I--I ***AM*** READY.
WAIT. WHAT?
I'VE BEEN AN ***IDIOT,*** MARK. YOU'RE RIGHT.
NO MORE HIDING.

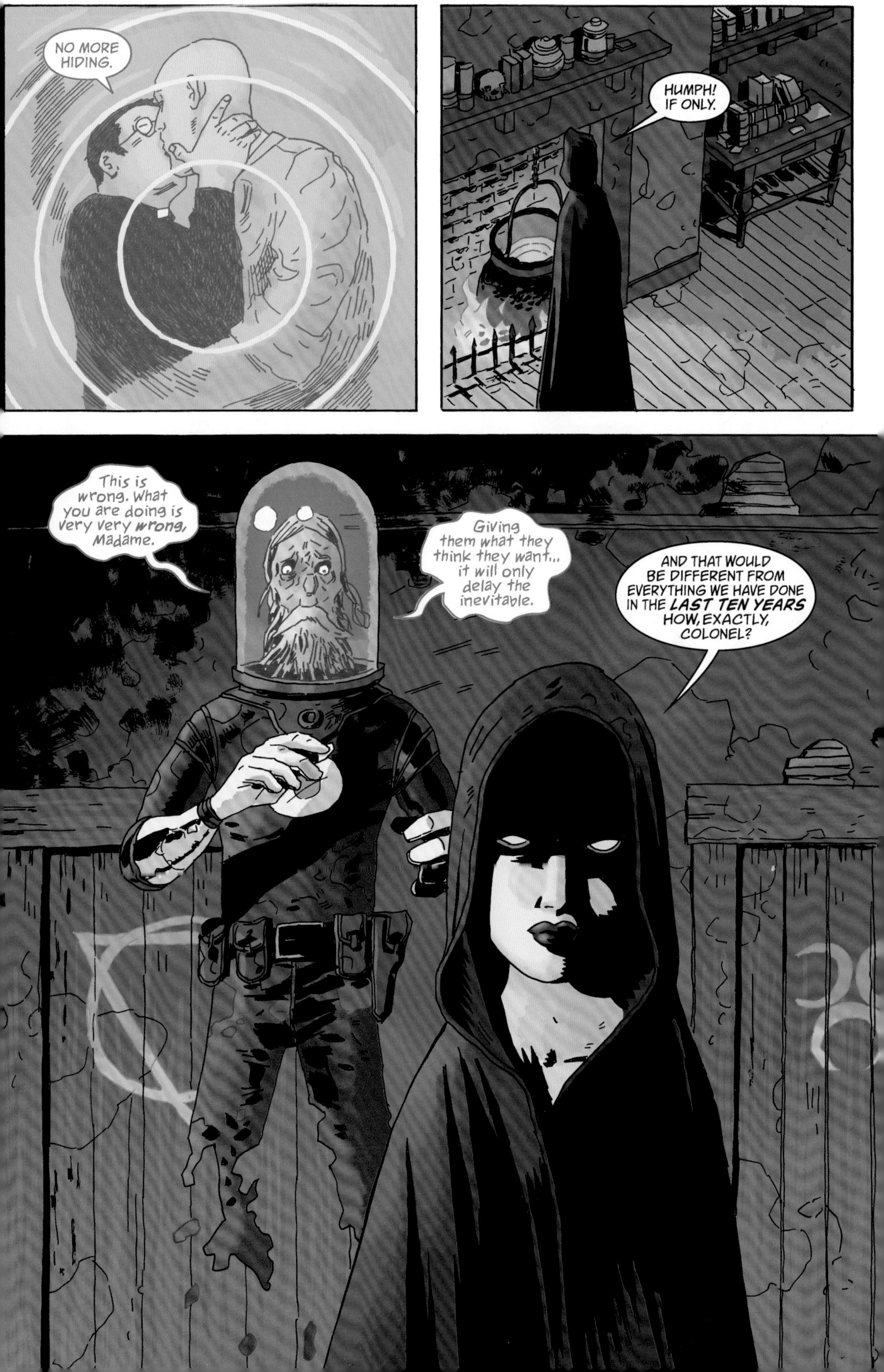
NO MORE HIDING.
HUMPH! IF ONLY.
This is wrong. What you are doing is very very wrong, Madame.
Giving them what they think they want... it will only delay the inevitable.
AND THAT WOULD BE DIFFERENT FROM EVERYTHING WE HAVE DONE IN THE LAST TEN YEARS HOW, EXACTLY, COLONEL?

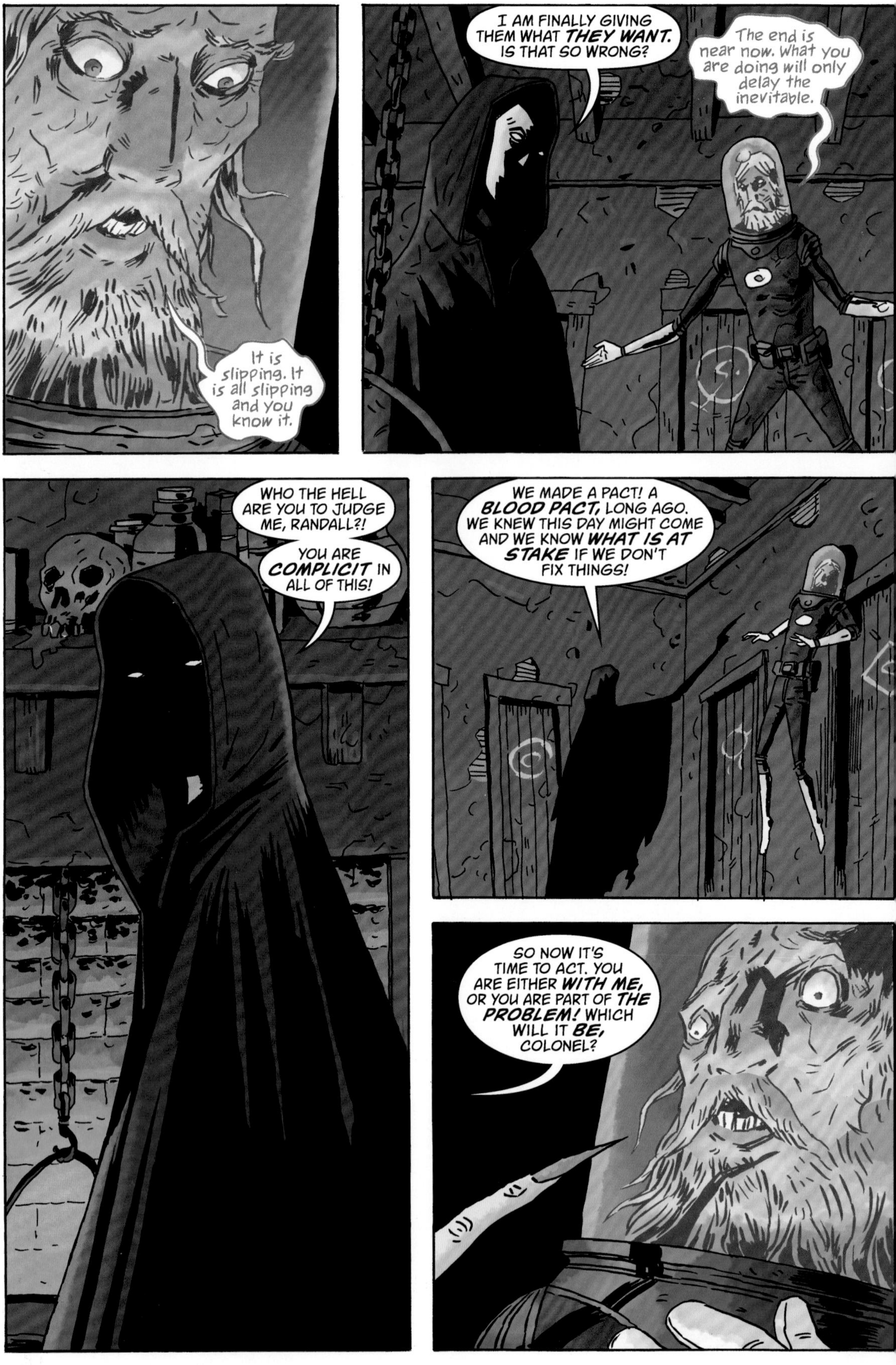
It is slipping. It is all slipping and you know it.
I AM FINALLY GIVING THEM WHAT THEY WANT. IS THAT SO WRONG?
The end is near now. What you are doing will only delay the inevitable.
WHO THE HELL ARE YOU TO JUDGE ME, RANDALL?!
YOU ARE COMPLICIT IN ALL OF THIS!
WE MADE A PACT! A BLOOD PACT, LONG AGO. WE KNEW THIS DAY MIGHT COME AND WE KNOW WHAT IS AT STAKE IF WE DON'T FIX THINGS!
SO NOW IT'S TIME TO ACT. YOU ARE EITHER WITH ME, OR YOU ARE PART OF THE PROBLEM! WHICH WILL IT BE, COLONEL?

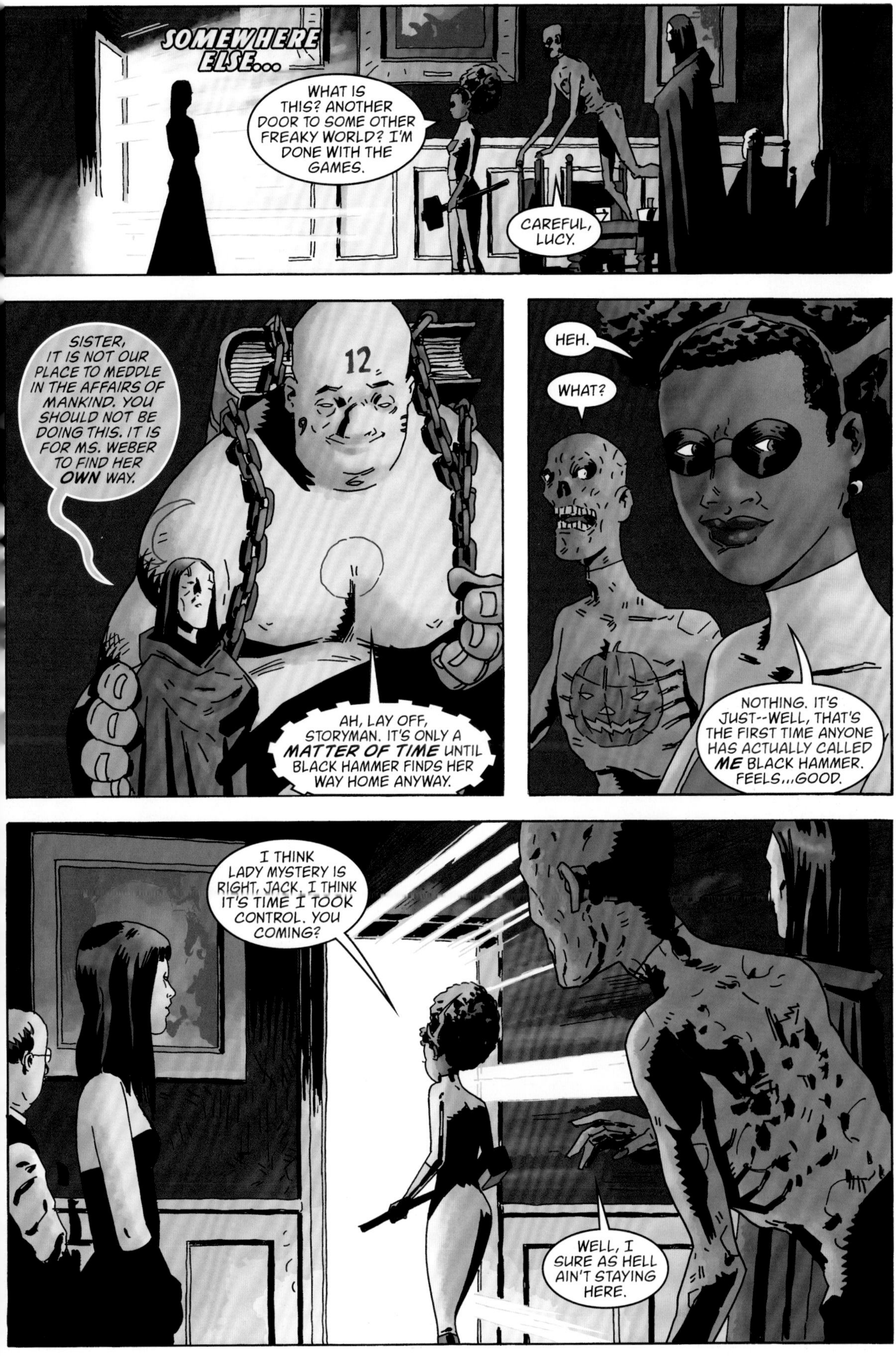
SOMEWHERE ELSE...
WHAT IS THIS? ANOTHER DOOR TO SOME OTHER FREAKY WORLD? I'M DONE WITH THE GAMES.
CAREFUL, LUCY.
SISTER, IT IS NOT OUR PLACE TO MEDDLE IN THE AFFAIRS OF MANKIND. YOU SHOULD NOT BE DOING THIS. IT IS FOR MS. WEBER TO FIND HER OWN WAY.
AH, LAY OFF, STORYMAN. IT'S ONLY A MATTER OF TIME UNTIL BLACK HAMMER FINDS HER WAY HOME ANYWAY.
HEH.
WHAT?
NOTHING. IT'S JUST--WELL, THAT'S THE FIRST TIME ANYONE HAS ACTUALLY CALLED ME BLACK HAMMER. FEELS...GOOD.
I THINK LADY MYSTERY IS RIGHT, JACK. I THINK IT'S TIME I TOOK CONTROL. YOU COMING?
WELL, I SURE AS HELL AIN'T STAYING HERE.

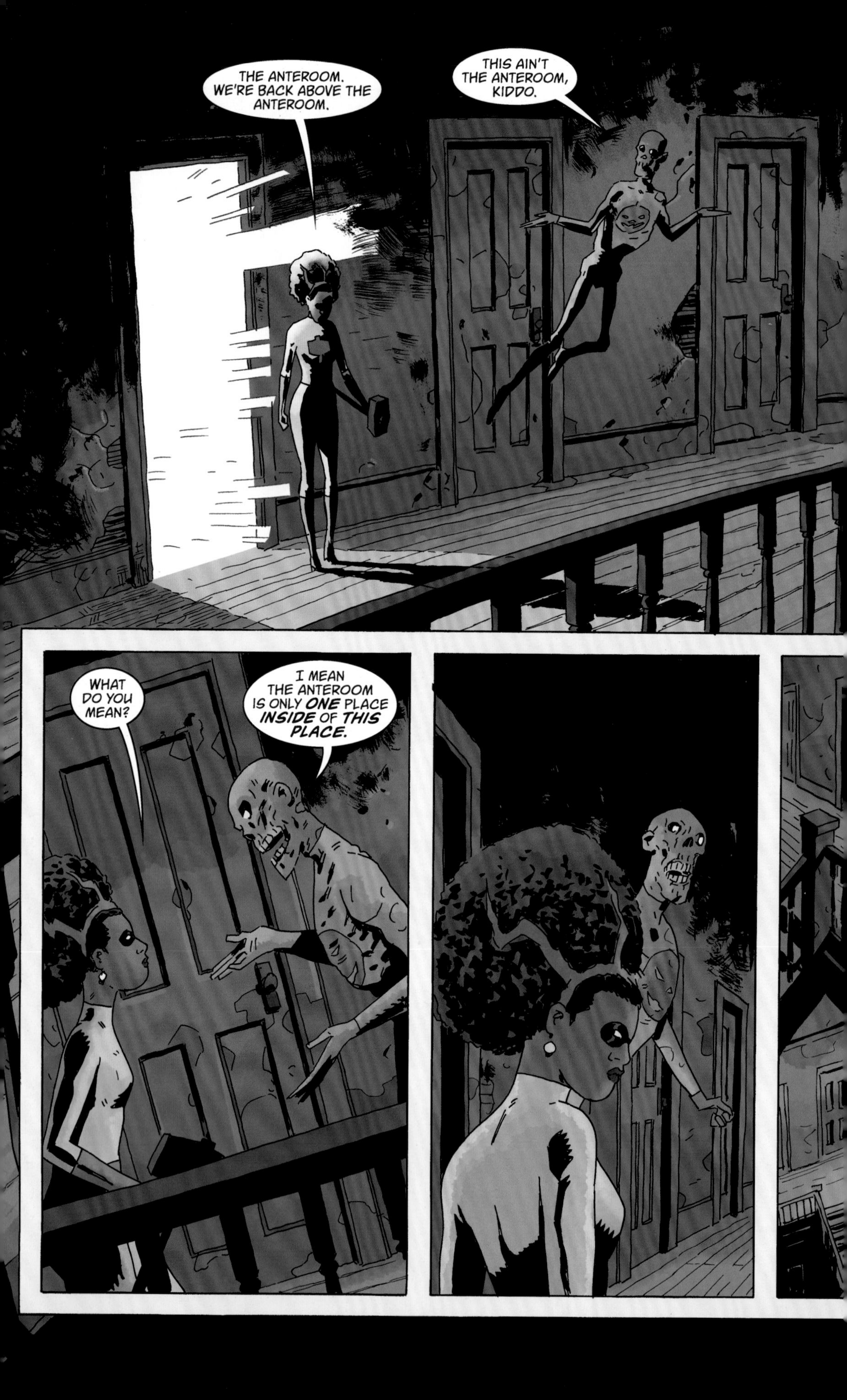
THE ANTEROOM. WE'RE BACK ABOVE THE ANTEROOM.
THIS AIN'T THE ANTEROOM, KIDDO.
WHAT DO YOU MEAN?
I MEAN THE ANTEROOM IS ONLY ONE PLACE INSIDE OF THIS PLACE.

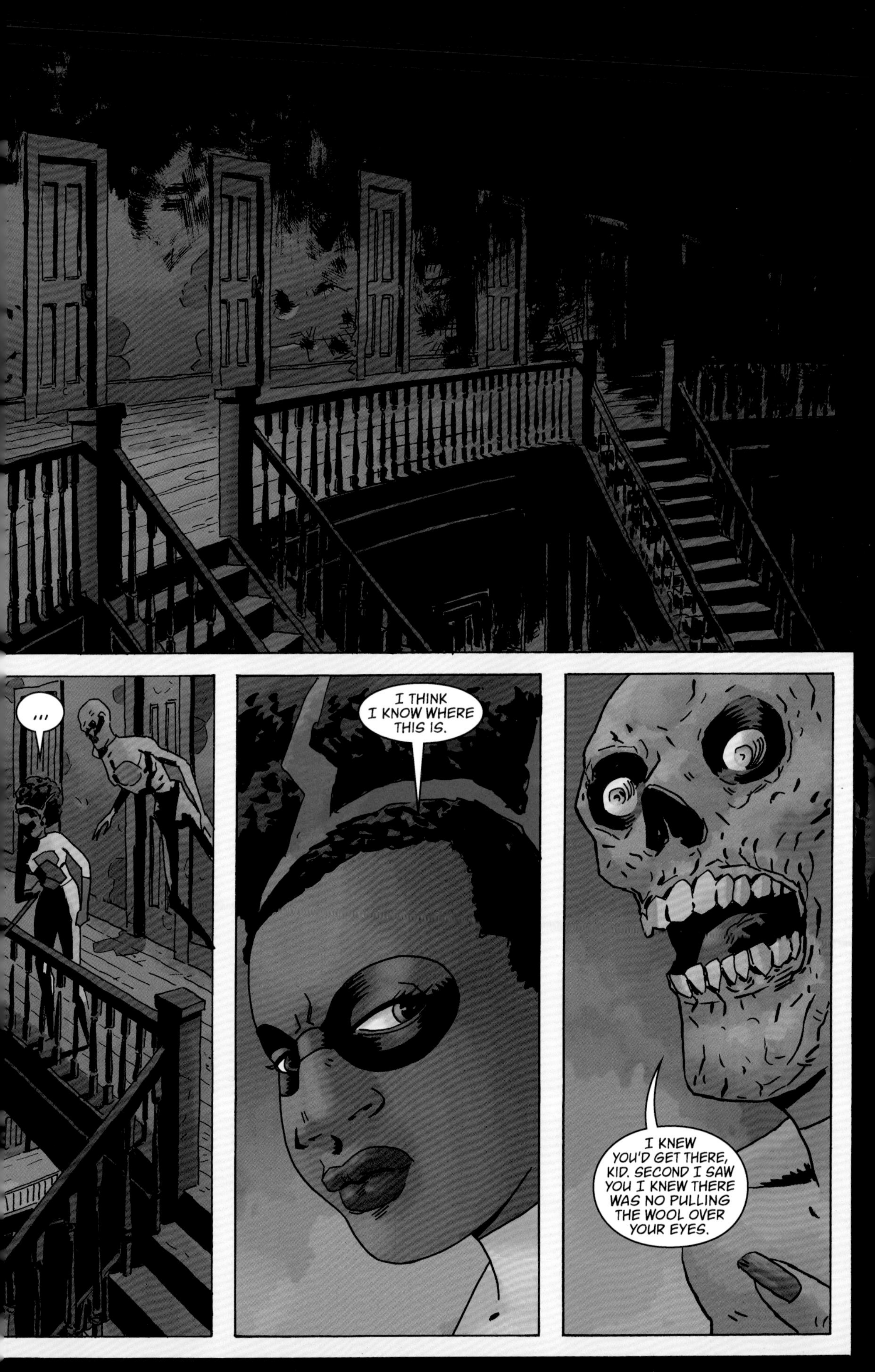
...
I THINK I KNOW WHERE THIS IS.
I KNEW YOU'D GET THERE, KID. SECOND I SAW YOU I KNEW THERE WAS NO PULLING THE WOOL OVER YOUR EYES.

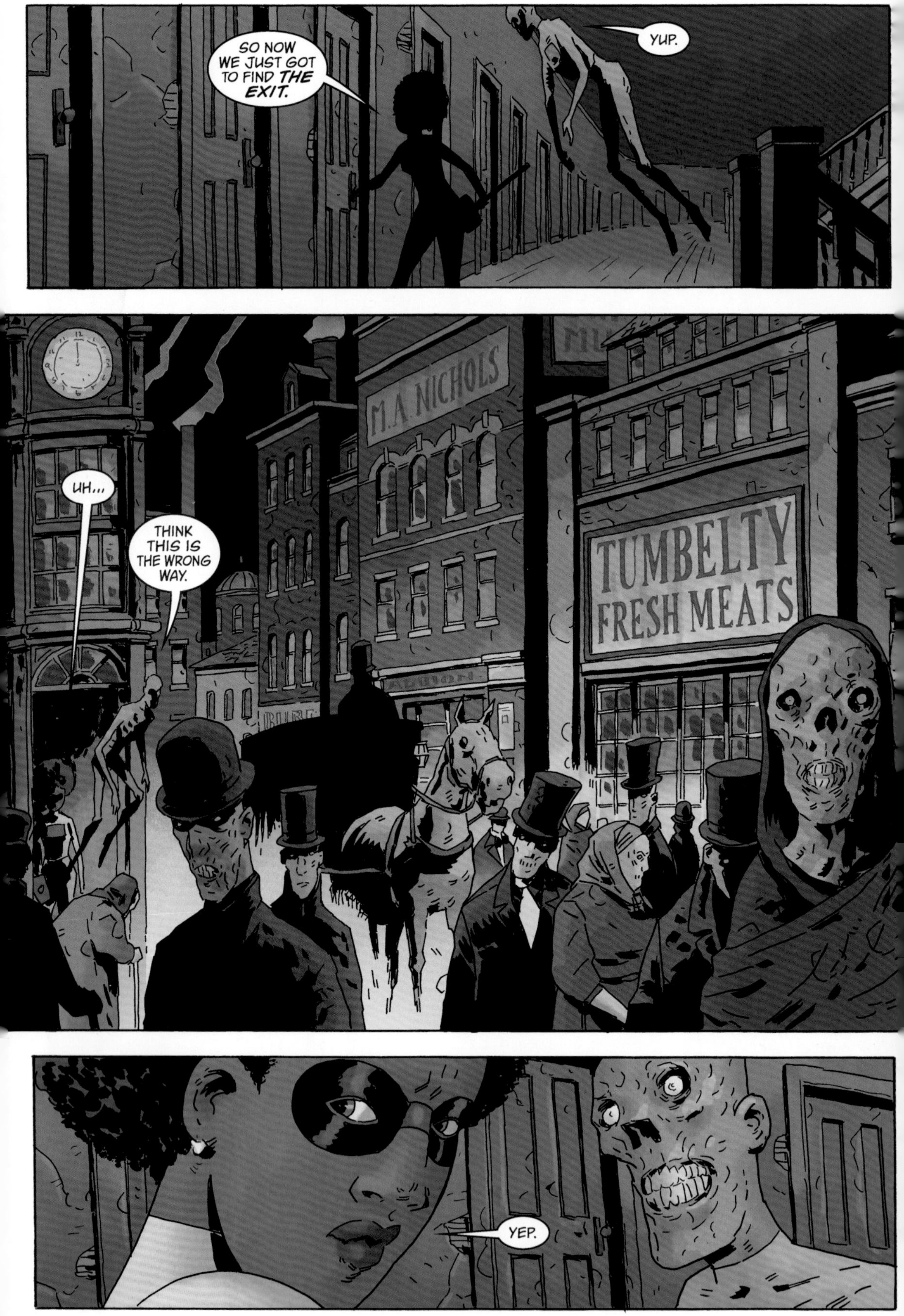
SO NOW WE JUST GOT TO FIND THE EXIT.
YUP.
M.A. NICHOLS
TUMBELTY FRESH MEATS
UH...
THINK THIS IS THE WRONG WAY.
YEP.

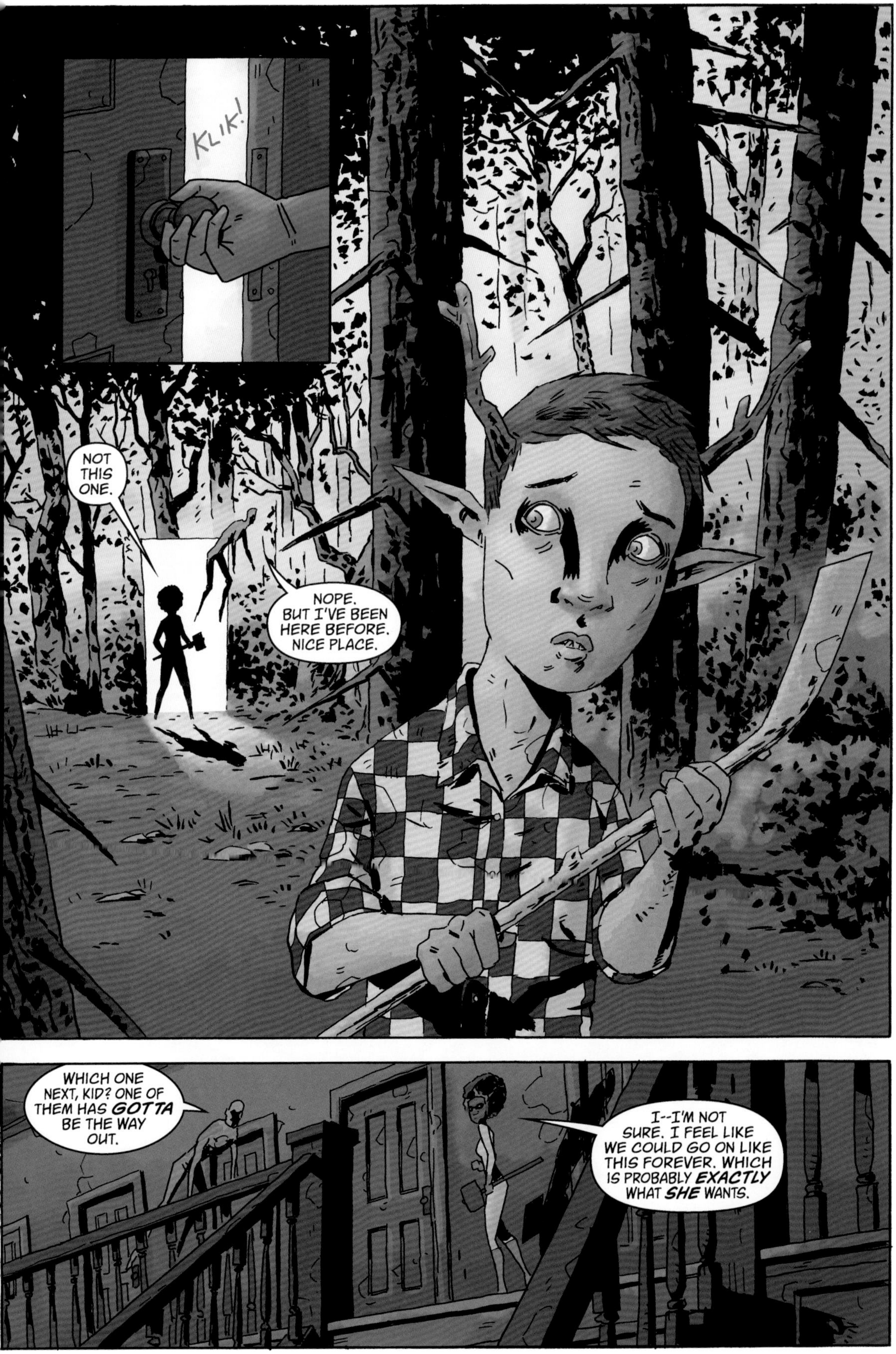
KLIK!
NOT THIS ONE.
NOPE. BUT I'VE BEEN HERE BEFORE. NICE PLACE.
WHICH ONE NEXT, KID? ONE OF THEM HAS GOTTA BE THE WAY OUT.
I--I'M NOT SURE. I FEEL LIKE WE COULD GO ON LIKE THIS FOREVER. WHICH IS PROBABLY EXACTLY WHAT SHE WANTS.

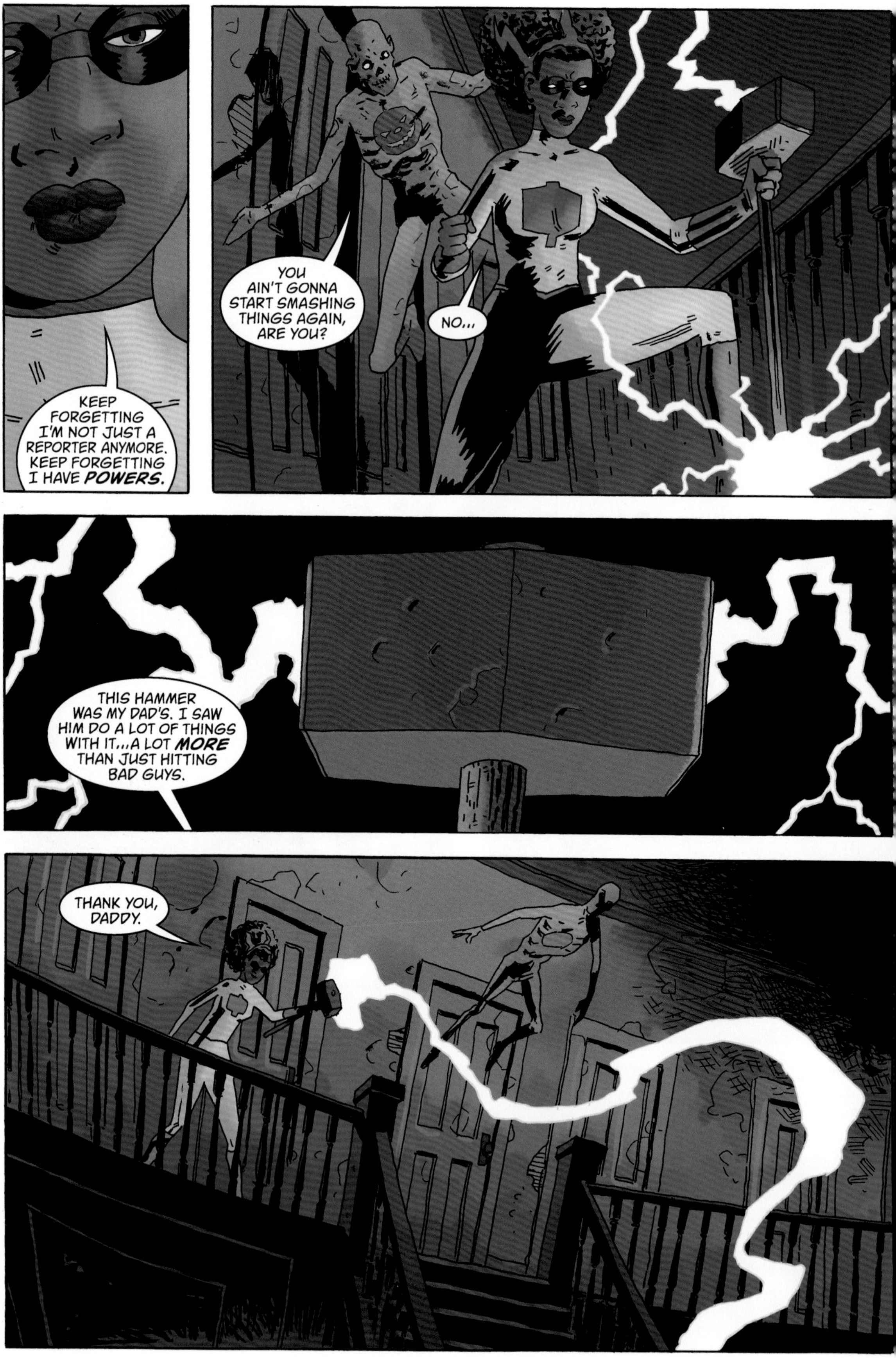
KEEP FORGETTING I'M NOT JUST A REPORTER ANYMORE. KEEP FORGETTING I HAVE **POWERS**.
YOU AIN'T GONNA START SMASHING THINGS AGAIN, ARE YOU?
NO...
THIS HAMMER WAS MY DAD'S. I SAW HIM DO A LOT OF THINGS WITH IT...A LOT **MORE** THAN JUST HITTING BAD GUYS.
THANK YOU, DADDY.

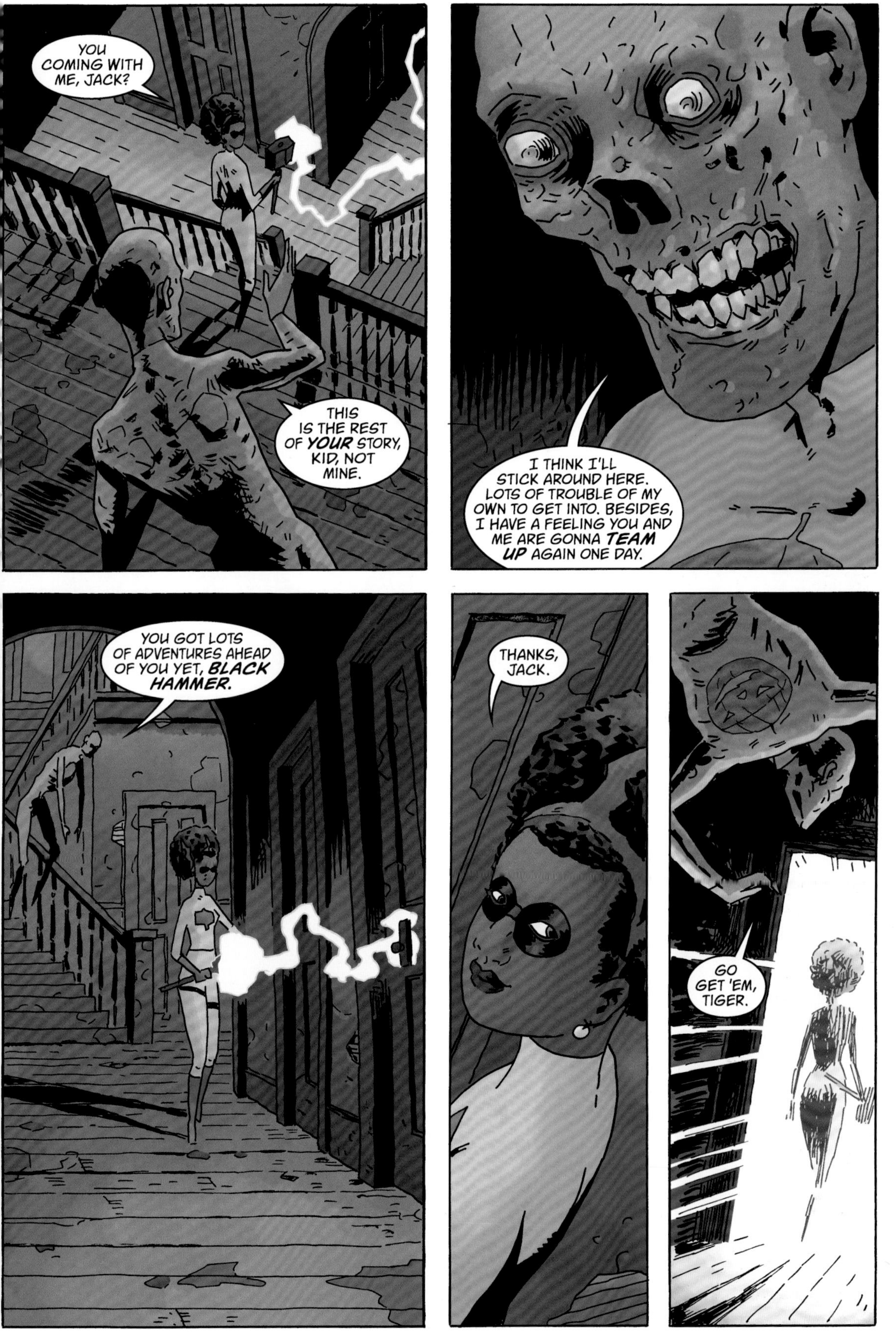
YOU COMING WITH ME, JACK?
THIS IS THE REST OF YOUR STORY, KID, NOT MINE.
I THINK I'LL STICK AROUND HERE. LOTS OF TROUBLE OF MY OWN TO GET INTO. BESIDES, I HAVE A FEELING YOU AND ME ARE GONNA TEAM UP AGAIN ONE DAY.
YOU GOT LOTS OF ADVENTURES AHEAD OF YOU YET, BLACK HAMMER.
THANKS, JACK.
GO GET 'EM, TIGER.

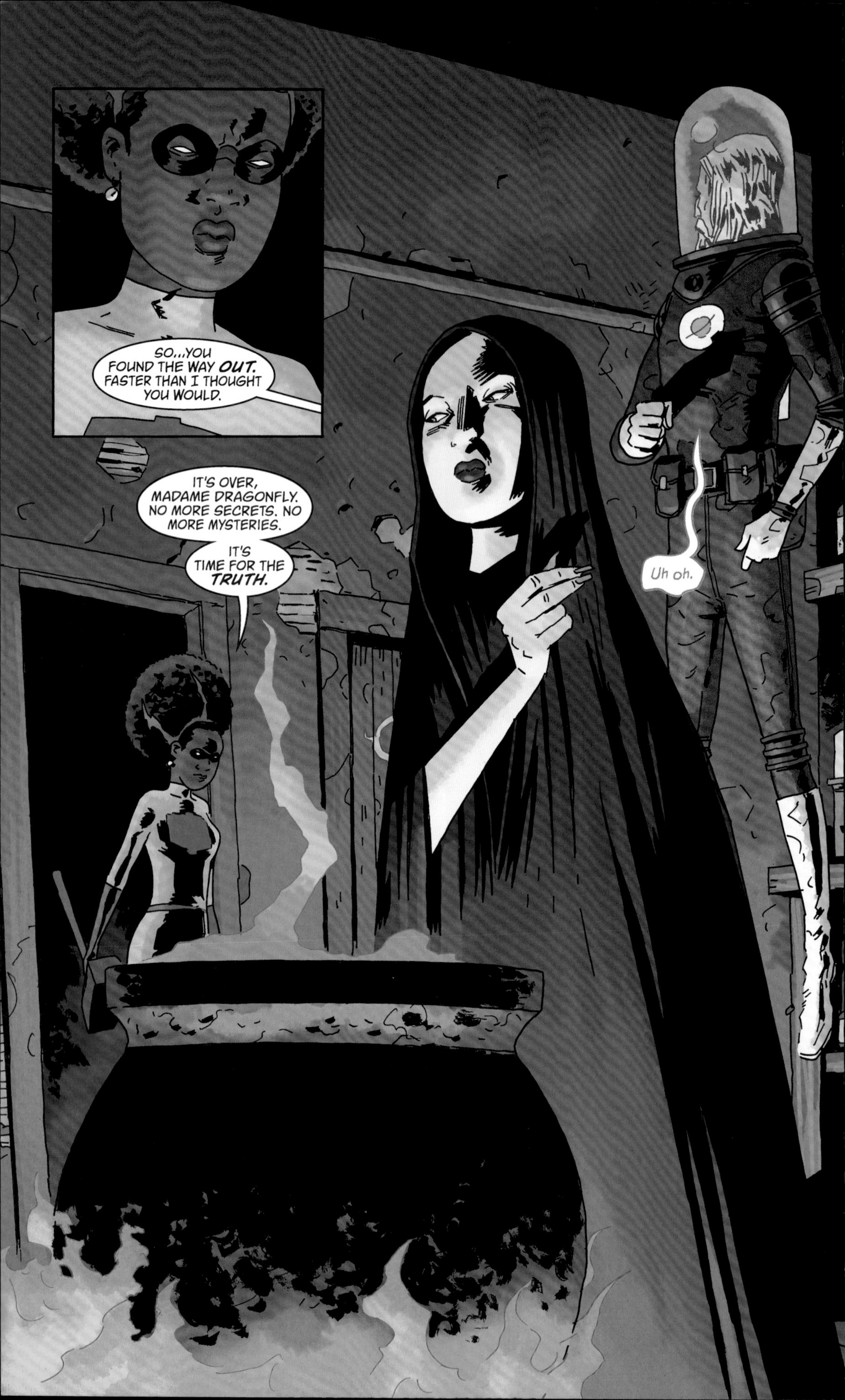
SO...YOU FOUND THE WAY OUT. FASTER THAN I THOUGHT YOU WOULD.
IT'S OVER, MADAME DRAGONFLY. NO MORE SECRETS. NO MORE MYSTERIES.
IT'S TIME FOR THE TRUTH.
Uh oh.

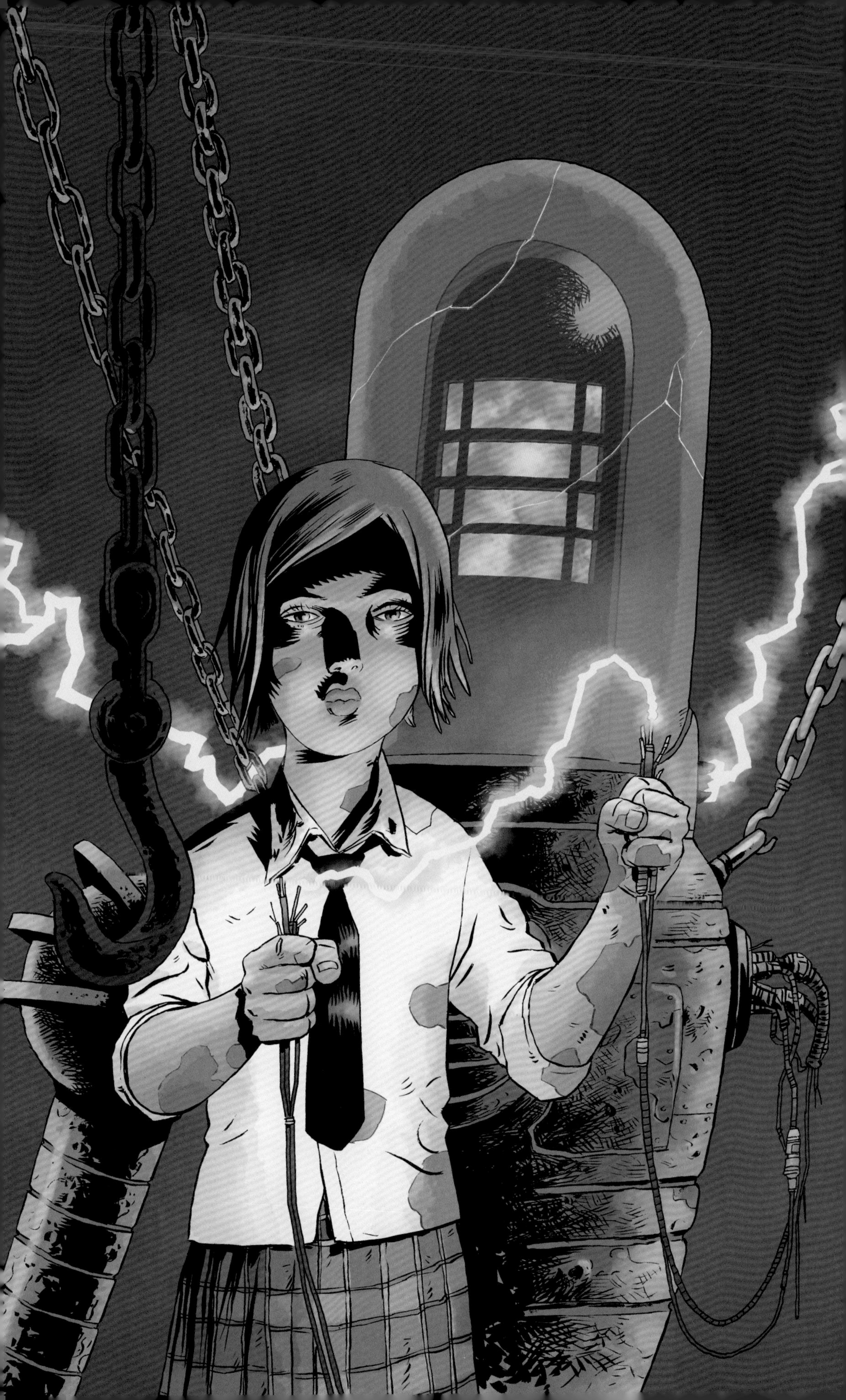

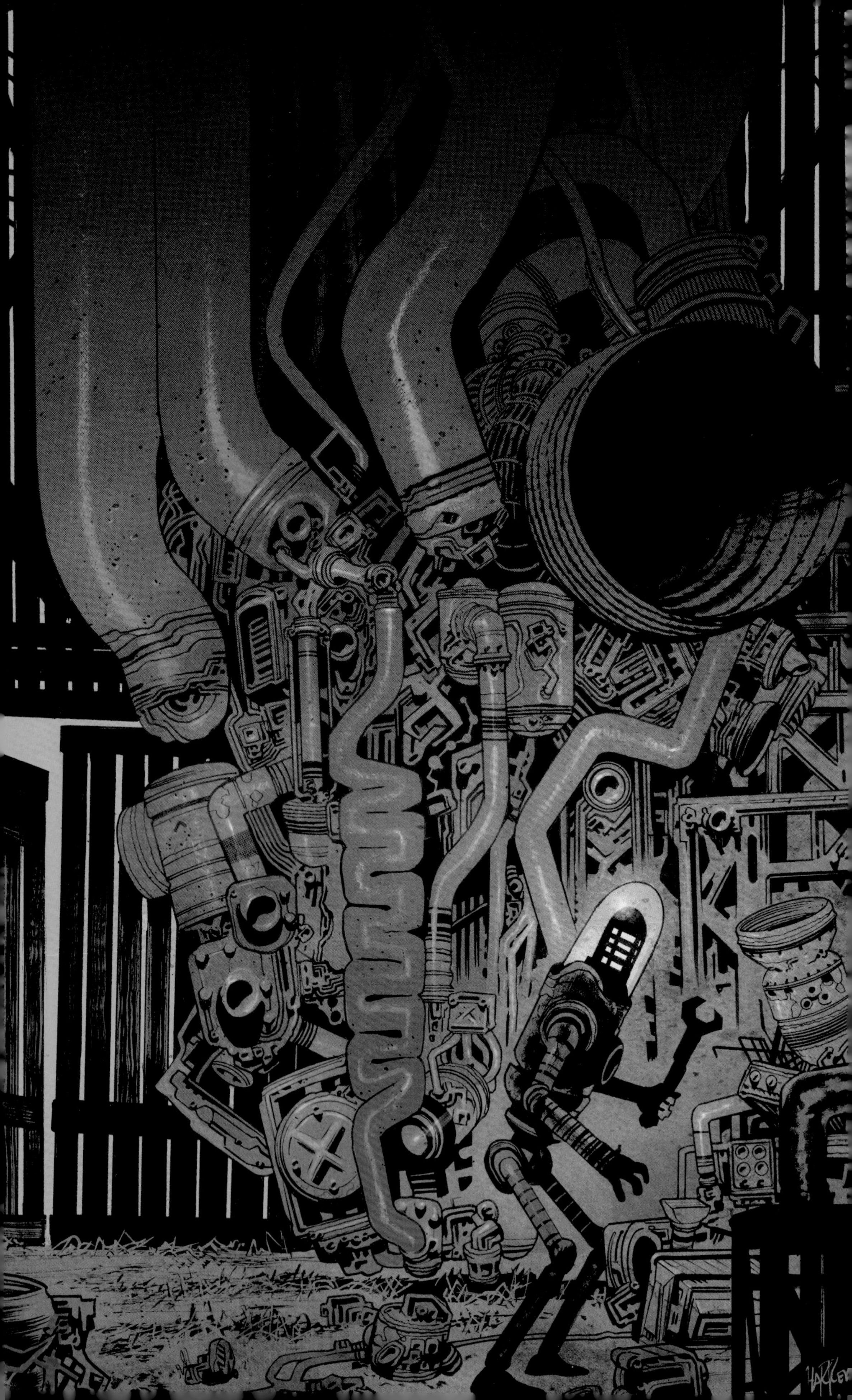

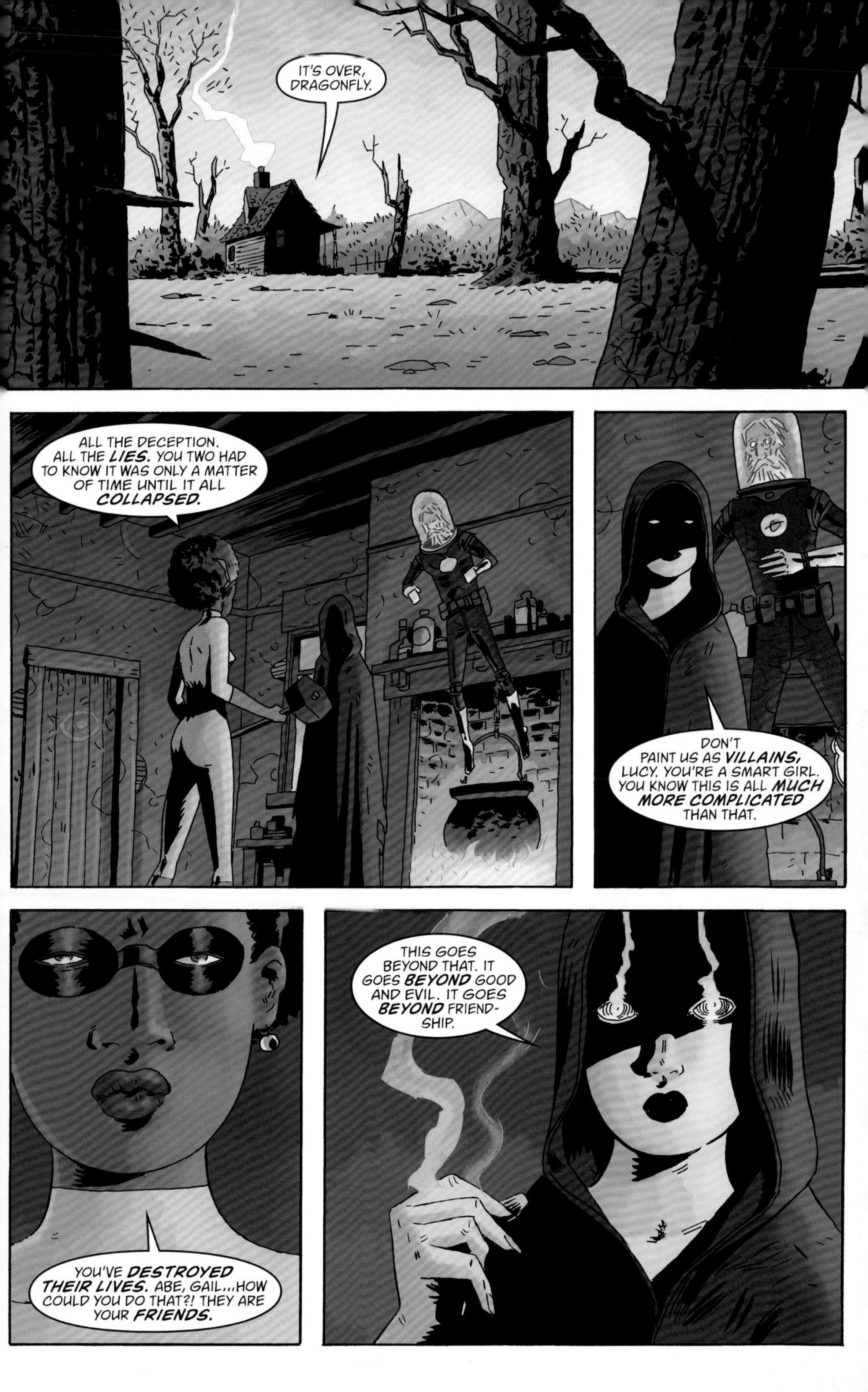
IT'S OVER, DRAGONFLY.
ALL THE DECEPTION. ALL THE LIES. YOU TWO HAD TO KNOW IT WAS ONLY A MATTER OF TIME UNTIL IT ALL COLLAPSED.
DON'T PAINT US AS VILLAINS, LUCY. YOU'RE A SMART GIRL. YOU KNOW THIS IS ALL MUCH MORE COMPLICATED THAN THAT.
YOU'VE DESTROYED THEIR LIVES. ABE, GAIL...HOW COULD YOU DO THAT?! THEY ARE YOUR FRIENDS.
THIS GOES BEYOND THAT. IT GOES BEYOND GOOD AND EVIL. IT GOES BEYOND FRIEND-SHIP.

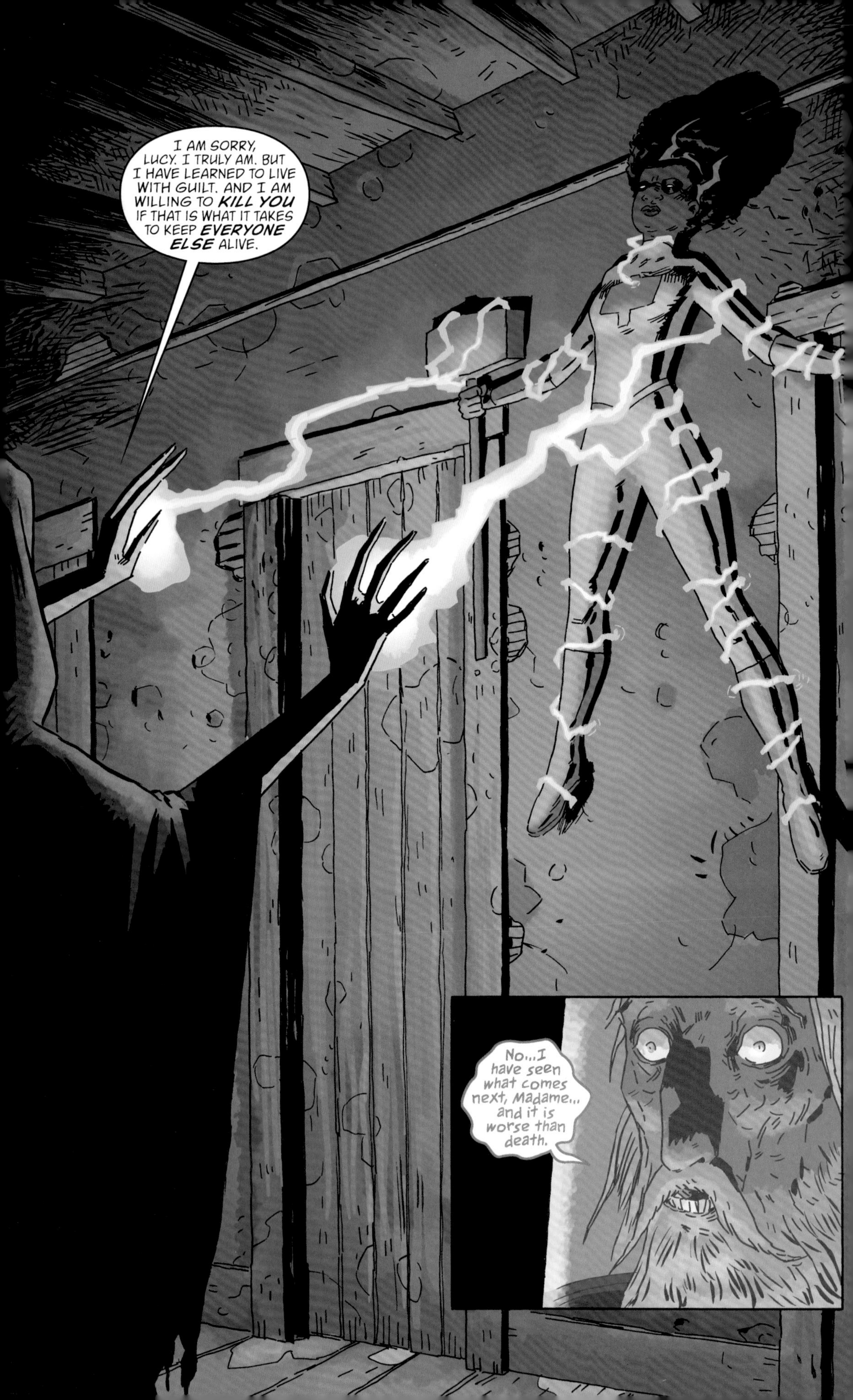
I AM SORRY, LUCY. I TRULY AM. BUT I HAVE LEARNED TO LIVE WITH GUILT. AND I AM WILLING TO KILL YOU IF THAT IS WHAT IT TAKES TO KEEP EVERYONE ELSE ALIVE.
No...I have seen what comes next, Madame... and it is worse than death.

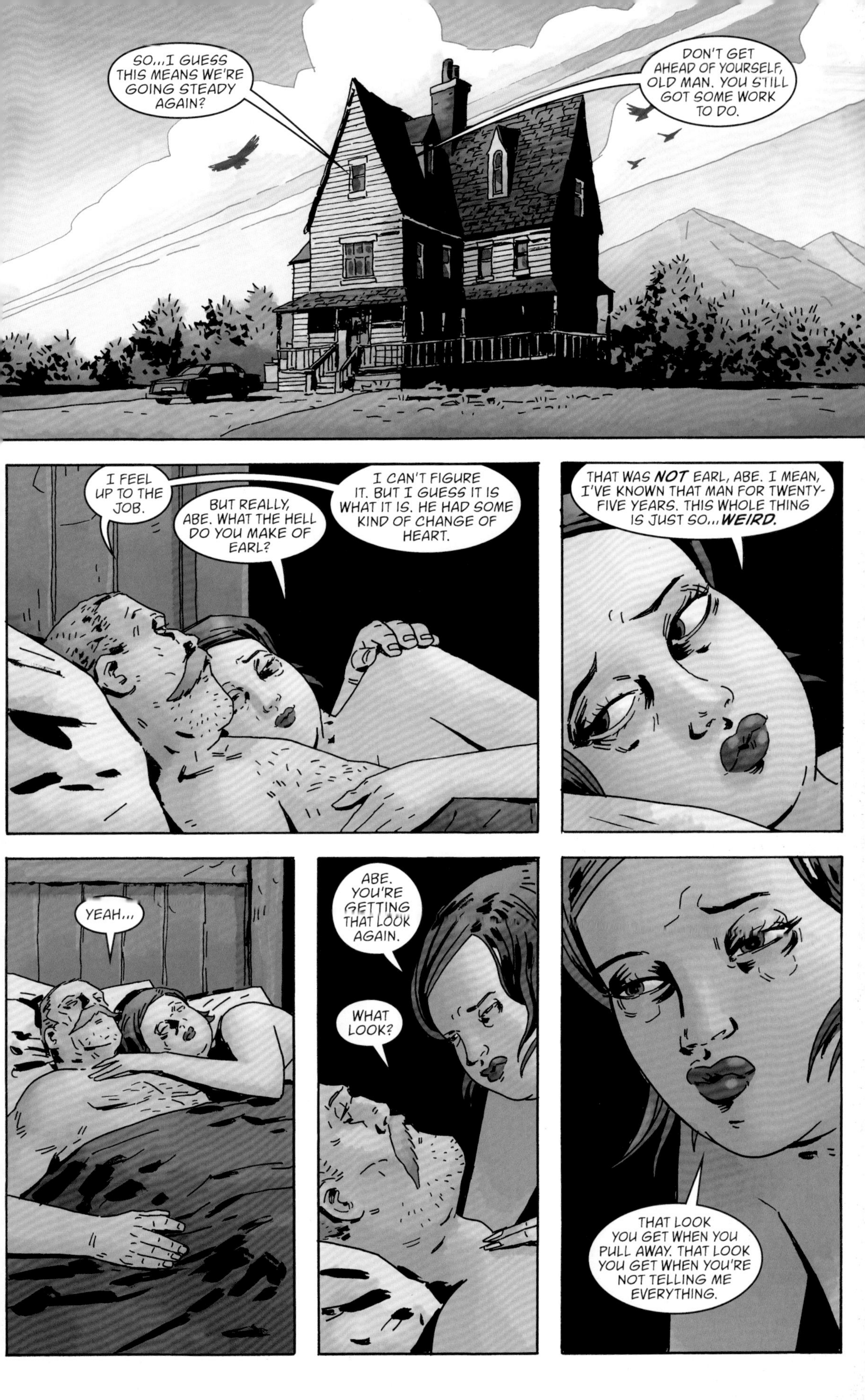
SO... I GUESS THIS MEANS WE'RE GOING STEADY AGAIN?
DON'T GET AHEAD OF YOURSELF, OLD MAN. YOU STILL GOT SOME WORK TO DO.
I FEEL UP TO THE JOB.
BUT REALLY, ABE. WHAT THE HELL DO YOU MAKE OF EARL?
I CAN'T FIGURE IT. BUT I GUESS IT IS WHAT IT IS. HE HAD SOME KIND OF CHANGE OF HEART.
THAT WAS NOT EARL, ABE. I MEAN, I'VE KNOWN THAT MAN FOR TWENTY-FIVE YEARS. THIS WHOLE THING IS JUST SO... WEIRD.
YEAH...
ABE. YOU'RE GETTING THAT LOOK AGAIN.
WHAT LOOK?
THAT LOOK YOU GET WHEN YOU PULL AWAY. THAT LOOK YOU GET WHEN YOU'RE NOT TELLING ME EVERYTHING.

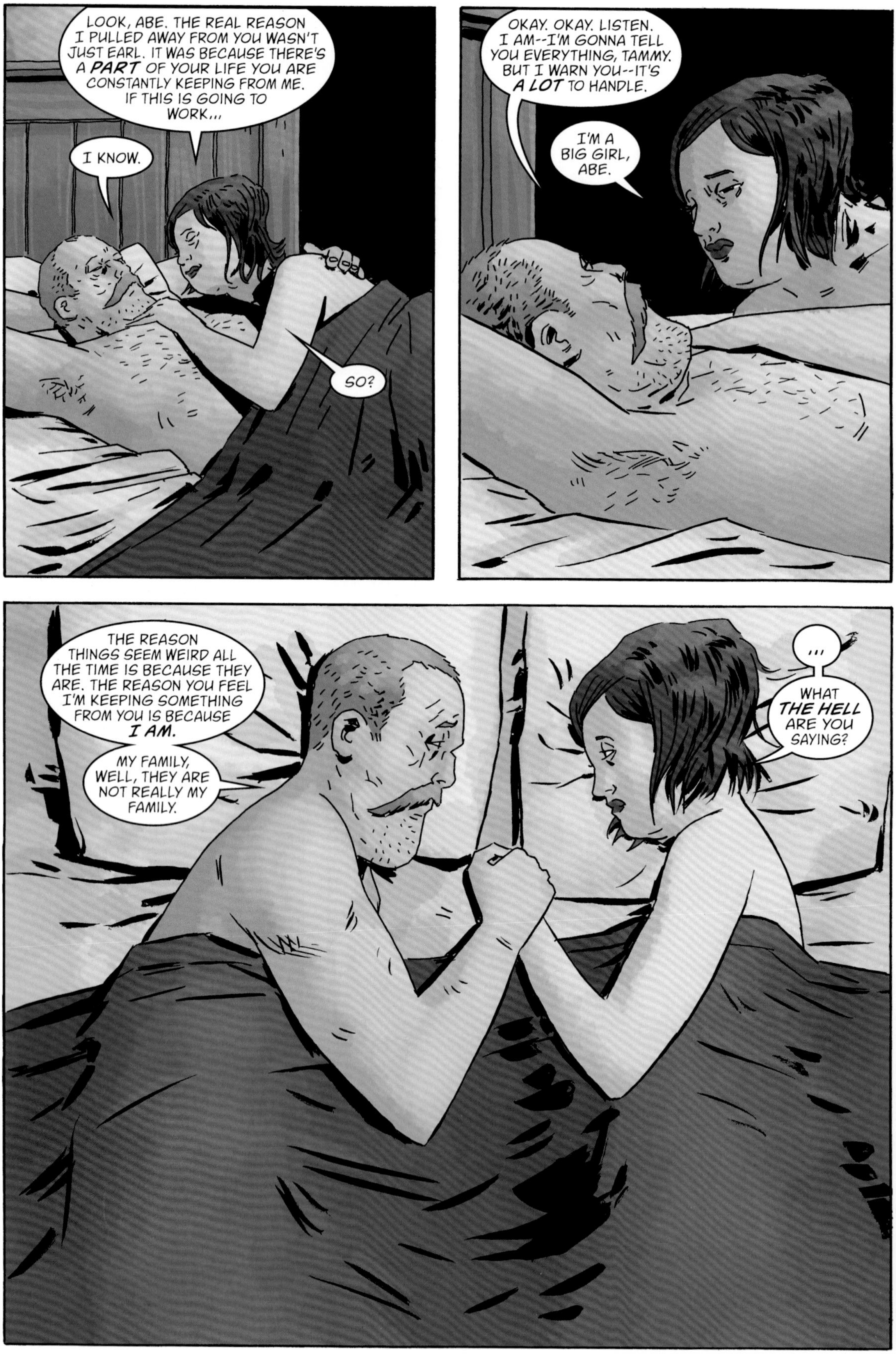
LOOK, ABE. THE REAL REASON I PULLED AWAY FROM YOU WASN'T JUST EARL. IT WAS BECAUSE THERE'S A PART OF YOUR LIFE YOU ARE CONSTANTLY KEEPING FROM ME. IF THIS IS GOING TO WORK...
I KNOW.
SO?
OKAY. OKAY. LISTEN. I AM--I'M GONNA TELL YOU EVERYTHING, TAMMY. BUT I WARN YOU--IT'S A LOT TO HANDLE.
I'M A BIG GIRL, ABE.
THE REASON THINGS SEEM WEIRD ALL THE TIME IS BECAUSE THEY ARE. THE REASON YOU FEEL I'M KEEPING SOMETHING FROM YOU IS BECAUSE I AM.
MY FAMILY, WELL, THEY ARE NOT REALLY MY FAMILY.
...
WHAT THE HELL ARE YOU SAYING?

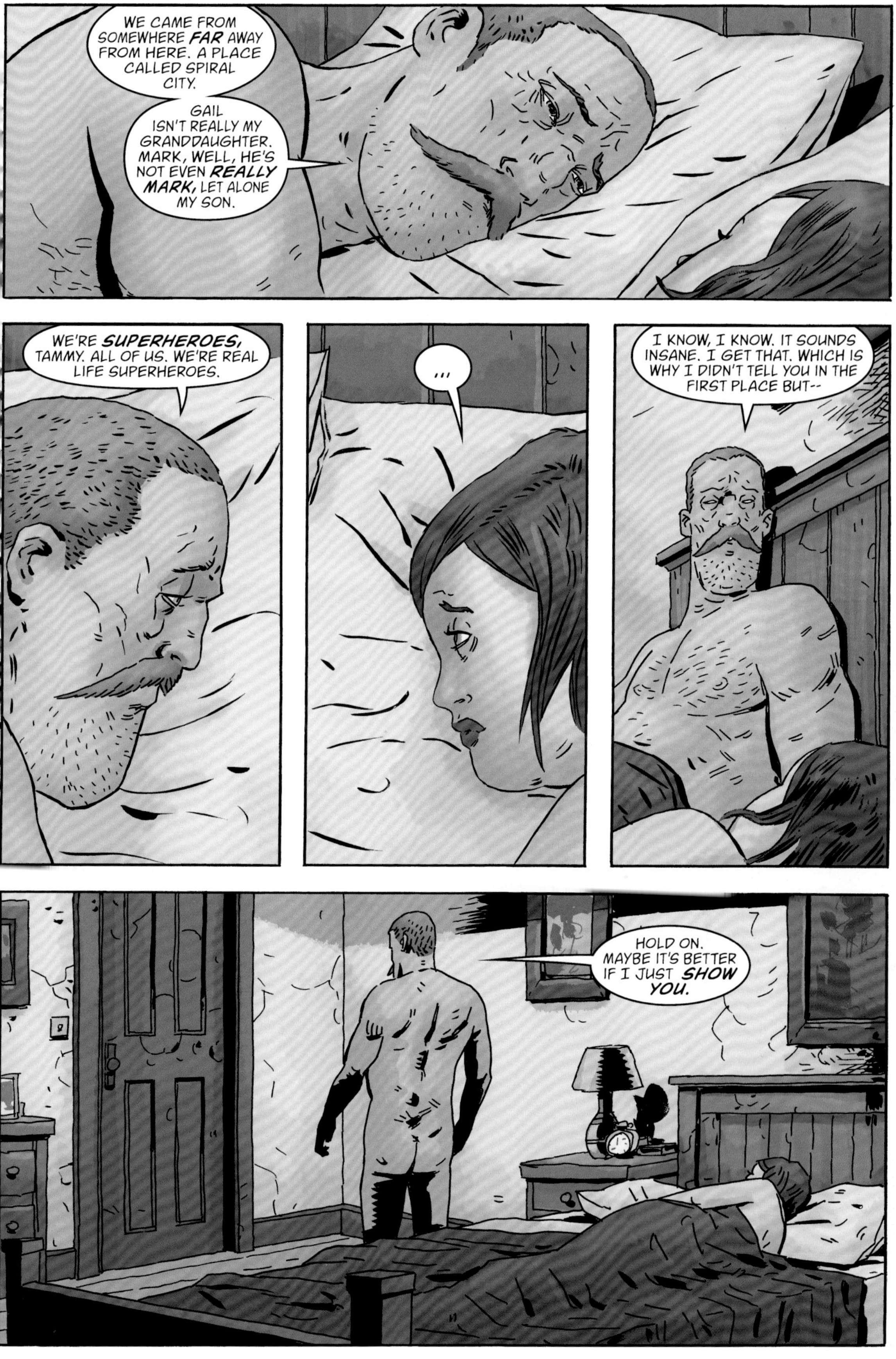
WE CAME FROM SOMEWHERE **FAR** AWAY FROM HERE. A PLACE CALLED SPIRAL CITY.
GAIL ISN'T REALLY MY GRANDDAUGHTER. MARK, WELL, HE'S NOT EVEN **REALLY MARK,** LET ALONE MY SON.
WE'RE **SUPERHEROES,** TAMMY. ALL OF US. WE'RE REAL LIFE SUPERHEROES.
...
I KNOW, I KNOW. IT SOUNDS INSANE. I GET THAT. WHICH IS WHY I DIDN'T TELL YOU IN THE FIRST PLACE BUT--
HOLD ON. MAYBE IT'S BETTER IF I JUST **SHOW YOU.**

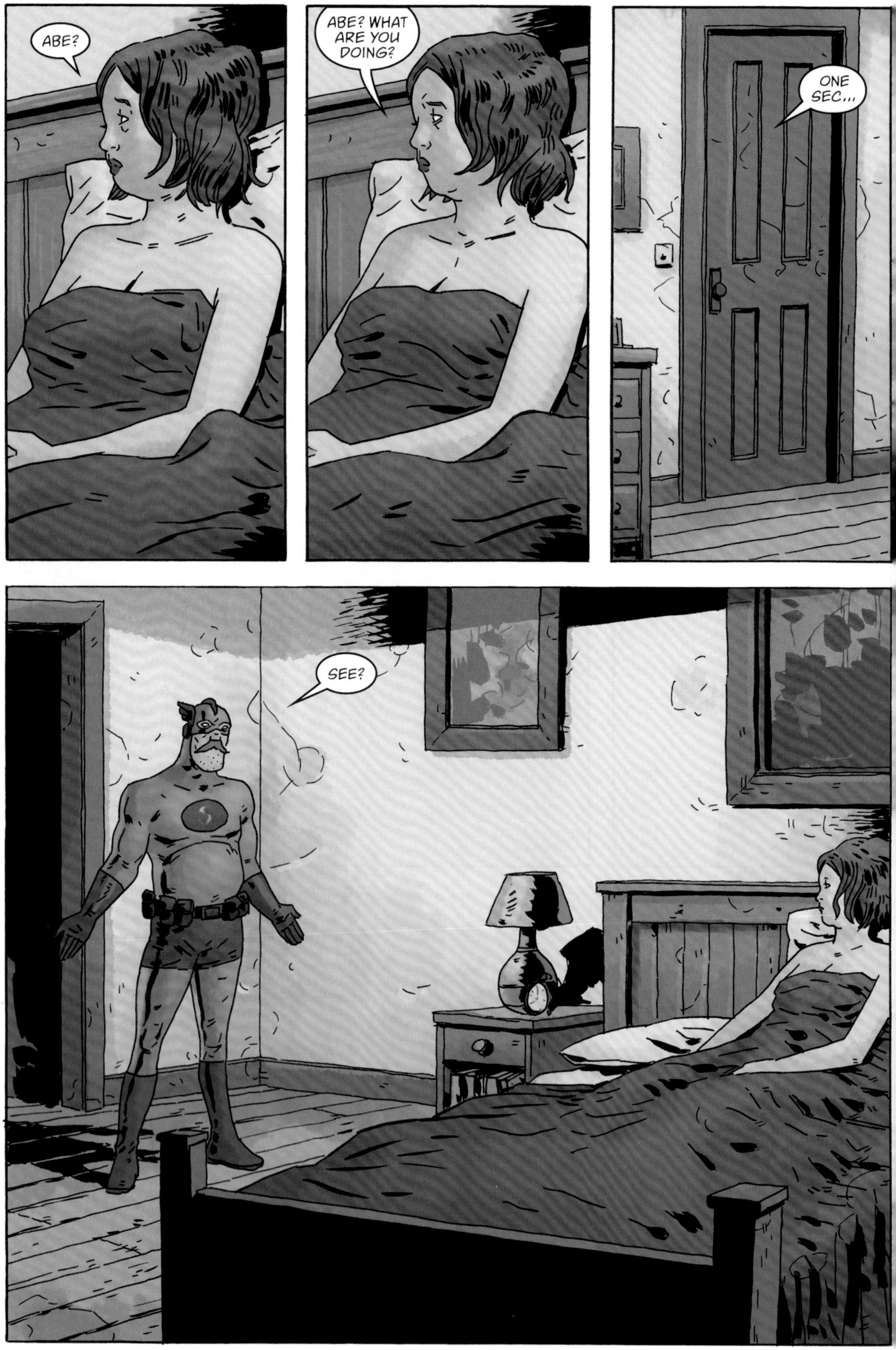
ABE?
ABE? WHAT ARE YOU DOING?
ONE SEC...
SEE?

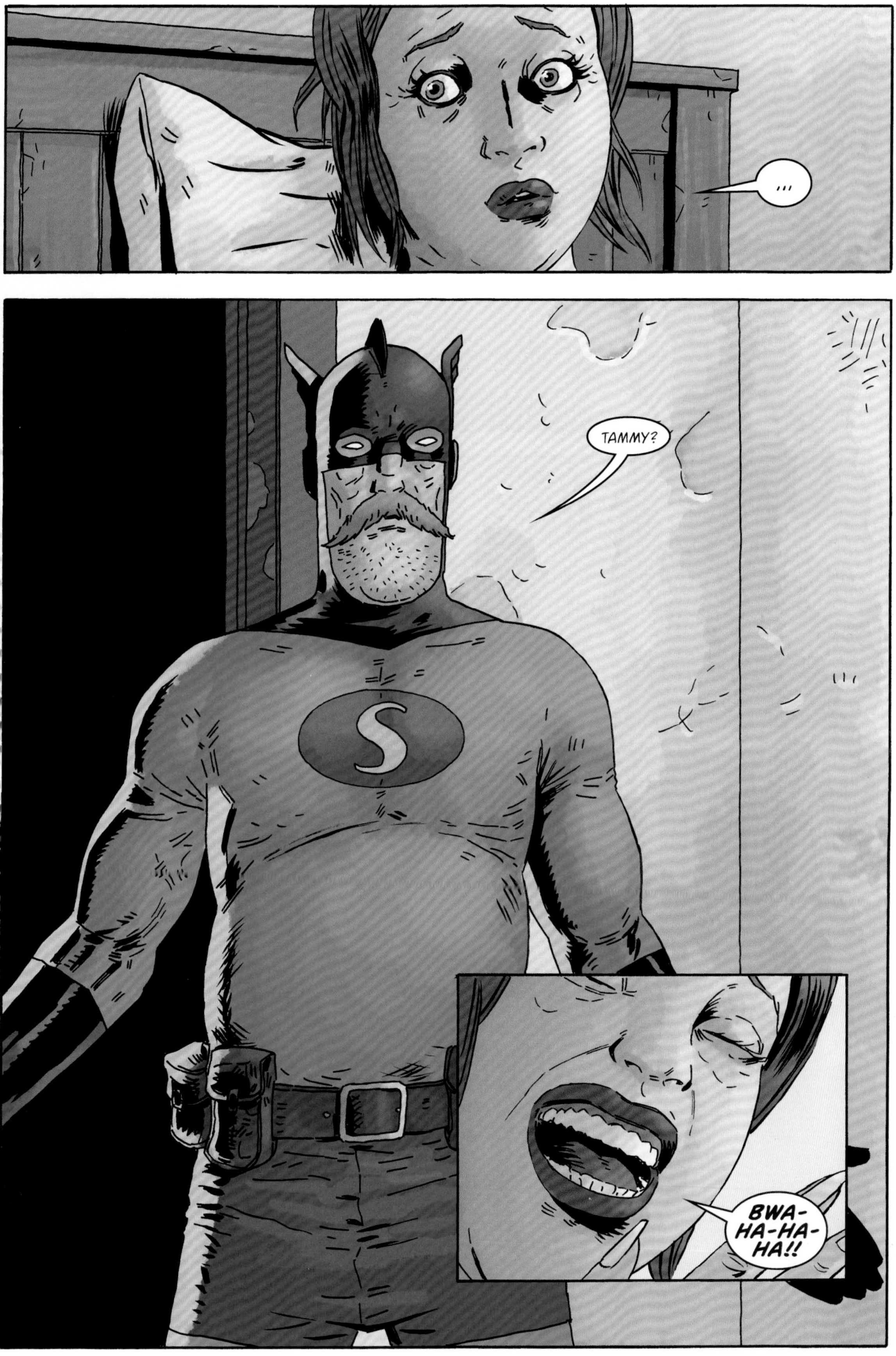
...
TAMMY?
BWA-HA-HA-HA!!

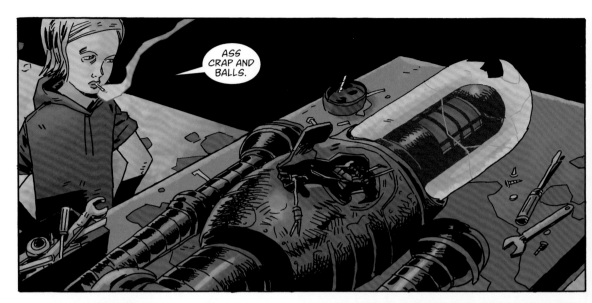

ASS CRAP AND BALLS.

I WAS NEVER MUCH WITH MACHINES, TALKY. I SURE COULD USE THE *WISDOM OF ZAFRAM* RIGHT ABOUT NOW.

LET'S SEE, BLUE WIRE CONNECTED TO THE RED WIRE...

KZAP!

GAH!

--ZZZT-- 10101010101-- ZZZTKT!

TALKY?!

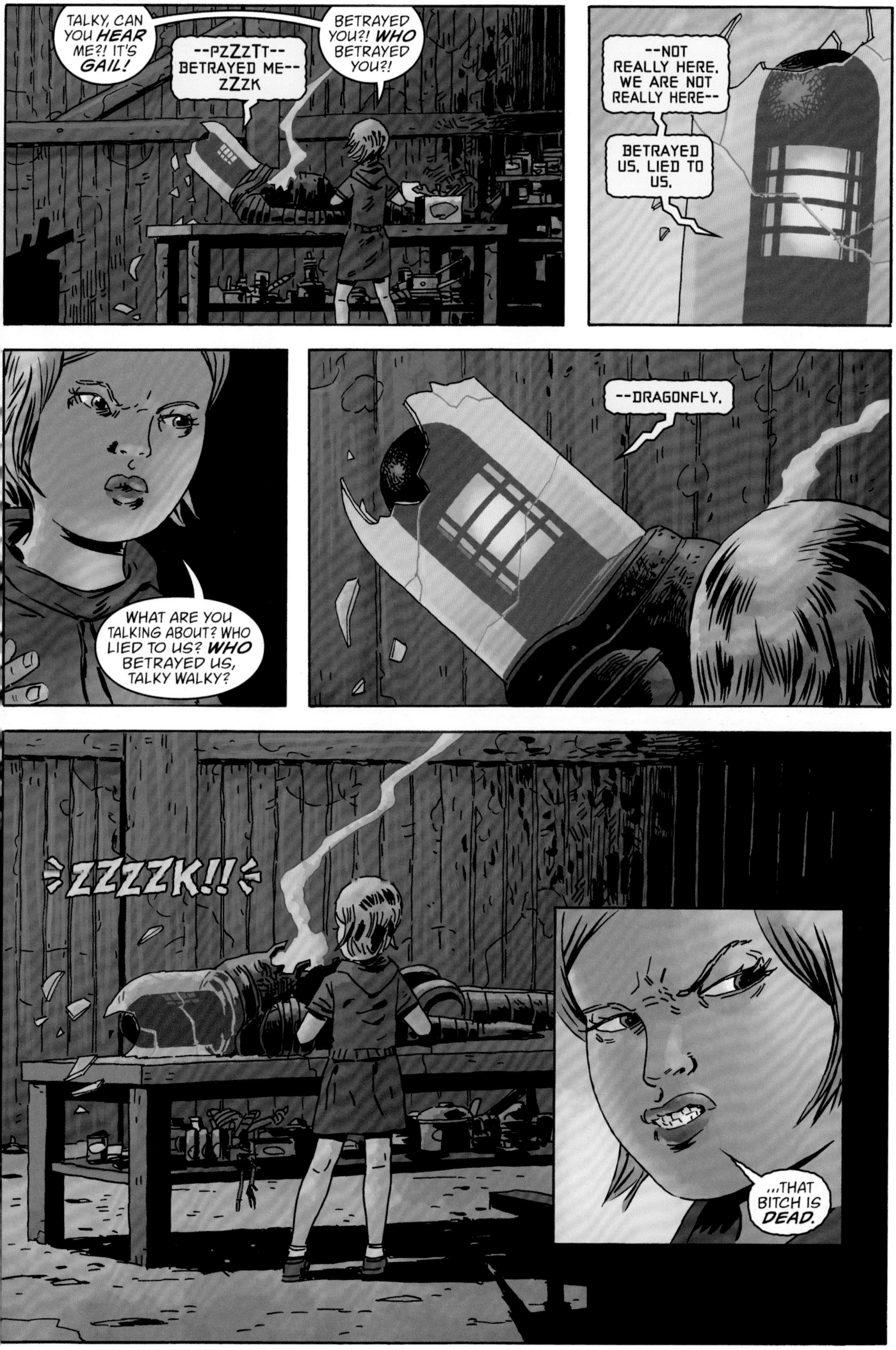
TALKY, CAN YOU HEAR ME?! IT'S GAIL!
--PZZZTT-- BETRAYED ME-- ZZZK
BETRAYED YOU?! WHO BETRAYED YOU?!
--NOT REALLY HERE. WE ARE NOT REALLY HERE--
BETRAYED US. LIED TO US.
WHAT ARE YOU TALKING ABOUT? WHO LIED TO US? WHO BETRAYED US, TALKY WALKY?
--DRAGONFLY.
ZZZZK!!
...THAT BITCH IS DEAD.

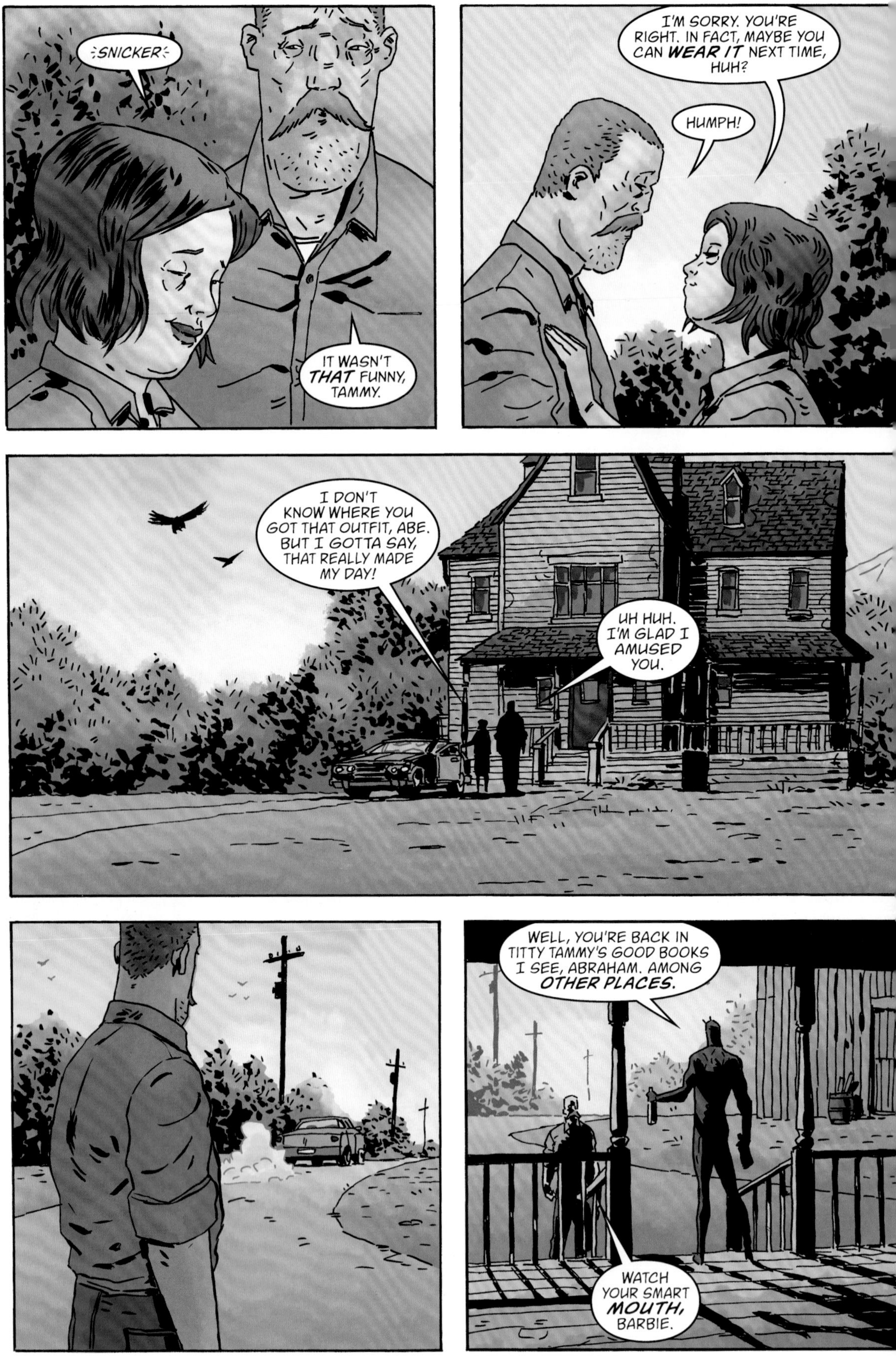

SNICKER
IT WASN'T THAT FUNNY, TAMMY.
I'M SORRY. YOU'RE RIGHT. IN FACT, MAYBE YOU CAN WEAR IT NEXT TIME, HUH?
HUMPH!
I DON'T KNOW WHERE YOU GOT THAT OUTFIT, ABE. BUT I GOTTA SAY, THAT REALLY MADE MY DAY!
UH HUH. I'M GLAD I AMUSED YOU.
WELL, YOU'RE BACK IN TITTY TAMMY'S GOOD BOOKS I SEE, ABRAHAM. AMONG OTHER PLACES.
WATCH YOUR SMART MOUTH, BARBIE.

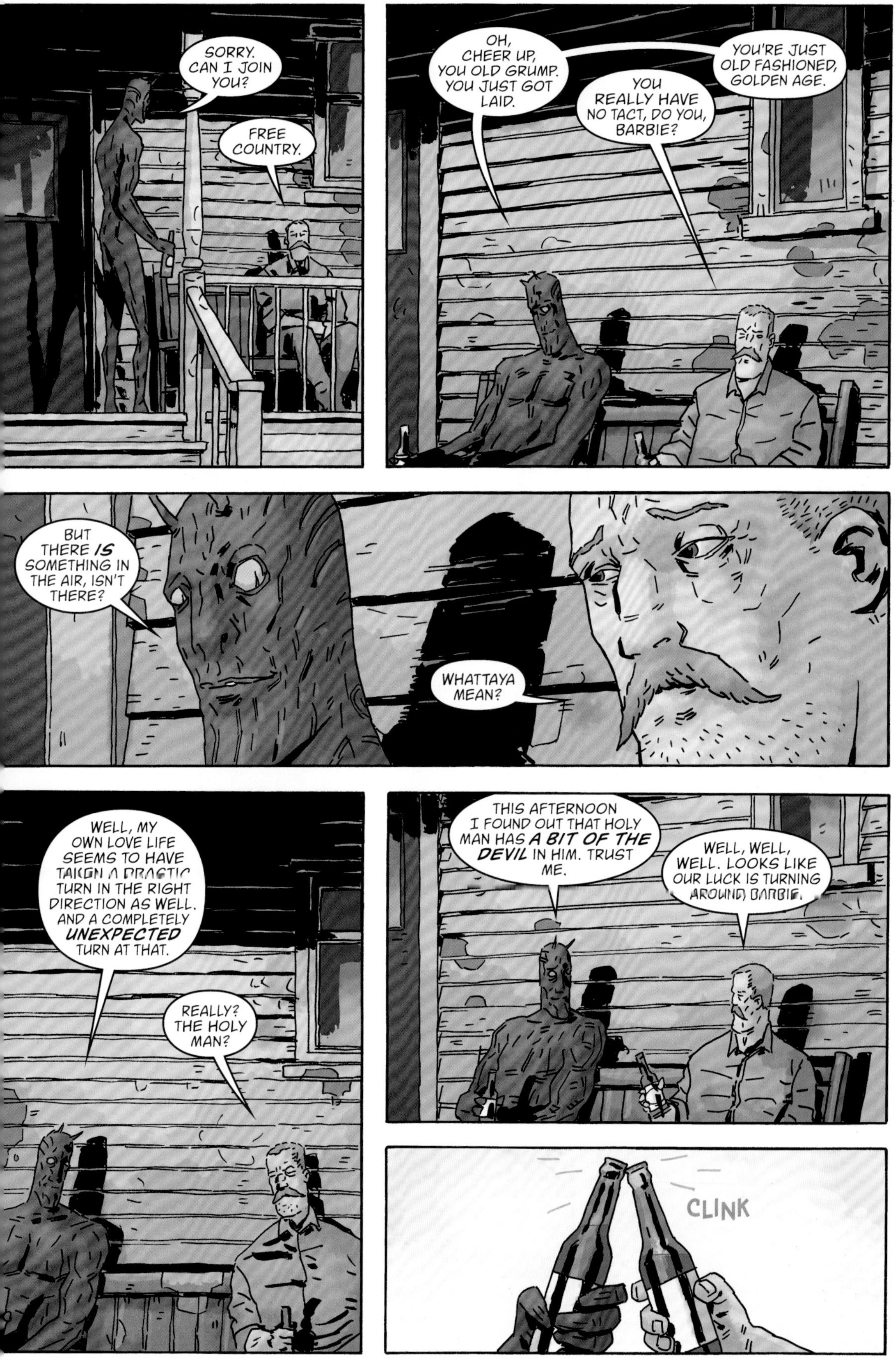
SORRY. CAN I JOIN YOU?
FREE COUNTRY.
OH, CHEER UP, YOU OLD GRUMP. YOU JUST GOT LAID.
YOU'RE JUST OLD FASHIONED, GOLDEN AGE.
YOU REALLY HAVE NO TACT, DO YOU, BARBIE?
BUT THERE *IS* SOMETHING IN THE AIR, ISN'T THERE?
WHATTAYA MEAN?
WELL, MY OWN LOVE LIFE SEEMS TO HAVE TAKEN A DRASTIC TURN IN THE RIGHT DIRECTION AS WELL. AND A COMPLETELY ***UNEXPECTED*** TURN AT THAT.
REALLY? THE HOLY MAN?
THIS AFTERNOON I FOUND OUT THAT HOLY MAN HAS ***A BIT OF THE DEVIL*** IN HIM. TRUST ME.
WELL, WELL, WELL. LOOKS LIKE OUR LUCK IS TURNING AROUND, BARBIE.
CLINK

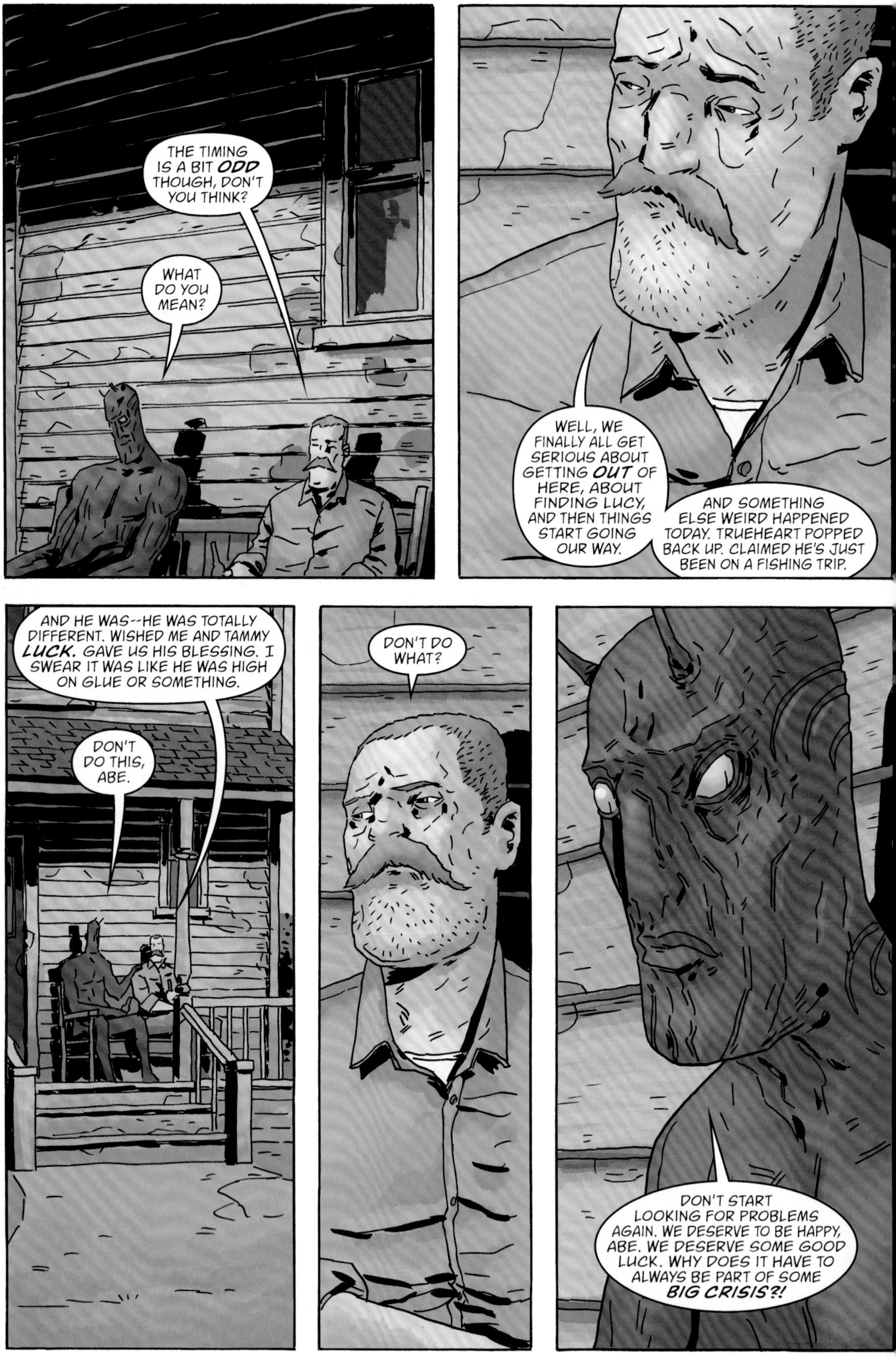

THE TIMING IS A BIT ODD THOUGH, DON'T YOU THINK?
WHAT DO YOU MEAN?
WELL, WE FINALLY ALL GET SERIOUS ABOUT GETTING OUT OF HERE, ABOUT FINDING LUCY, AND THEN THINGS START GOING OUR WAY.
AND SOMETHING ELSE WEIRD HAPPENED TODAY. TRUEHEART POPPED BACK UP. CLAIMED HE'S JUST BEEN ON A FISHING TRIP.
AND HE WAS--HE WAS TOTALLY DIFFERENT. WISHED ME AND TAMMY LUCK. GAVE US HIS BLESSING. I SWEAR IT WAS LIKE HE WAS HIGH ON GLUE OR SOMETHING.
DON'T DO THIS, ABE.
DON'T DO WHAT?
DON'T START LOOKING FOR PROBLEMS AGAIN. WE DESERVE TO BE HAPPY, ABE. WE DESERVE SOME GOOD LUCK. WHY DOES IT HAVE TO ALWAYS BE PART OF SOME BIG CRISIS?!

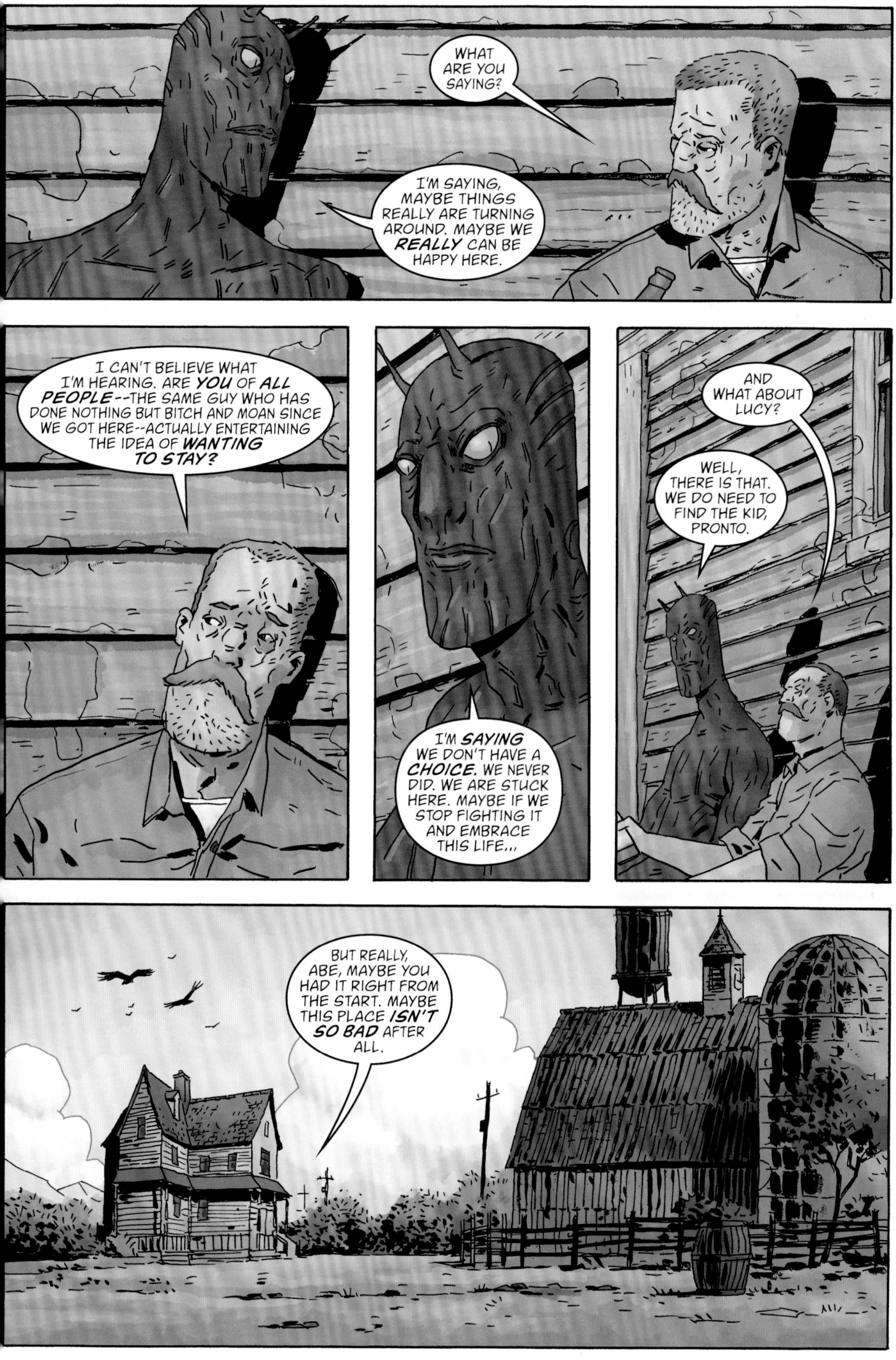
WHAT ARE YOU SAYING?
I'M SAYING, MAYBE THINGS REALLY ARE TURNING AROUND. MAYBE WE REALLY CAN BE HAPPY HERE.
I CAN'T BELIEVE WHAT I'M HEARING. ARE YOU OF ALL PEOPLE--THE SAME GUY WHO HAS DONE NOTHING BUT BITCH AND MOAN SINCE WE GOT HERE--ACTUALLY ENTERTAINING THE IDEA OF WANTING TO STAY?
I'M SAYING WE DON'T HAVE A CHOICE. WE NEVER DID. WE ARE STUCK HERE. MAYBE IF WE STOP FIGHTING IT AND EMBRACE THIS LIFE...
AND WHAT ABOUT LUCY?
WELL, THERE IS THAT. WE DO NEED TO FIND THE KID, PRONTO.
BUT REALLY, ABE, MAYBE YOU HAD IT RIGHT FROM THE START. MAYBE THIS PLACE ISN'T SO BAD AFTER ALL.

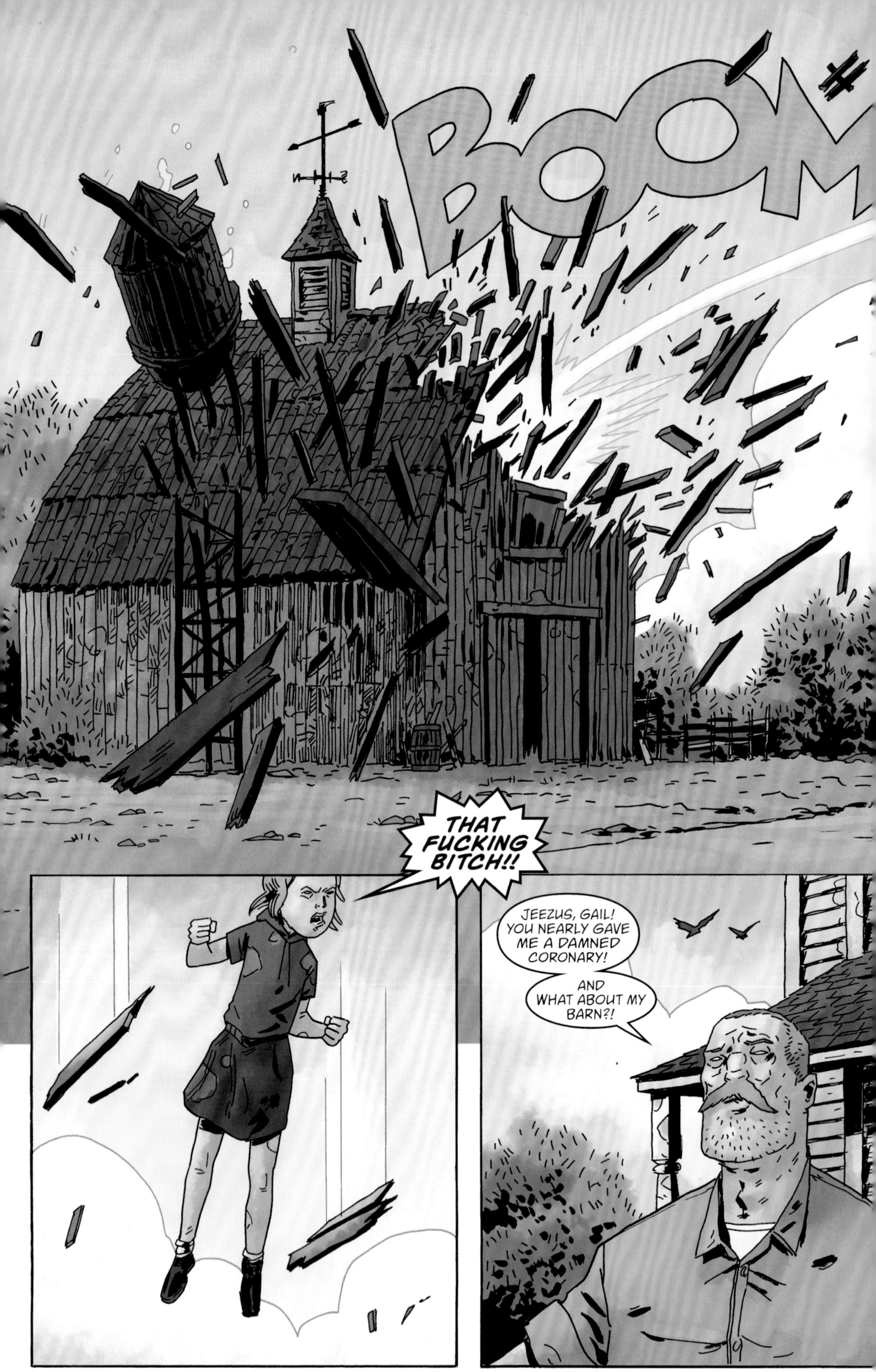
BOOM
THAT FUCKING BITCH!!
JEEZUS, GAIL! YOU NEARLY GAVE ME A DAMNED CORONARY!
AND WHAT ABOUT MY BARN?!

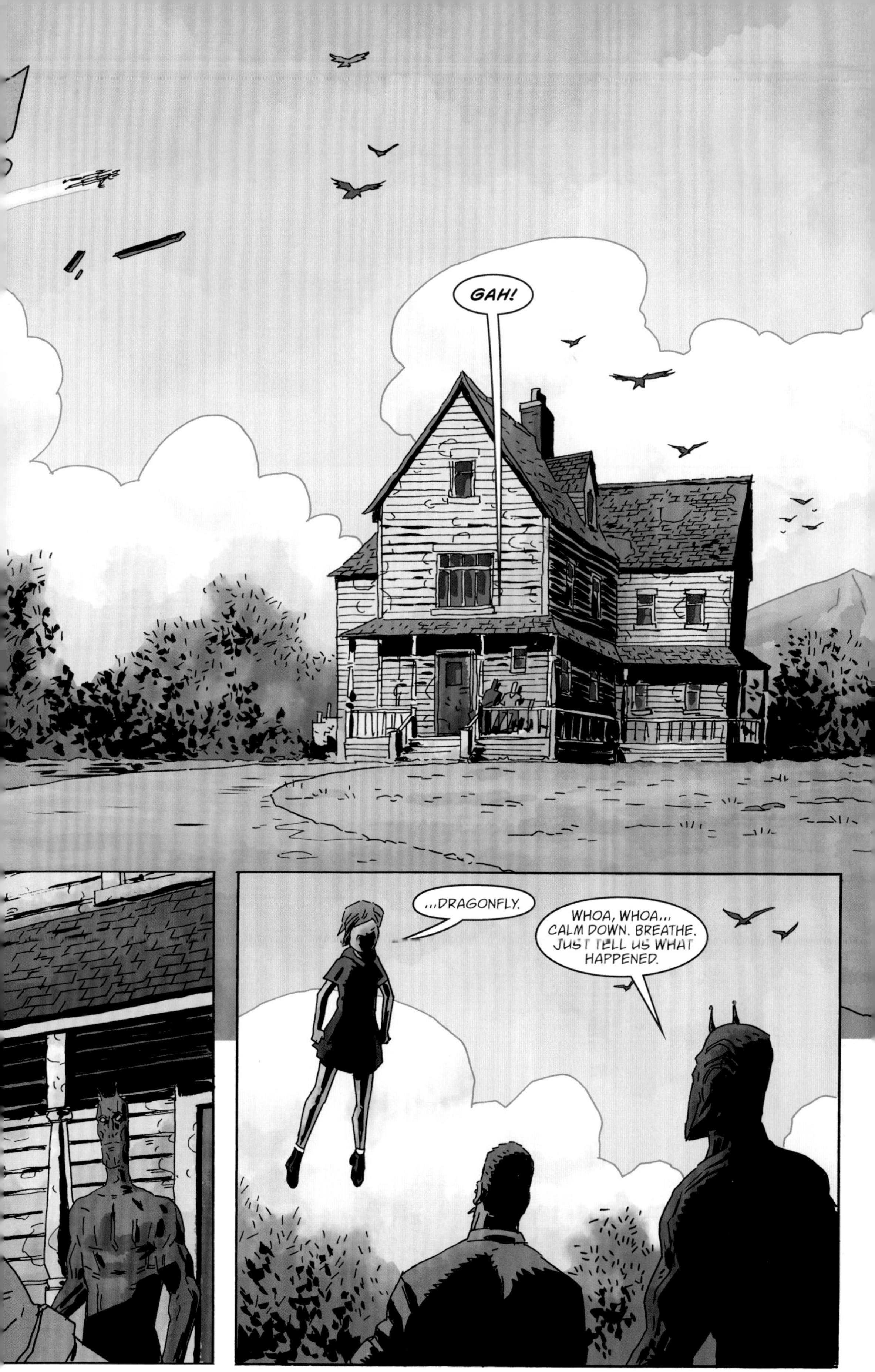
GAH!
...DRAGONFLY.
WHOA, WHOA... CALM DOWN. BREATHE. JUST TELL US WHAT HAPPENED.

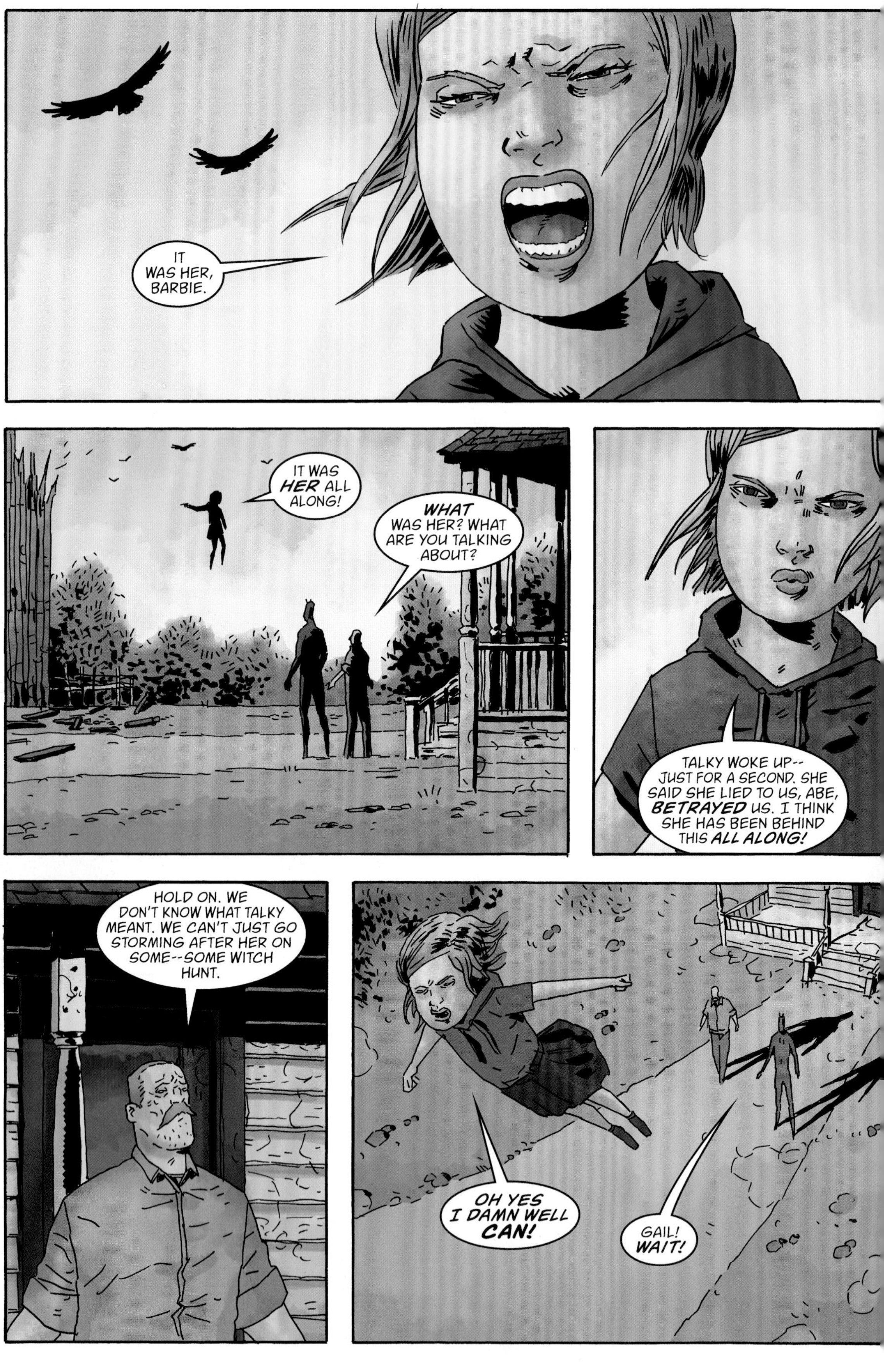
IT WAS HER, BARBIE.
IT WAS HER ALL ALONG!
WHAT WAS HER? WHAT ARE YOU TALKING ABOUT?
TALKY WOKE UP-- JUST FOR A SECOND. SHE SAID SHE LIED TO US, ABE, BETRAYED US. I THINK SHE HAS BEEN BEHIND THIS ALL ALONG!
HOLD ON. WE DON'T KNOW WHAT TALKY MEANT. WE CAN'T JUST GO STORMING AFTER HER ON SOME--SOME WITCH HUNT.
OH YES I DAMN WELL CAN!
GAIL! WAIT!

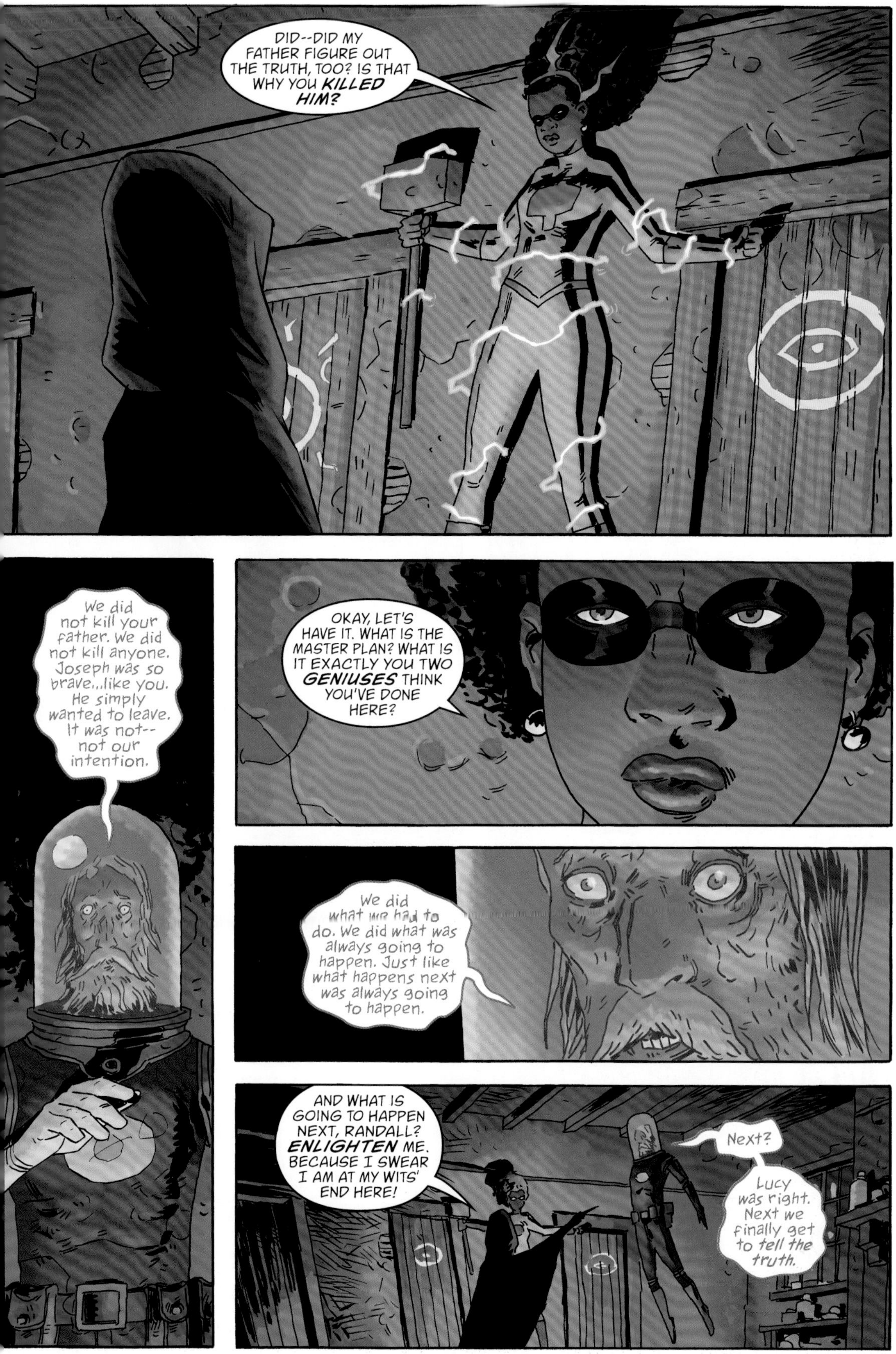
DID--DID MY FATHER FIGURE OUT THE TRUTH, TOO? IS THAT WHY YOU KILLED HIM?
We did not kill your father. We did not kill anyone. Joseph was so brave...like you. He simply wanted to leave. It was not--not our intention.
OKAY, LET'S HAVE IT. WHAT IS THE MASTER PLAN? WHAT IS IT EXACTLY YOU TWO GENIUSES THINK YOU'VE DONE HERE?
We did what we had to do. We did what was always going to happen. Just like what happens next was always going to happen.
AND WHAT IS GOING TO HAPPEN NEXT, RANDALL? ENLIGHTEN ME. BECAUSE I SWEAR I AM AT MY WITS' END HERE!
Next?
Lucy was right. Next we finally get to tell the truth.

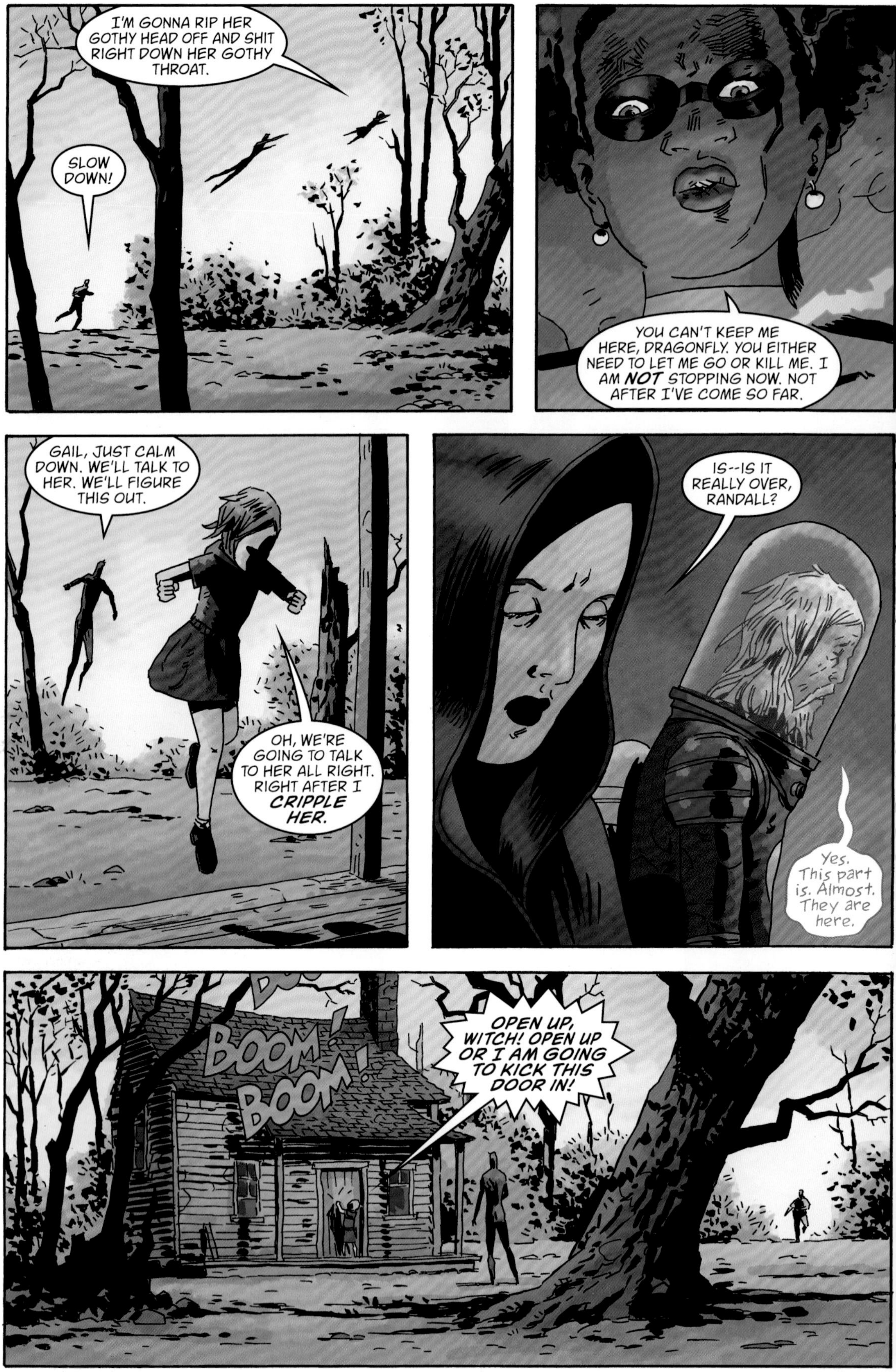

I'M GONNA RIP HER GOTHY HEAD OFF AND SHIT RIGHT DOWN HER GOTHY THROAT.
SLOW DOWN!
YOU CAN'T KEEP ME HERE, DRAGONFLY. YOU EITHER NEED TO LET ME GO OR KILL ME. I AM **NOT** STOPPING NOW. NOT AFTER I'VE COME SO FAR.
GAIL, JUST CALM DOWN. WE'LL TALK TO HER. WE'LL FIGURE THIS OUT.
OH, WE'RE GOING TO TALK TO HER ALL RIGHT. RIGHT AFTER I **CRIPPLE HER.**
IS--IS IT REALLY OVER, RANDALL?
Yes. This part is. Almost. They are here.
BOOM! BOOM!
OPEN UP, WITCH! OPEN UP OR I AM GOING TO KICK THIS DOOR IN!

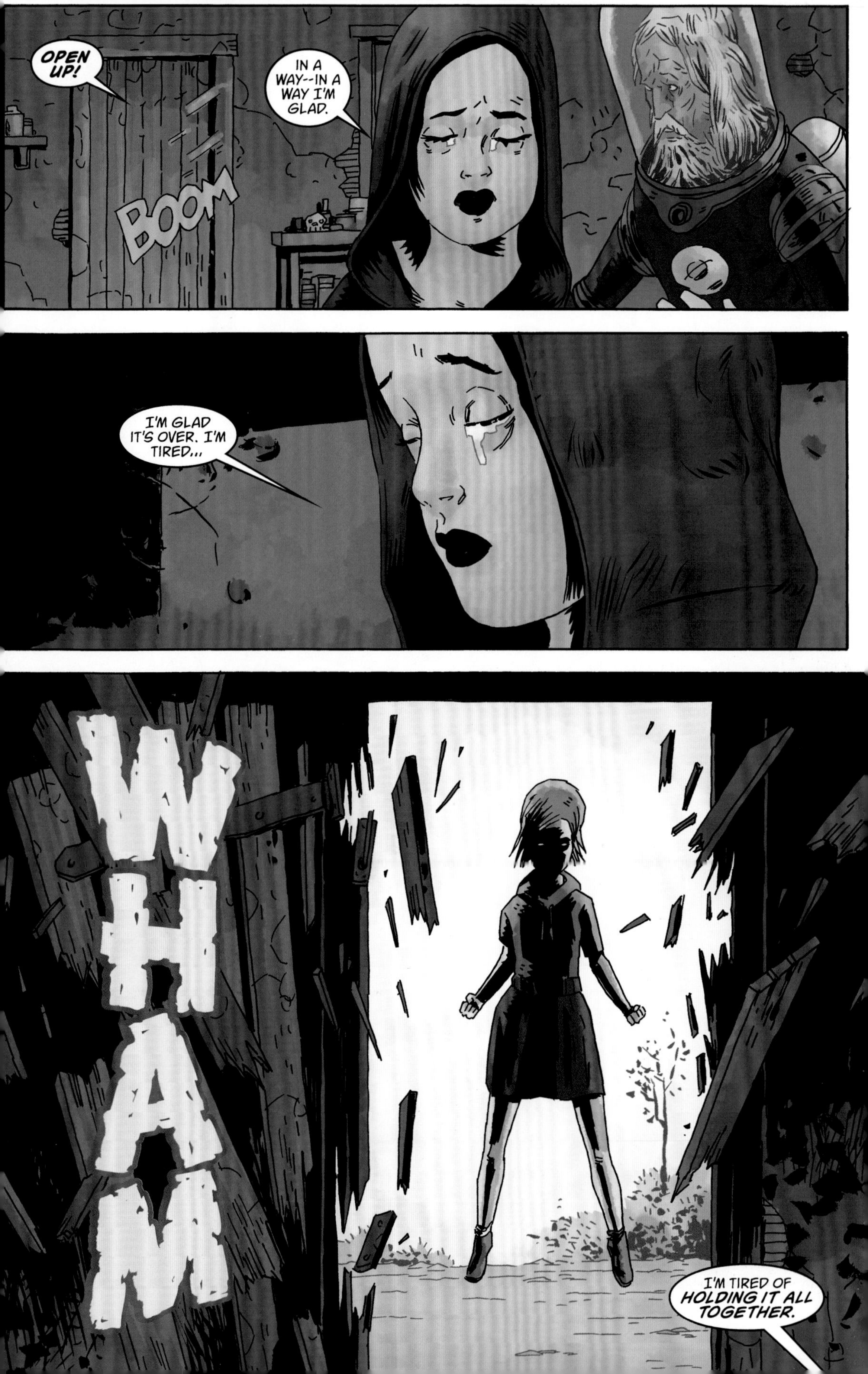
OPEN UP!
BOOM
IN A WAY--IN A WAY I'M GLAD.
I'M GLAD IT'S OVER. I'M TIRED...
WHAM
I'M TIRED OF HOLDING IT ALL TOGETHER.

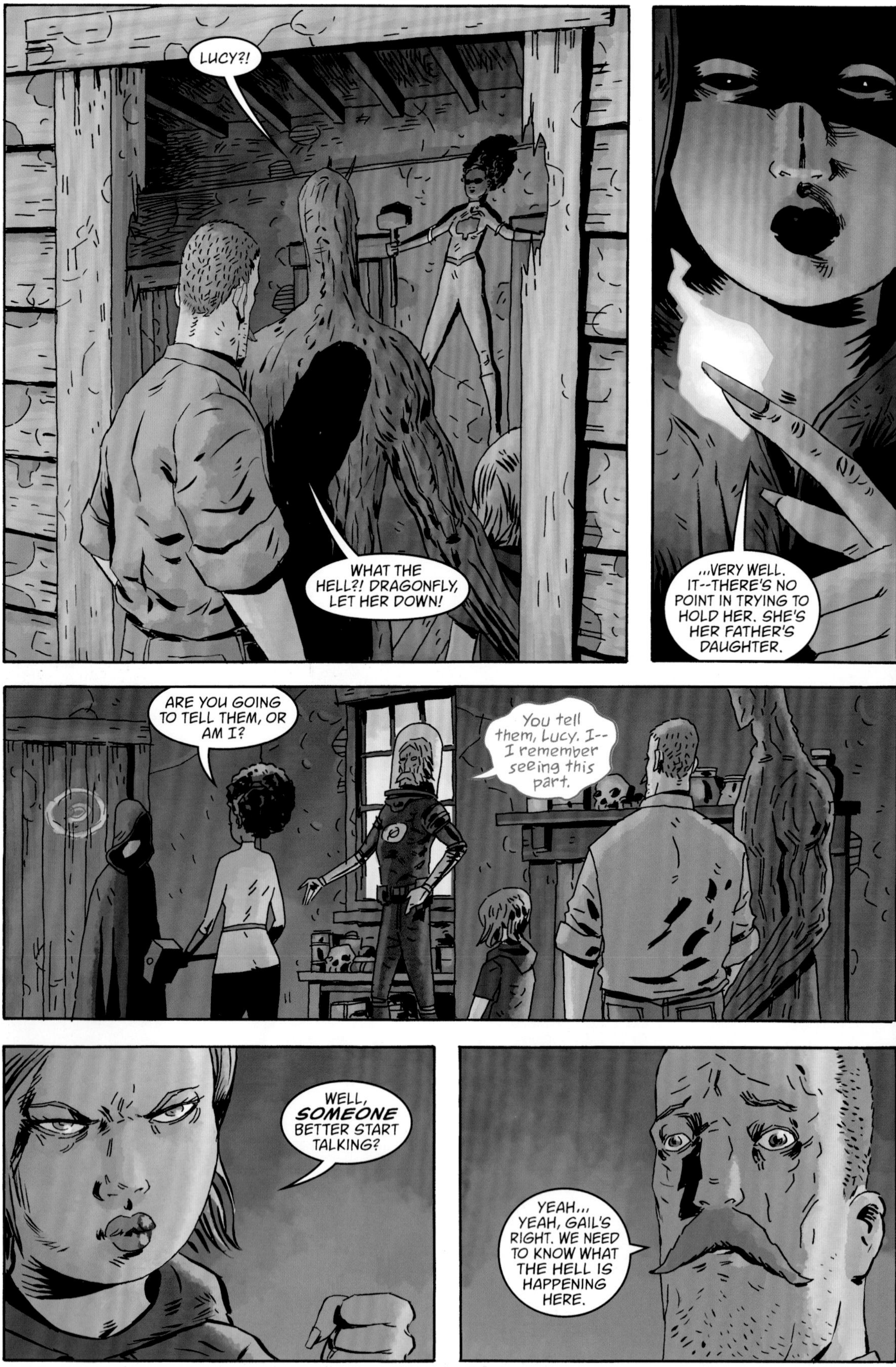
LUCY?!
WHAT THE HELL?! DRAGONFLY, LET HER DOWN!
...VERY WELL. IT--THERE'S NO POINT IN TRYING TO HOLD HER. SHE'S HER FATHER'S DAUGHTER.
ARE YOU GOING TO TELL THEM, OR AM I?
You tell them, Lucy. I-- I remember seeing this part.
WELL, SOMEONE BETTER START TALKING?
YEAH... YEAH, GAIL'S RIGHT. WE NEED TO KNOW WHAT THE HELL IS HAPPENING HERE.

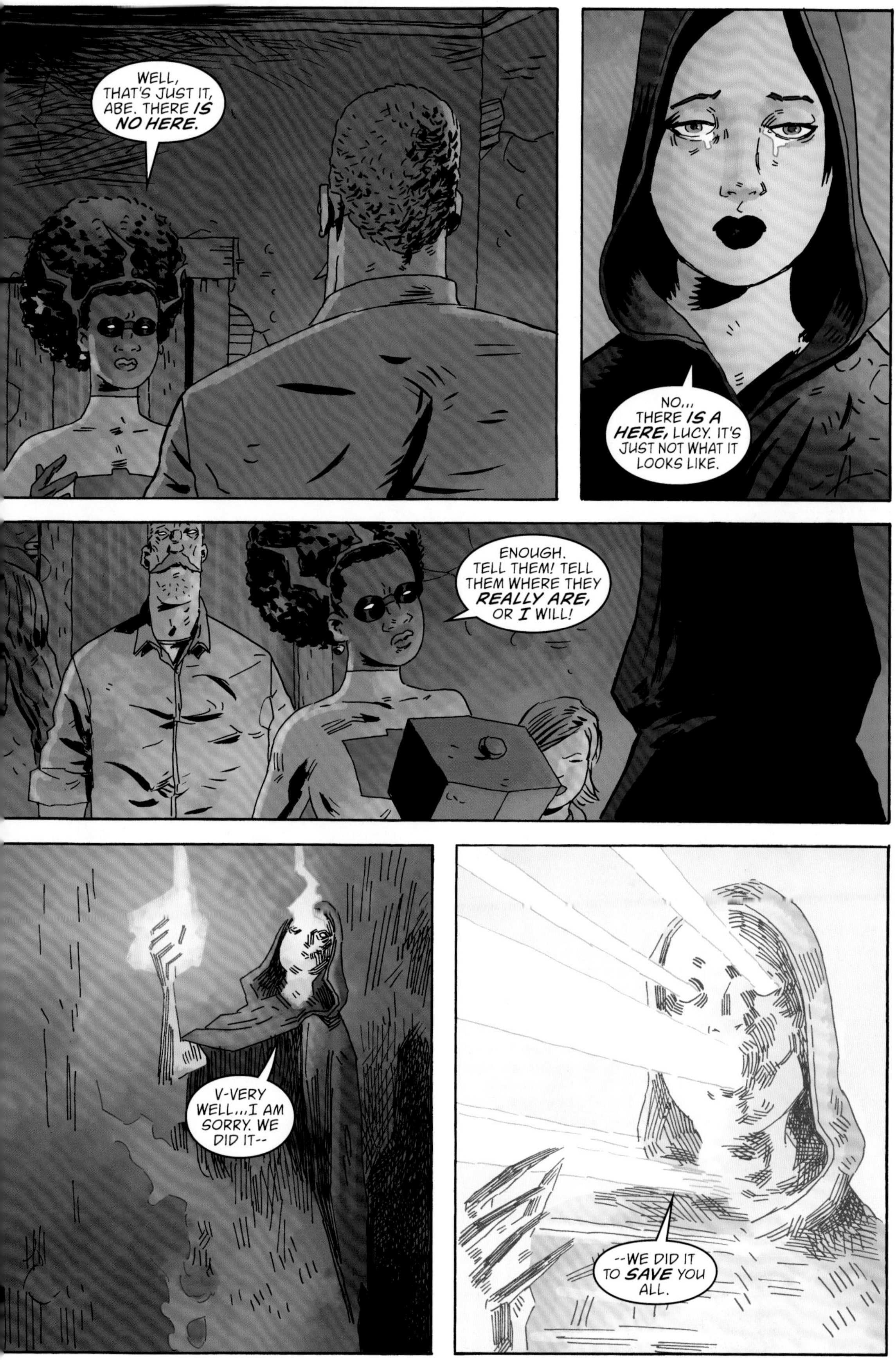
WELL, THAT'S JUST IT, ABE. THERE *IS* *NO HERE*.
NO... THERE *IS A HERE,* LUCY. IT'S JUST NOT WHAT IT LOOKS LIKE.
ENOUGH. TELL THEM! TELL THEM WHERE THEY *REALLY ARE,* OR *I* WILL!
V-VERY WELL... I AM SORRY. WE DID IT--
--WE DID IT TO *SAVE* YOU ALL.

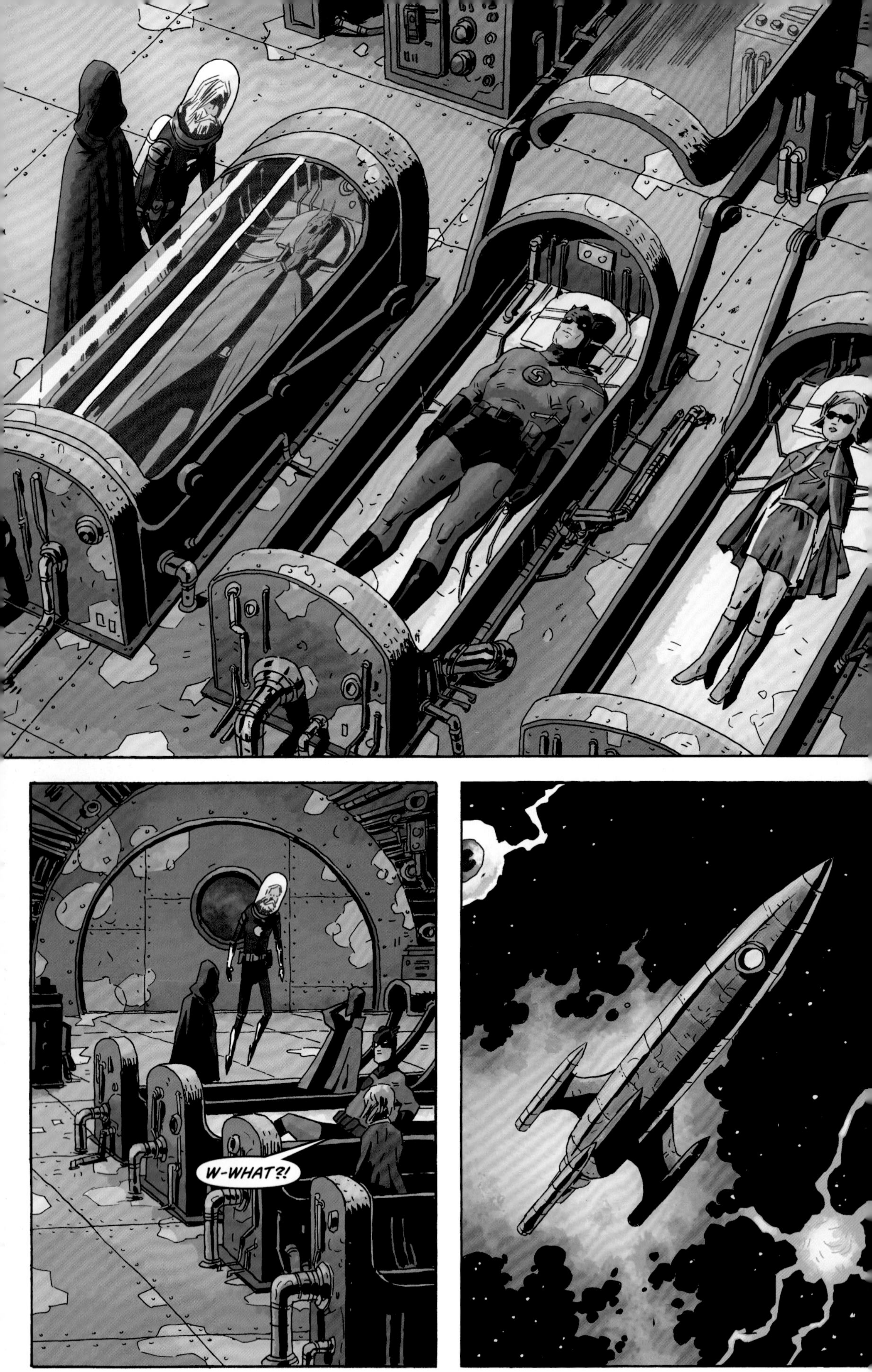
W-WHAT?!

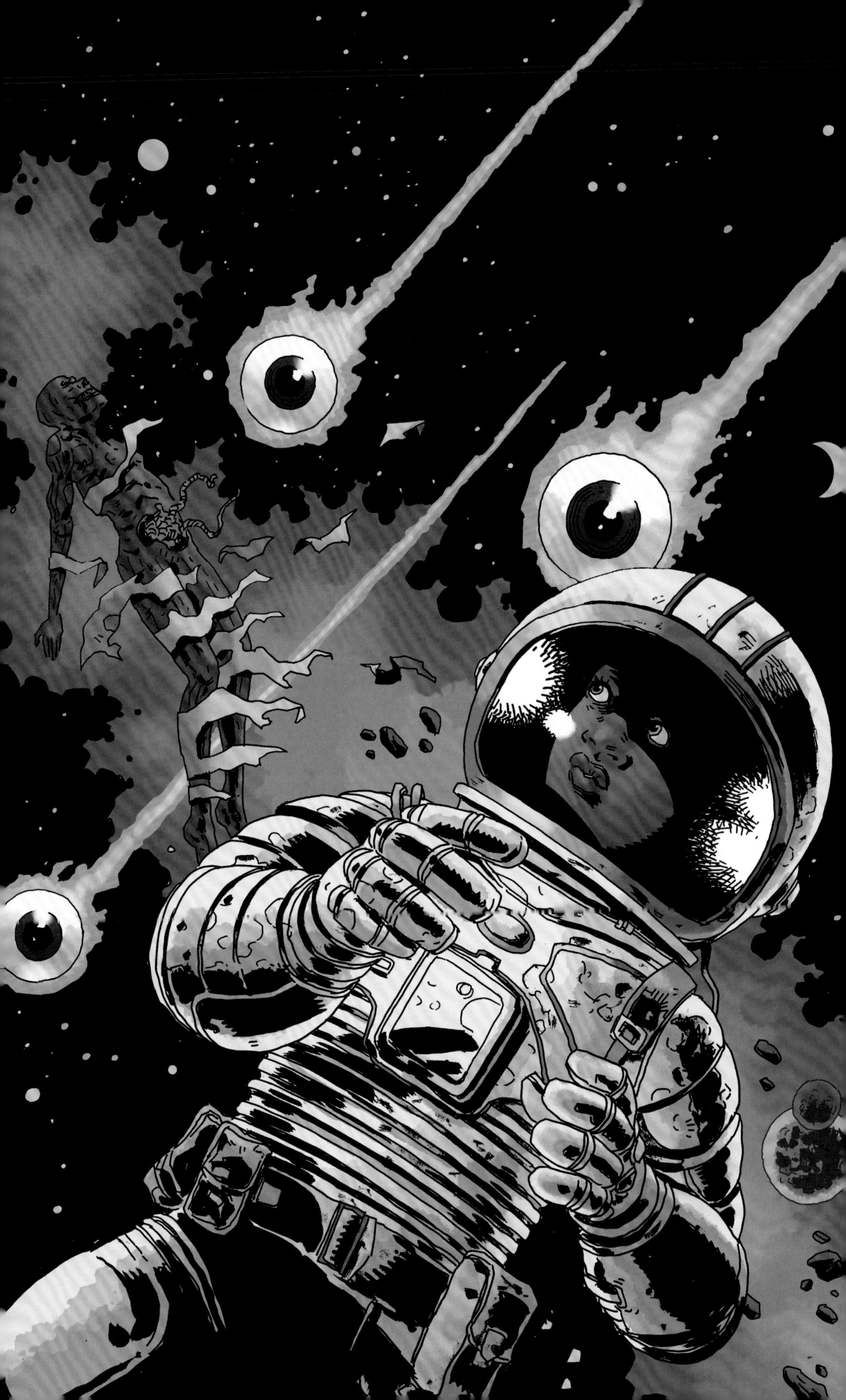

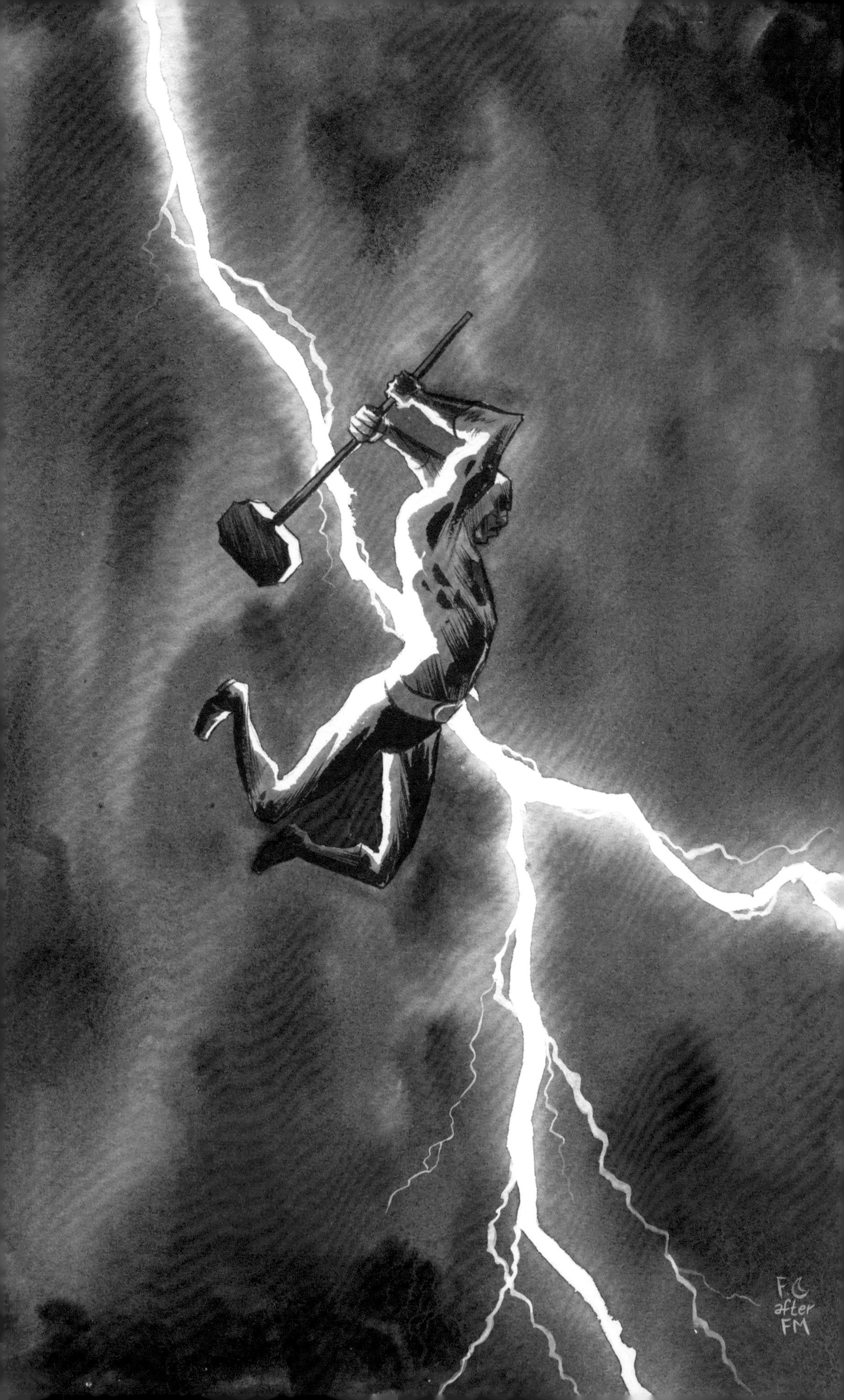
F.C
after
FM

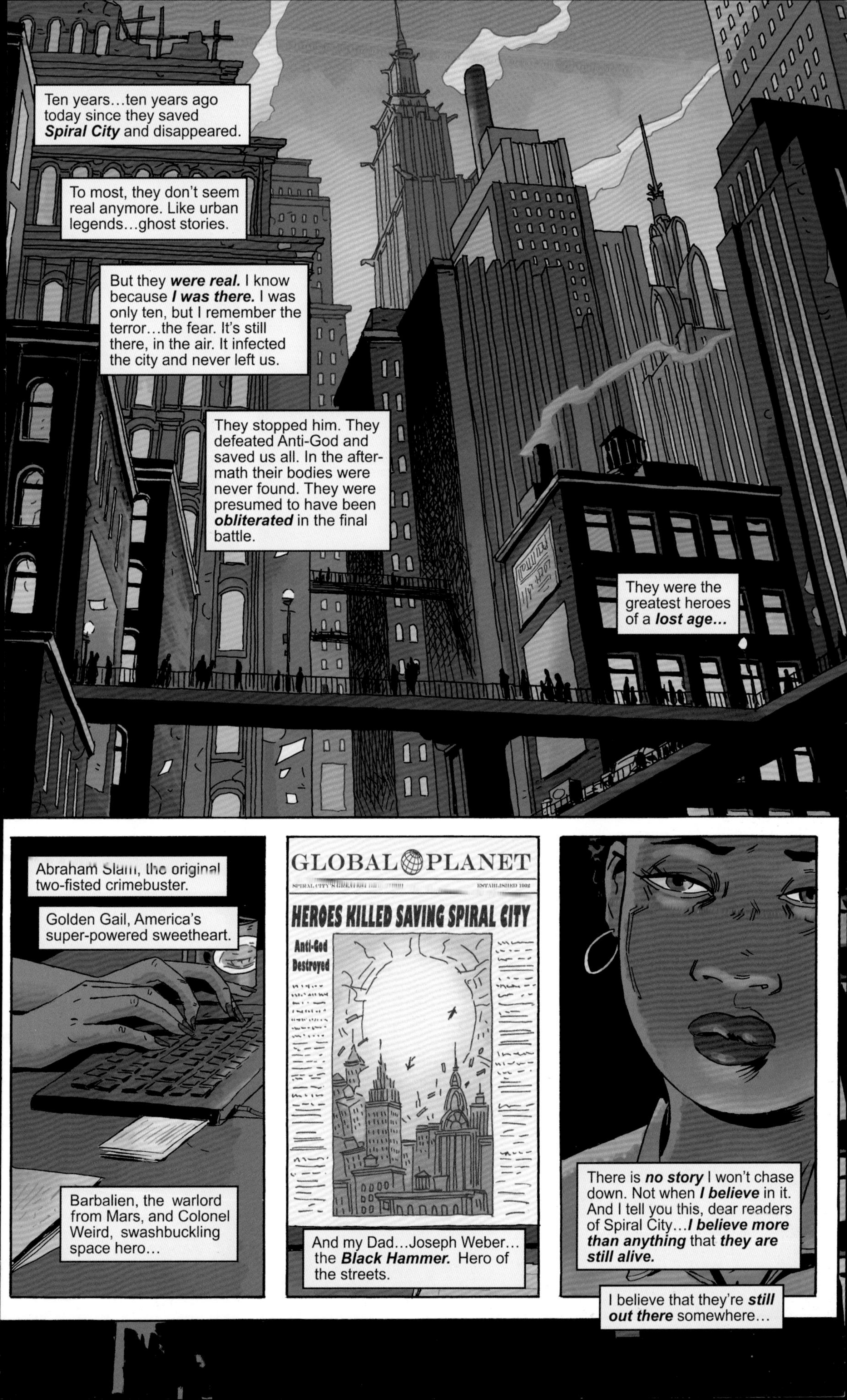
Ten years…ten years ago today since they saved ***Spiral City*** and disappeared.
To most, they don't seem real anymore. Like urban legends…ghost stories.
But they ***were real.*** I know because ***I was there.*** I was only ten, but I remember the terror…the fear. It's still there, in the air. It infected the city and never left us.
They stopped him. They defeated Anti-God and saved us all. In the aftermath their bodies were never found. They were presumed to have been ***obliterated*** in the final battle.
They were the greatest heroes of a ***lost age…***
Abraham Slam, the original two-fisted crimebuster.
Golden Gail, America's super-powered sweetheart.
Barbalien, the warlord from Mars, and Colonel Weird, swashbuckling space hero…
GLOBAL PLANET
ESTABLISHED 1902
HEROES KILLED SAVING SPIRAL CITY
Anti-God Destroyed
And my Dad…Joseph Weber…the ***Black Hammer.*** Hero of the streets.
There is ***no story*** I won't chase down. Not when ***I believe*** in it. And I tell you this, dear readers of Spiral City…***I believe more than anything*** that ***they are still alive.***
I believe that they're ***still out there*** somewhere…

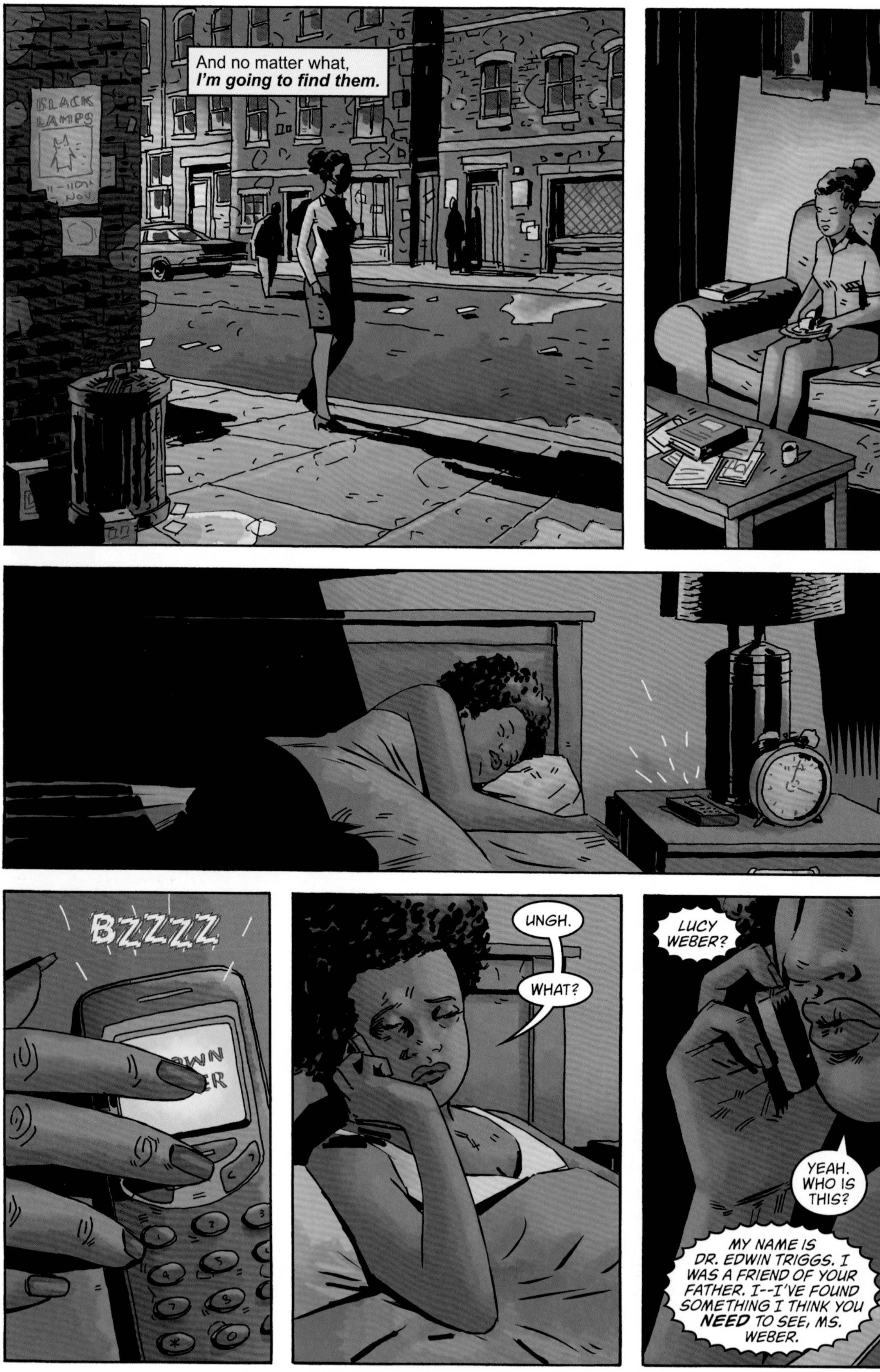

And no matter what,
I'm going to find them.
BLACK LAMPS
BZZZZ
UNGH.
WHAT?
LUCY WEBER?
YEAH. WHO IS THIS?
MY NAME IS DR. EDWIN TRIGGS. I WAS A FRIEND OF YOUR FATHER. I--I'VE FOUND SOMETHING I THINK YOU **NEED** TO SEE, MS. WEBER.

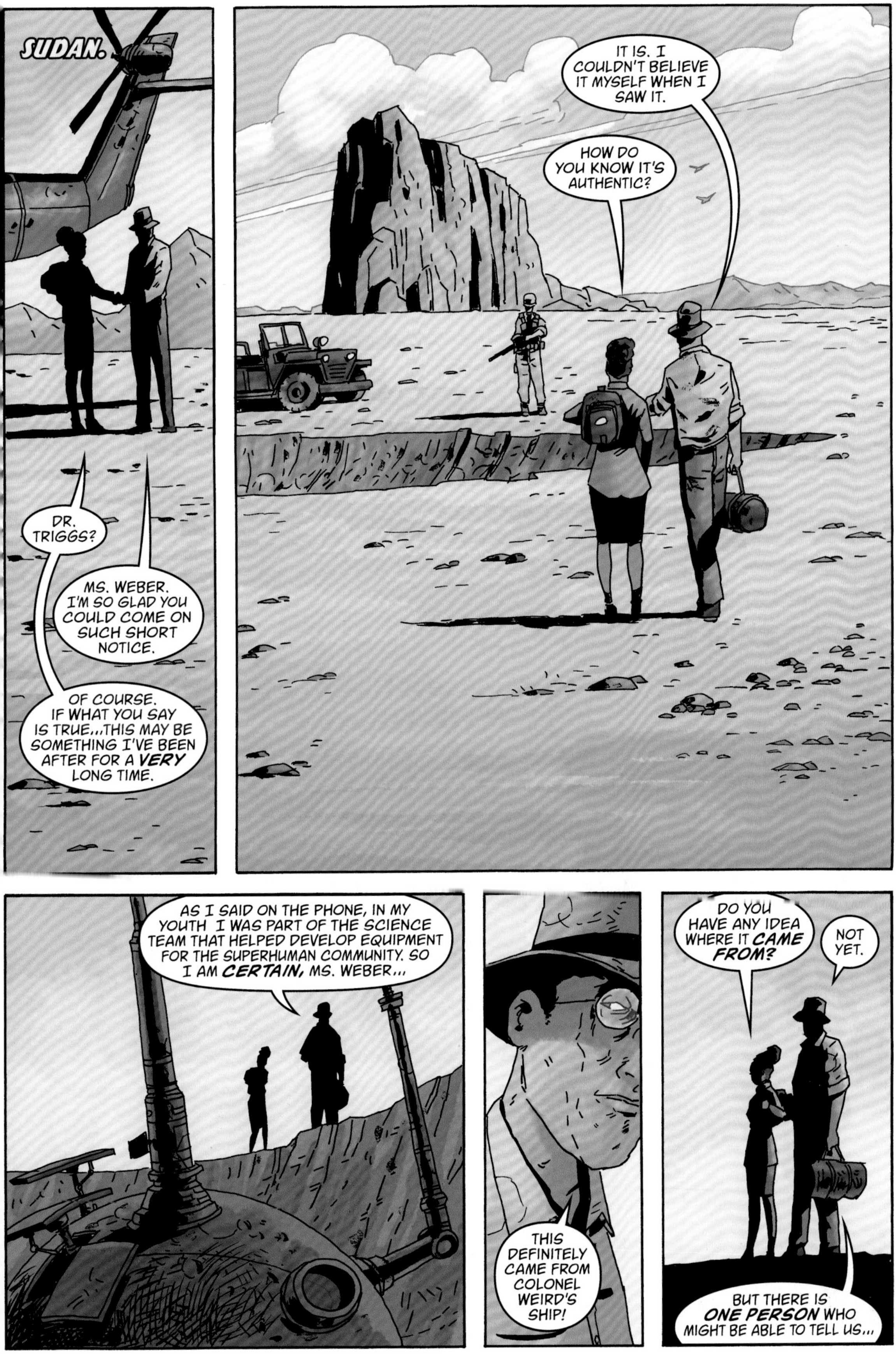
SUDAN.
DR. TRIGGS?
MS. WEBER. I'M SO GLAD YOU COULD COME ON SUCH SHORT NOTICE.
OF COURSE. IF WHAT YOU SAY IS TRUE...THIS MAY BE SOMETHING I'VE BEEN AFTER FOR A VERY LONG TIME.
HOW DO YOU KNOW IT'S AUTHENTIC?
IT IS. I COULDN'T BELIEVE IT MYSELF WHEN I SAW IT.
AS I SAID ON THE PHONE, IN MY YOUTH I WAS PART OF THE SCIENCE TEAM THAT HELPED DEVELOP EQUIPMENT FOR THE SUPERHUMAN COMMUNITY. SO I AM CERTAIN, MS. WEBER...
THIS DEFINITELY CAME FROM COLONEL WEIRD'S SHIP!
DO YOU HAVE ANY IDEA WHERE IT CAME FROM?
NOT YET.
BUT THERE IS ONE PERSON WHO MIGHT BE ABLE TO TELL US...

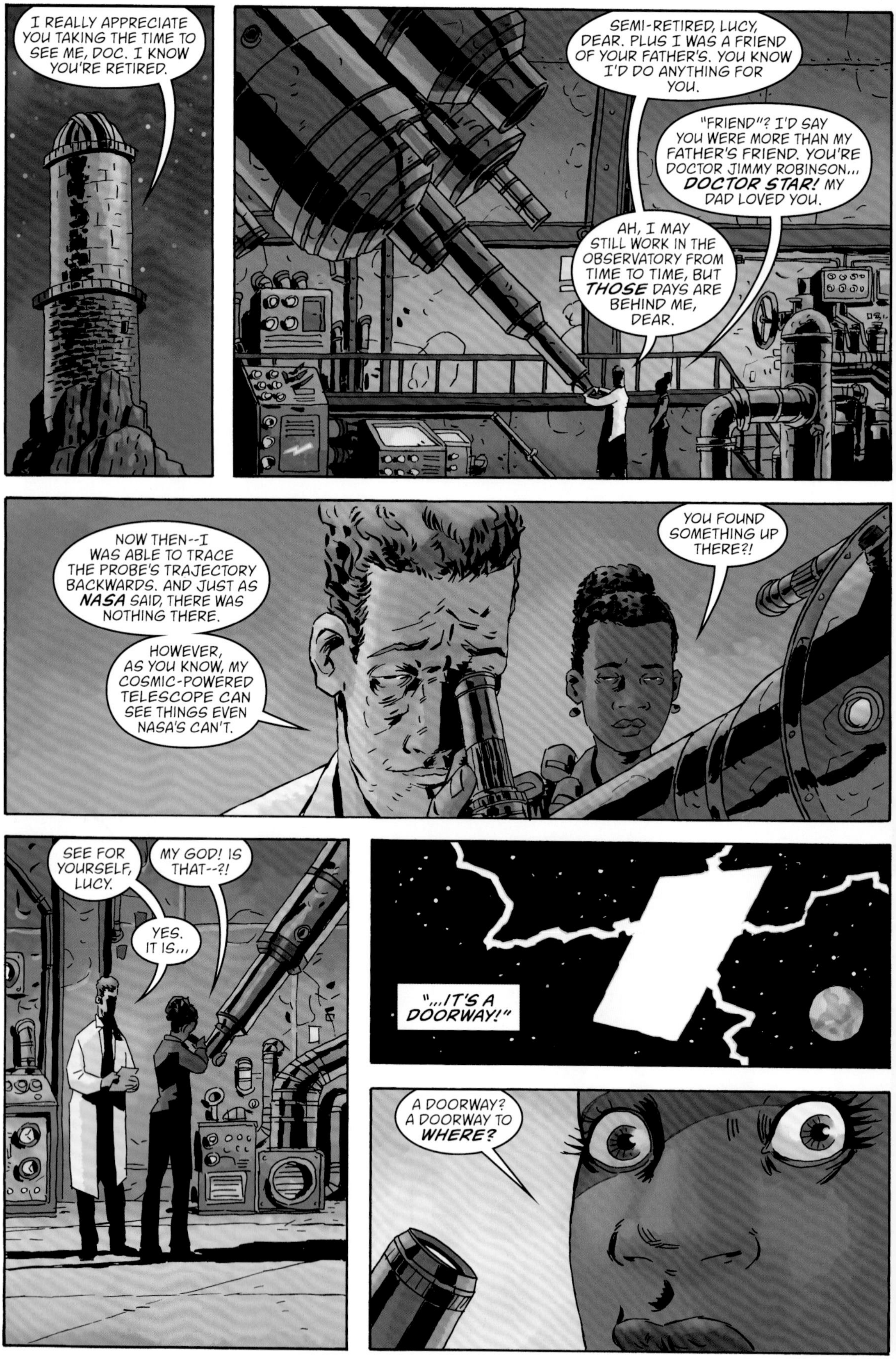
I REALLY APPRECIATE YOU TAKING THE TIME TO SEE ME, DOC. I KNOW YOU'RE RETIRED.
SEMI-RETIRED, LUCY, DEAR. PLUS I WAS A FRIEND OF YOUR FATHER'S. YOU KNOW I'D DO ANYTHING FOR YOU.
"FRIEND"? I'D SAY YOU WERE MORE THAN MY FATHER'S FRIEND. YOU'RE DOCTOR JIMMY ROBINSON... DOCTOR STAR! MY DAD LOVED YOU.
AH, I MAY STILL WORK IN THE OBSERVATORY FROM TIME TO TIME, BUT THOSE DAYS ARE BEHIND ME, DEAR.
NOW THEN--I WAS ABLE TO TRACE THE PROBE'S TRAJECTORY BACKWARDS. AND JUST AS NASA SAID, THERE WAS NOTHING THERE.
HOWEVER, AS YOU KNOW, MY COSMIC-POWERED TELESCOPE CAN SEE THINGS EVEN NASA'S CAN'T.
YOU FOUND SOMETHING UP THERE?!
SEE FOR YOURSELF, LUCY.
MY GOD! IS THAT--?!
YES. IT IS...
"...IT'S A DOORWAY!"
A DOORWAY? A DOORWAY TO WHERE?

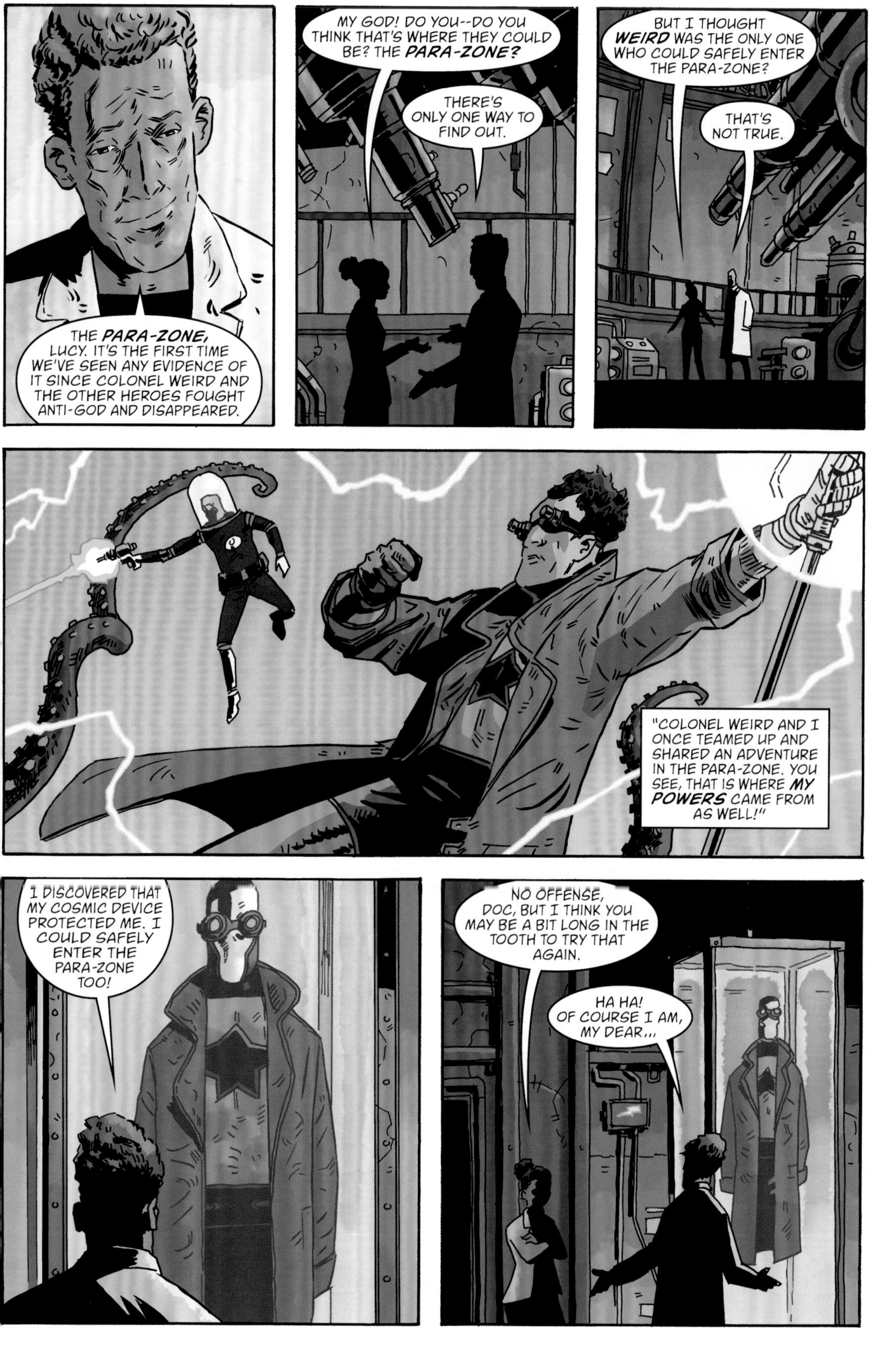
THE PARA-ZONE, LUCY. IT'S THE FIRST TIME WE'VE SEEN ANY EVIDENCE OF IT SINCE COLONEL WEIRD AND THE OTHER HEROES FOUGHT ANTI-GOD AND DISAPPEARED.
MY GOD! DO YOU--DO YOU THINK THAT'S WHERE THEY COULD BE? THE PARA-ZONE?
THERE'S ONLY ONE WAY TO FIND OUT.
BUT I THOUGHT WEIRD WAS THE ONLY ONE WHO COULD SAFELY ENTER THE PARA-ZONE?
THAT'S NOT TRUE.
"COLONEL WEIRD AND I ONCE TEAMED UP AND SHARED AN ADVENTURE IN THE PARA-ZONE. YOU SEE, THAT IS WHERE MY POWERS CAME FROM AS WELL!"
I DISCOVERED THAT MY COSMIC DEVICE PROTECTED ME. I COULD SAFELY ENTER THE PARA-ZONE TOO!
NO OFFENSE, DOC, BUT I THINK YOU MAY BE A BIT LONG IN THE TOOTH TO TRY THAT AGAIN.
HA HA! OF COURSE I AM, MY DEAR...

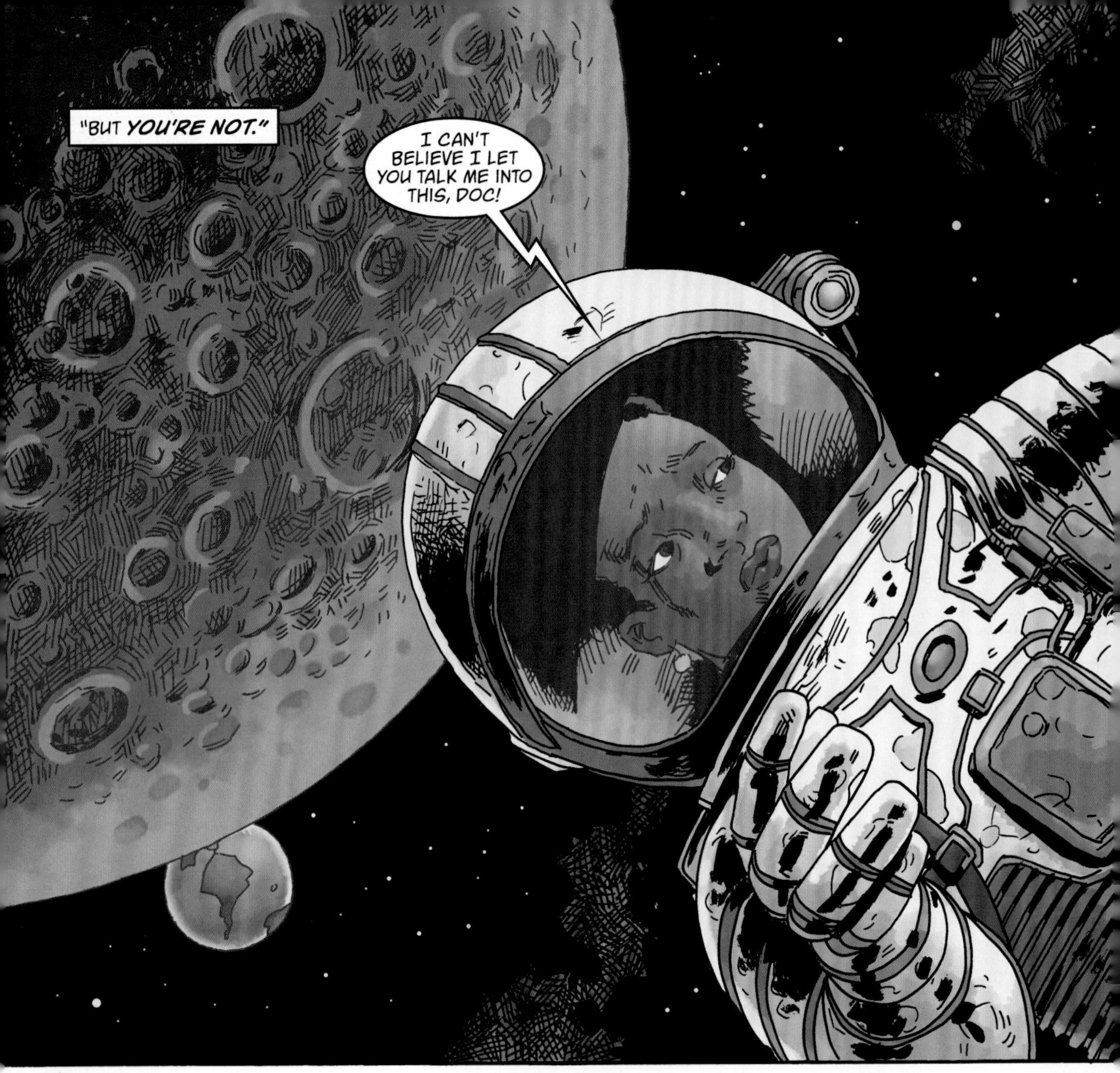
"BUT YOU'RE NOT."
I CAN'T BELIEVE I LET YOU TALK ME INTO THIS, DOC!

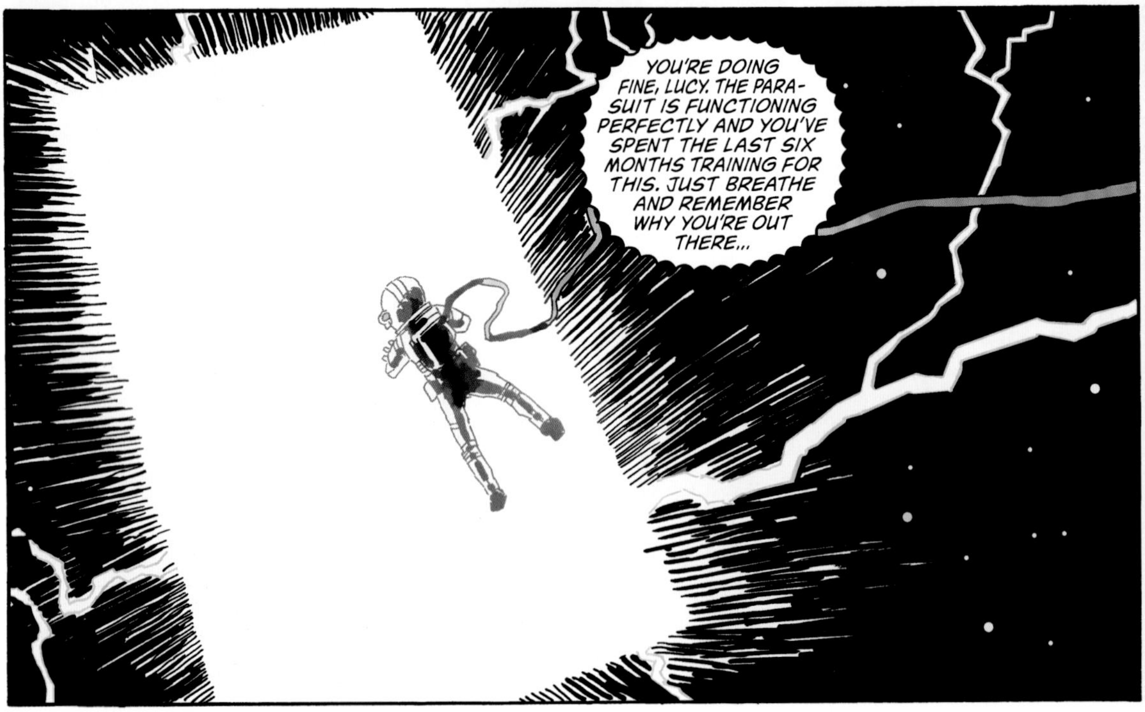
YOU'RE DOING FINE, LUCY. THE PARA-SUIT IS FUNCTIONING PERFECTLY AND YOU'VE SPENT THE LAST SIX MONTHS TRAINING FOR THIS. JUST BREATHE AND REMEMBER WHY YOU'RE OUT THERE...

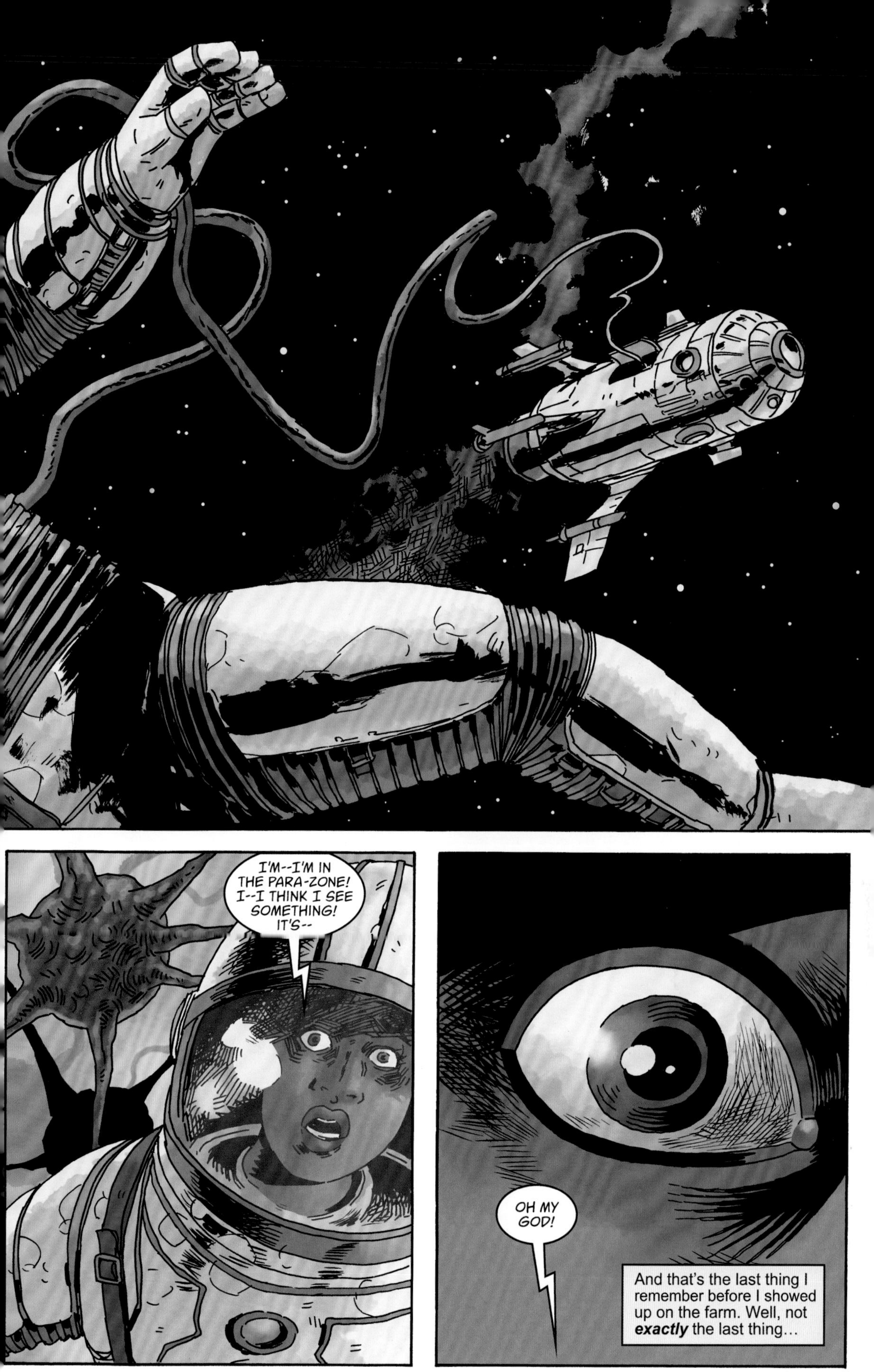
I'M--I'M IN THE PARA-ZONE! I--I THINK I SEE SOMETHING! IT'S--
OH MY GOD!
And that's the last thing I remember before I showed up on the farm. Well, not *exactly* the last thing…

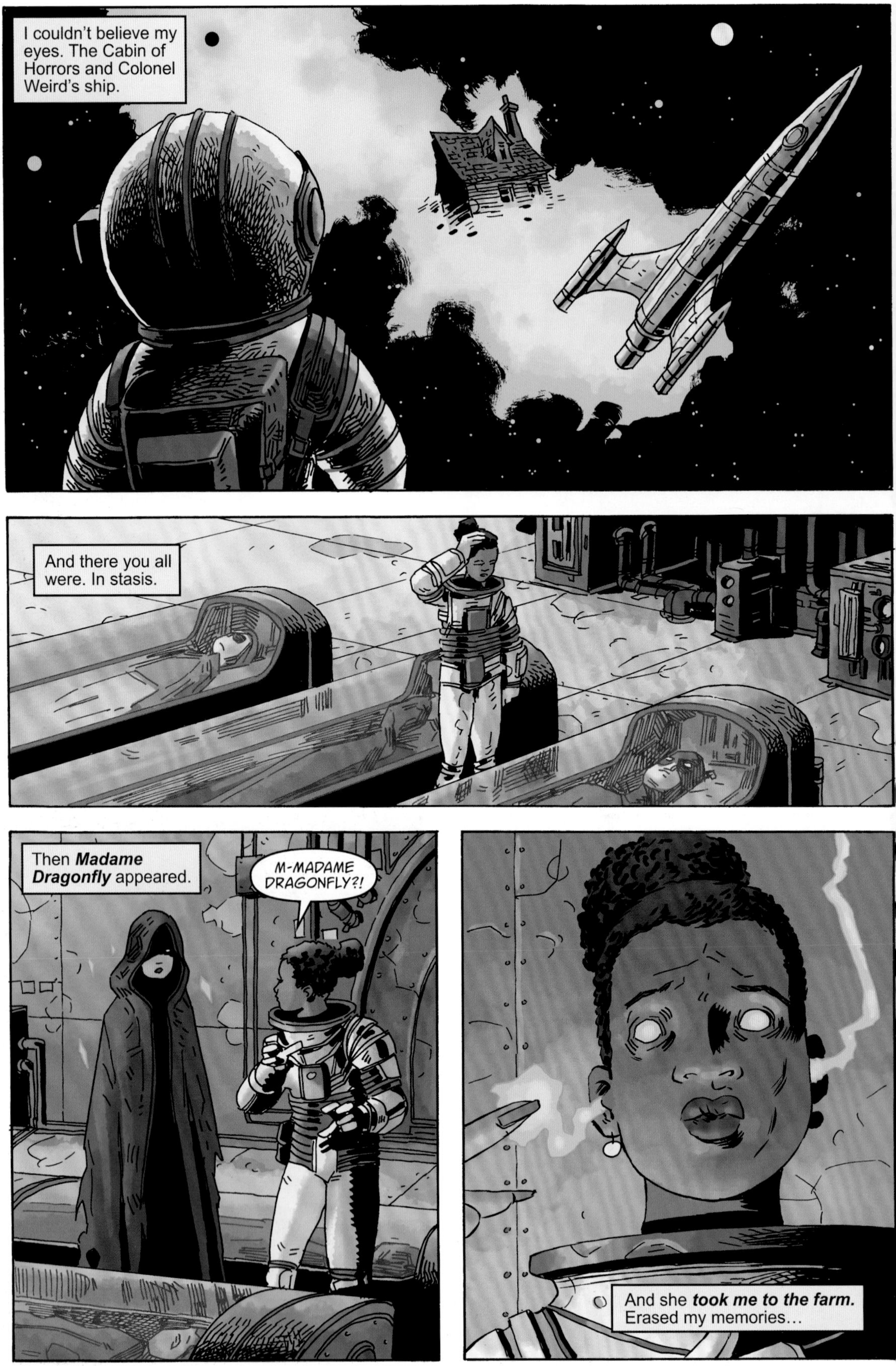
I couldn't believe my eyes. The Cabin of Horrors and Colonel Weird's ship.
And there you all were. In stasis.
Then ***Madame Dragonfly*** appeared.
M-MADAME DRAGONFLY?!
And she ***took me to the farm.*** Erased my memories…

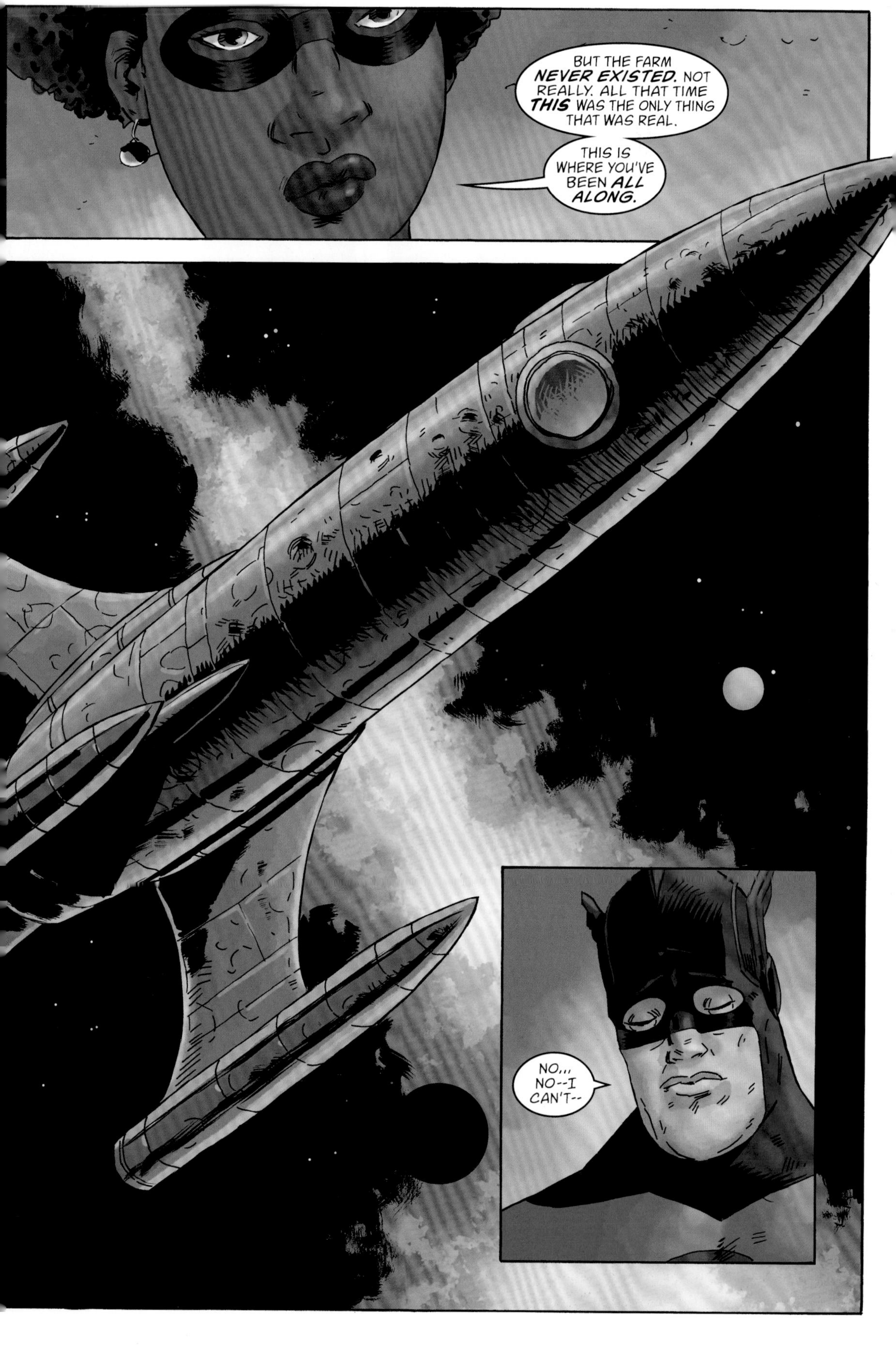

BUT THE FARM **NEVER EXISTED.** NOT REALLY. ALL THAT TIME **THIS** WAS THE ONLY THING THAT WAS REAL.
THIS IS WHERE YOU'VE BEEN **ALL ALONG.**
NO... NO--I CAN'T--

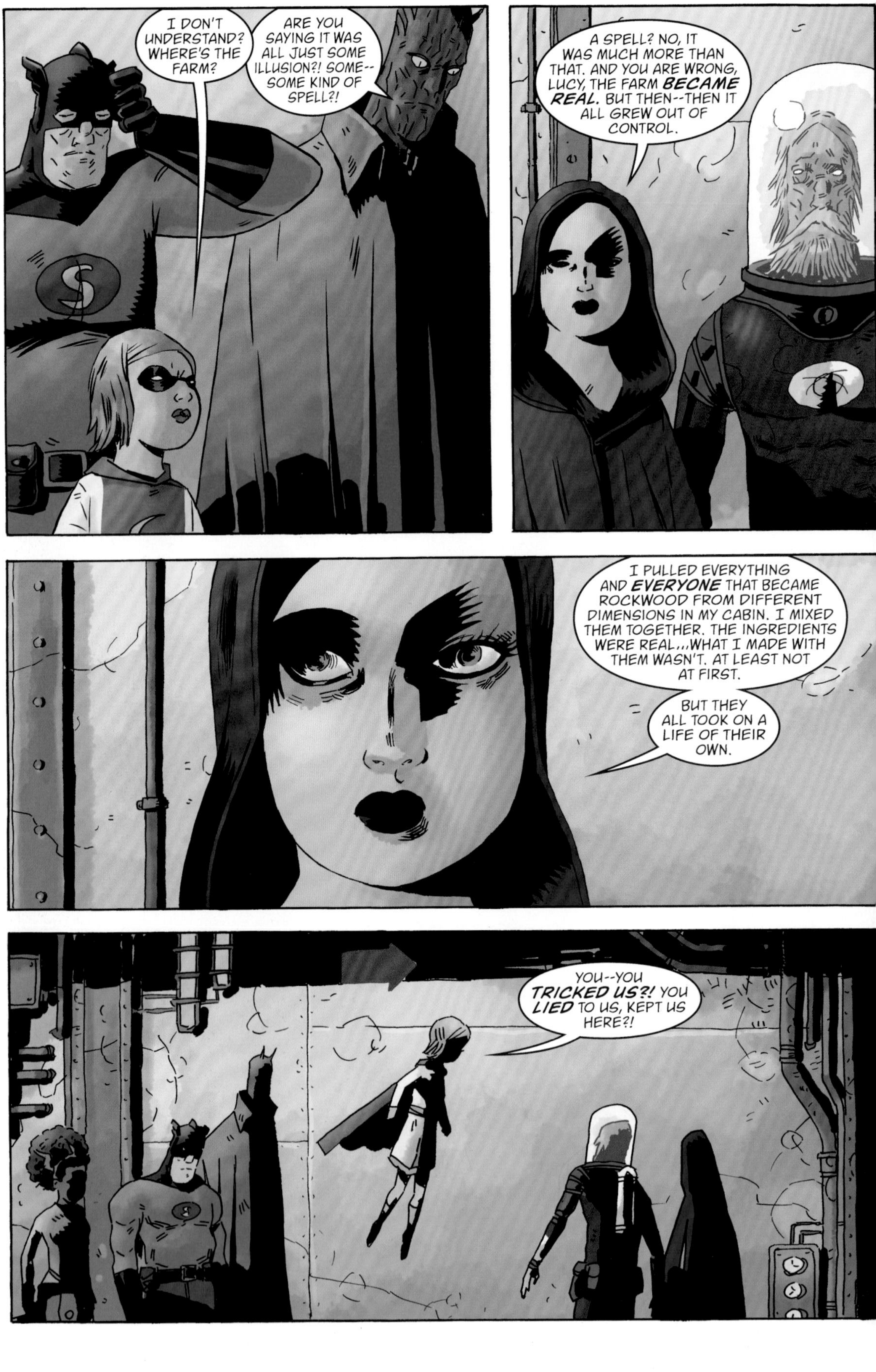
I DON'T UNDERSTAND? WHERE'S THE FARM?
ARE YOU SAYING IT WAS ALL JUST SOME ILLUSION?! SOME-- SOME KIND OF SPELL?!
A SPELL? NO, IT WAS MUCH MORE THAN THAT. AND YOU ARE WRONG, LUCY, THE FARM **BECAME REAL.** BUT THEN--THEN IT ALL GREW OUT OF CONTROL.
I PULLED EVERYTHING AND **EVERYONE** THAT BECAME ROCKWOOD FROM DIFFERENT DIMENSIONS IN MY CABIN. I MIXED THEM TOGETHER. THE INGREDIENTS WERE REAL...WHAT I MADE WITH THEM WASN'T. AT LEAST NOT AT FIRST.
BUT THEY ALL TOOK ON A LIFE OF THEIR OWN.
YOU--YOU **TRICKED US?!** YOU **LIED** TO US, KEPT US HERE?!

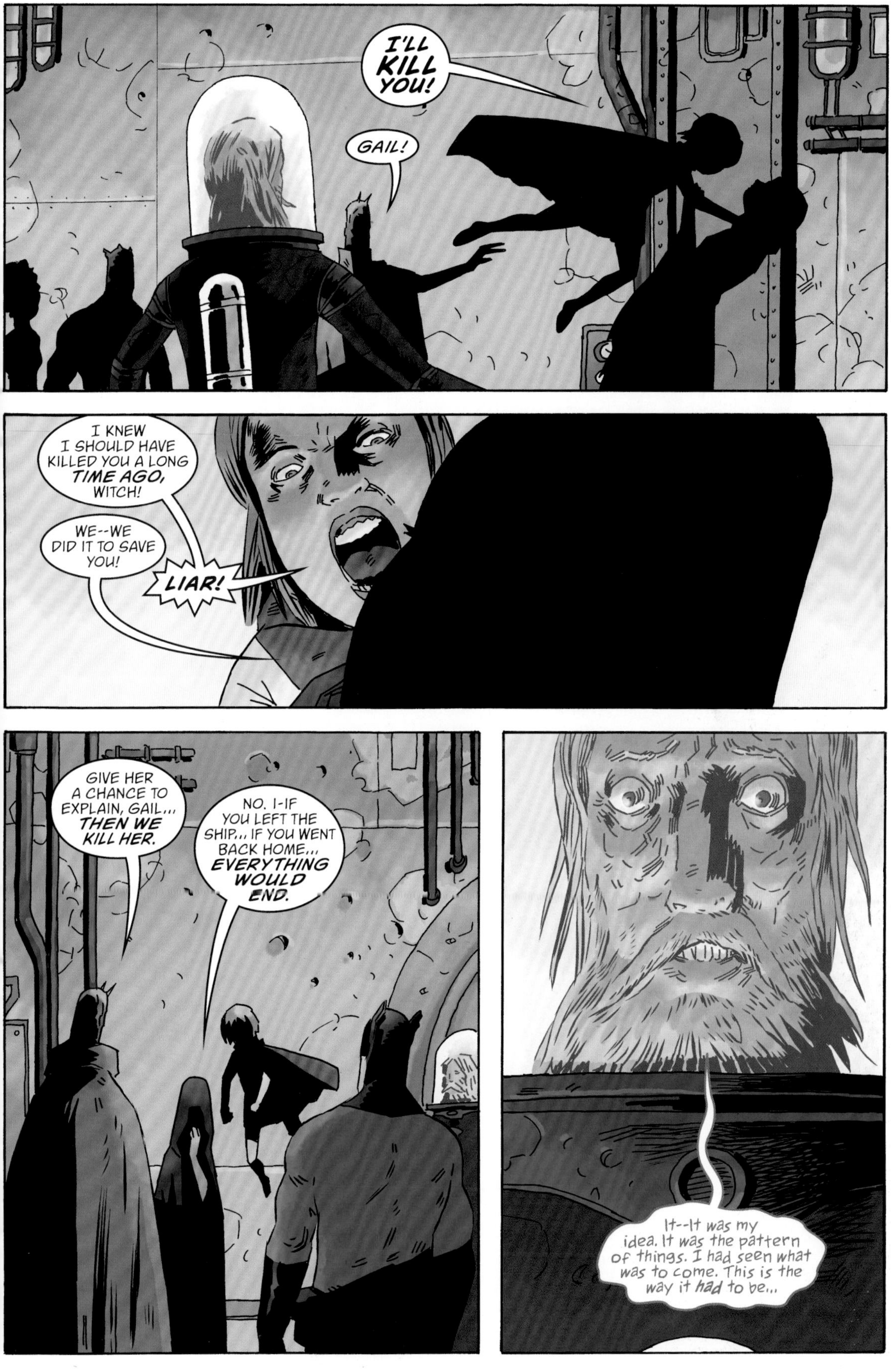
I'LL KILL YOU!
GAIL!
I KNEW I SHOULD HAVE KILLED YOU A LONG TIME AGO, WITCH!
WE--WE DID IT TO SAVE YOU!
LIAR!
GIVE HER A CHANCE TO EXPLAIN, GAIL... THEN WE KILL HER.
NO. I-IF YOU LEFT THE SHIP... IF YOU WENT BACK HOME... EVERYTHING WOULD END.
It--It was my idea. It was the pattern of things. I had seen what was to come. This is the way it had to be...

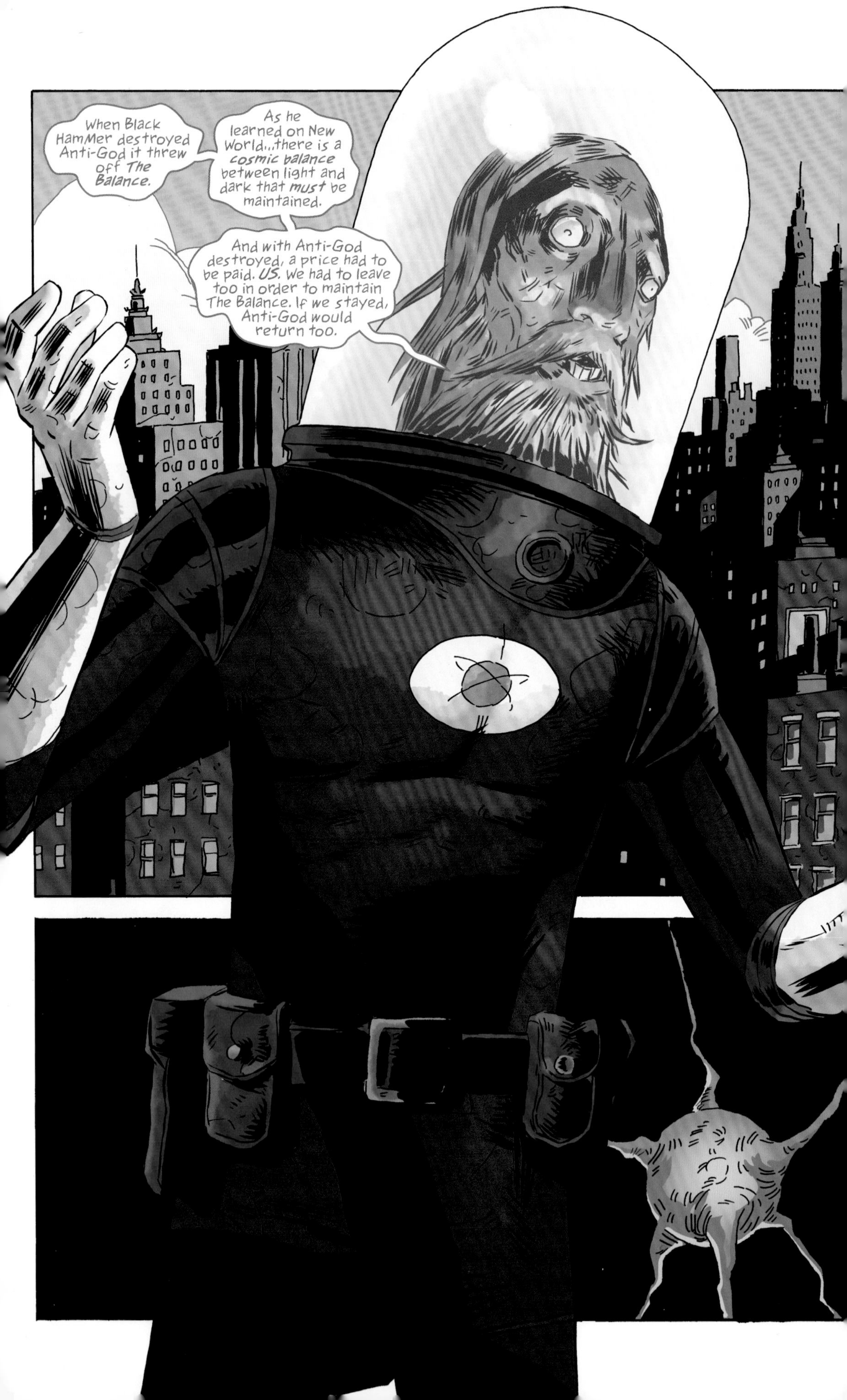
When Black HamMer destroyed Anti-God it threw off *The Balance.*
As he learned on New World...there is a *cosmic balance* between light and dark that *must* be maintained.
And with Anti-God destroyed, a price had to be paid. *US.* We had to leave too in order to maintain The Balance. If we stayed, Anti-God would return too.

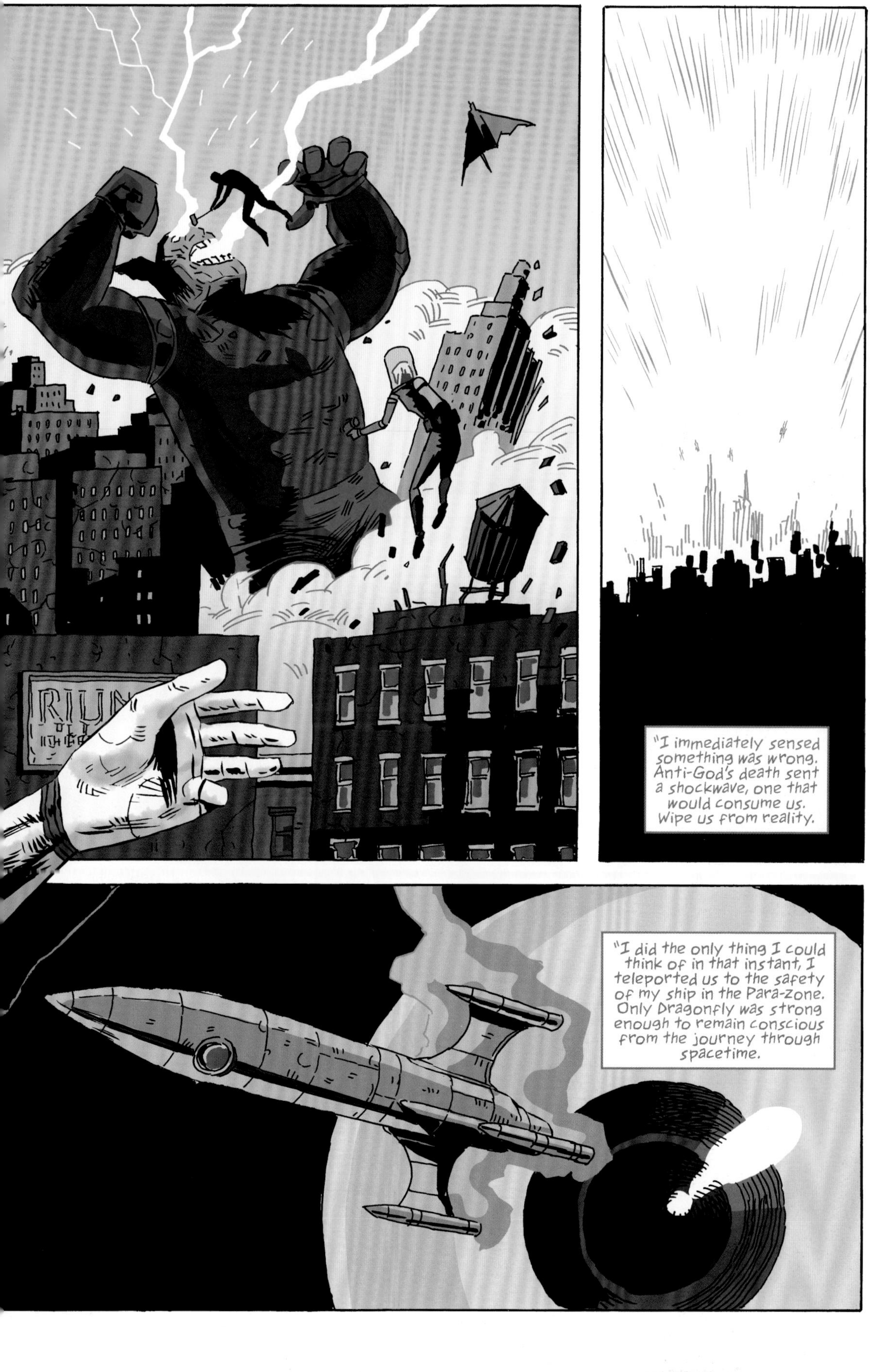
"I immediately sensed something was wrong. Anti-God's death sent a shockwave, one that would consume us. Wipe us from reality.
"I did the only thing I could think of in that instant, I teleported us to the safety of my ship in the Para-zone. Only Dragonfly was strong enough to remain conscious from the journey through spacetime.

"We had to act quickly. We knew if you woke we would all face the dilemma. Do we go back and risk Anti-God returning or...do we stay here forever."

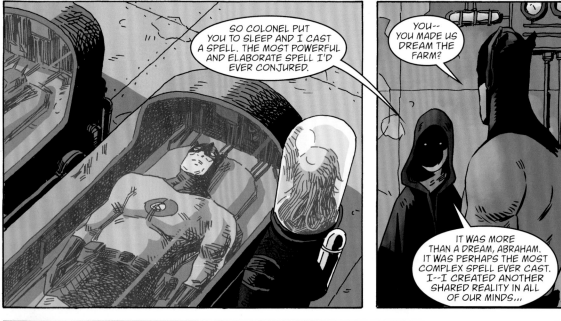

SO COLONEL PUT YOU TO SLEEP AND I CAST A SPELL. THE MOST POWERFUL AND ELABORATE SPELL I'D EVER CONJURED.

YOU-- YOU MADE US DREAM THE FARM?

IT WAS MORE THAN A DREAM, ABRAHAM. IT WAS PERHAPS THE MOST COMPLEX SPELL EVER CAST. I--I CREATED ANOTHER SHARED REALITY IN ALL OF OUR MINDS...

"IT WAS THE MOST NEUTRAL SETTING I COULD THINK OF. IF--IF WE HAD TO STAY THERE FOREVER I JUST WANTED YOU ALL TO BE HAPPY."

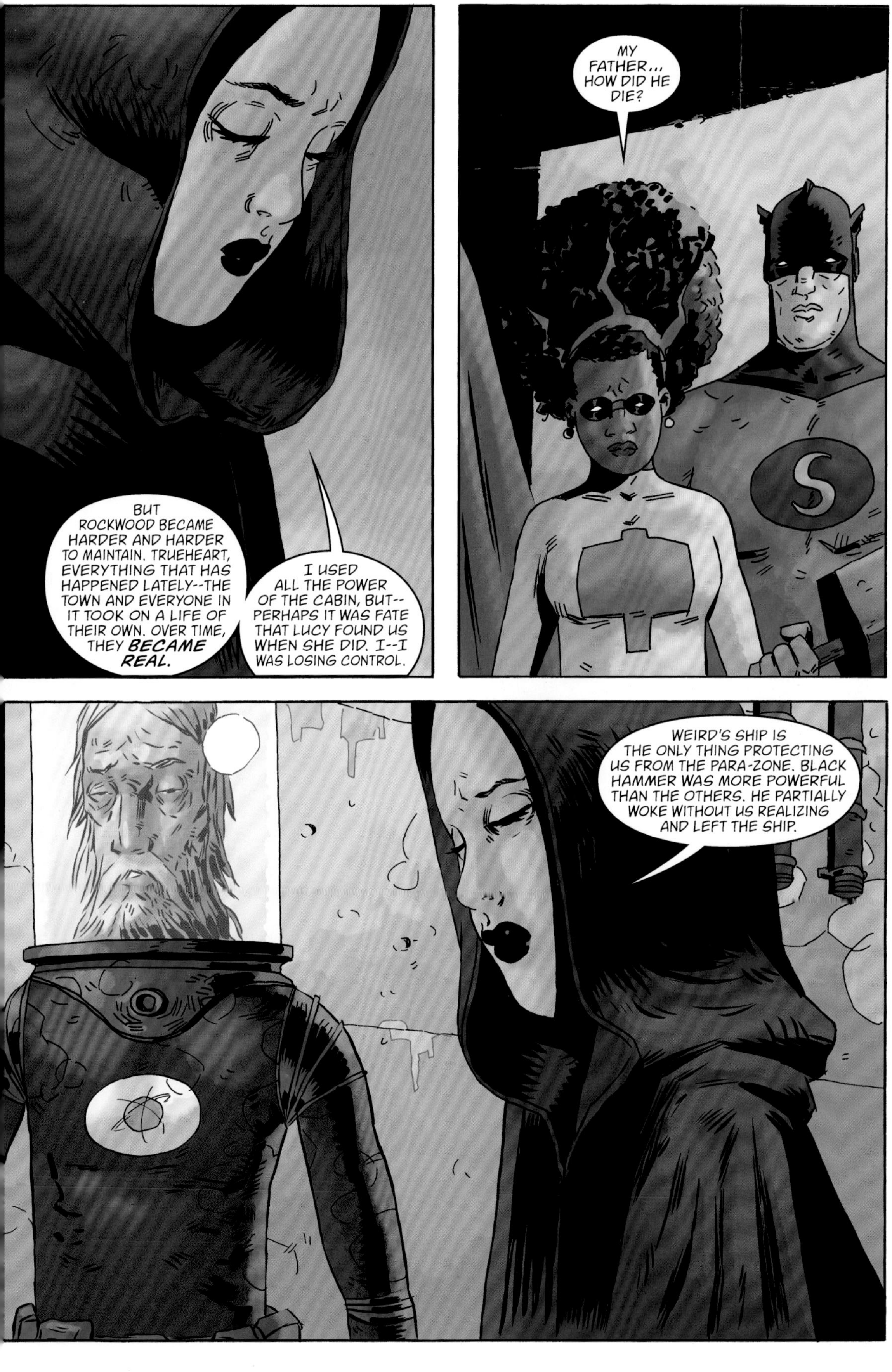

BUT ROCKWOOD BECAME HARDER AND HARDER TO MAINTAIN. TRUEHEART, EVERYTHING THAT HAS HAPPENED LATELY--THE TOWN AND EVERYONE IN IT TOOK ON A LIFE OF THEIR OWN. OVER TIME, THEY *BECAME REAL.*
I USED ALL THE POWER OF THE CABIN, BUT--PERHAPS IT WAS FATE THAT LUCY FOUND US WHEN SHE DID. I--I WAS LOSING CONTROL.
MY FATHER... HOW DID HE DIE?
WEIRD'S SHIP IS THE ONLY THING PROTECTING US FROM THE PARA-ZONE. BLACK HAMMER WAS MORE POWERFUL THAN THE OTHERS. HE PARTIALLY WOKE WITHOUT US REALIZING AND LEFT THE SHIP.

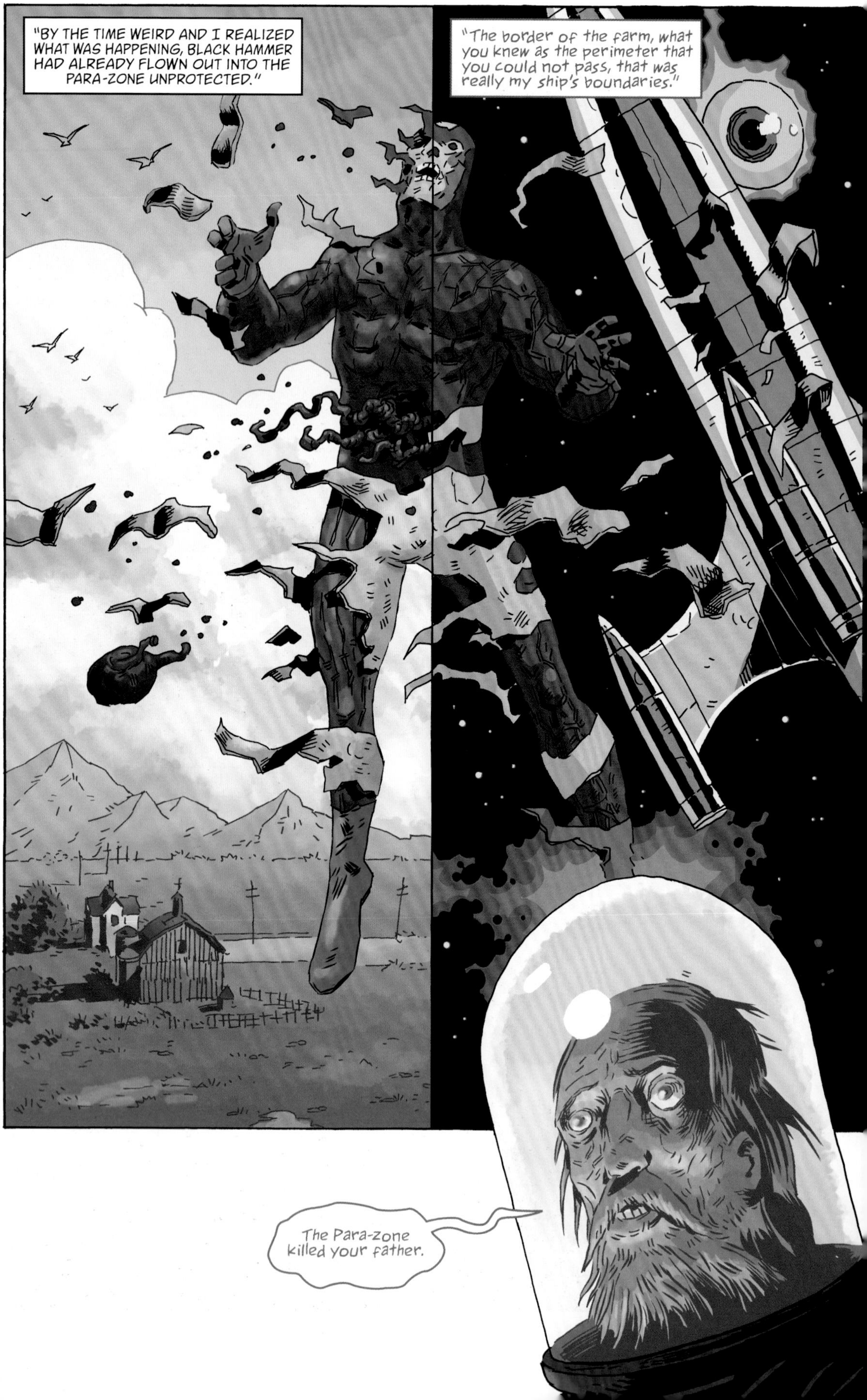
"BY THE TIME WEIRD AND I REALIZED WHAT WAS HAPPENING, BLACK HAMMER HAD ALREADY FLOWN OUT INTO THE PARA-ZONE UNPROTECTED."
"The border of the farm, what you knew as the perimeter that you could not pass, that was really my ship's boundaries."
The Para-zone killed your father.

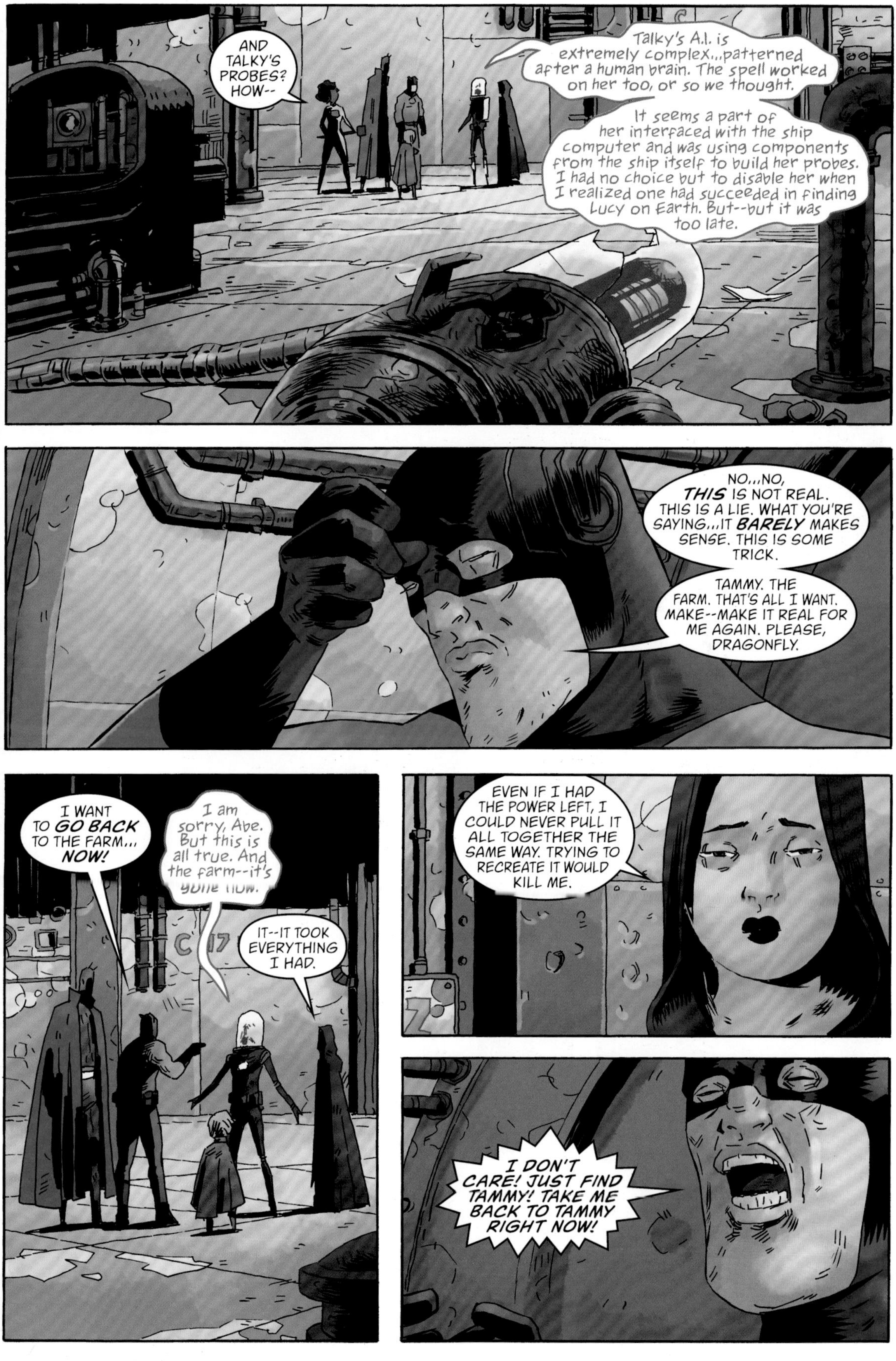
AND TALKY'S PROBES? HOW--
Talky's A.I. is extremely complex...patterned after a human brain. The spell worked on her too, or so we thought.
It seems a part of her interfaced with the ship computer and was using components from the ship itself to build her probes. I had no choice but to disable her when I realized one had succeeded in finding Lucy on Earth. But--but it was too late.
NO...NO, THIS IS NOT REAL. THIS IS A LIE. WHAT YOU'RE SAYING...IT BARELY MAKES SENSE. THIS IS SOME TRICK.
TAMMY. THE FARM. THAT'S ALL I WANT. MAKE--MAKE IT REAL FOR ME AGAIN. PLEASE, DRAGONFLY.
I WANT TO GO BACK TO THE FARM... NOW!
I am sorry, Abe. But this is all true. And the farm--it's gone now.
IT--IT TOOK EVERYTHING I HAD.
EVEN IF I HAD THE POWER LEFT, I COULD NEVER PULL IT ALL TOGETHER THE SAME WAY. TRYING TO RECREATE IT WOULD KILL ME.
I DON'T CARE! JUST FIND TAMMY! TAKE ME BACK TO TAMMY RIGHT NOW!

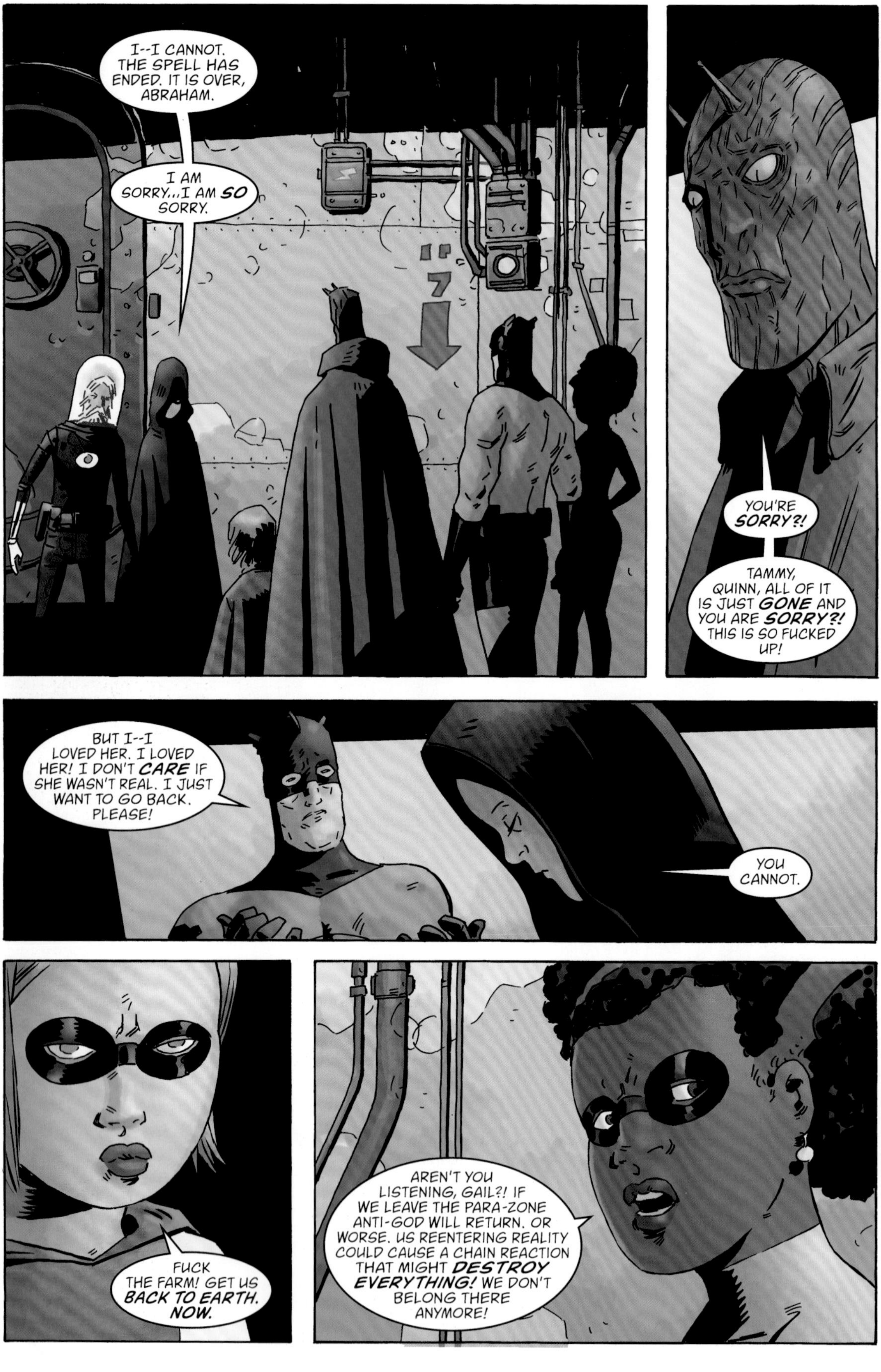
I--I CANNOT. THE SPELL HAS ENDED. IT IS OVER, ABRAHAM.
I AM SORRY...I AM **SO** SORRY.
YOU'RE ***SORRY?!***
TAMMY, QUINN, ALL OF IT IS JUST ***GONE*** AND YOU ARE ***SORRY?!*** THIS IS SO FUCKED UP!
BUT I--I LOVED HER. I LOVED HER! I DON'T ***CARE*** IF SHE WASN'T REAL. I JUST WANT TO GO BACK. PLEASE!
YOU CANNOT.
FUCK THE FARM! GET US ***BACK TO EARTH. NOW.***
AREN'T YOU LISTENING, GAIL?! IF WE LEAVE THE PARA-ZONE ANTI-GOD WILL RETURN. OR WORSE. US REENTERING REALITY COULD CAUSE A CHAIN REACTION THAT MIGHT ***DESTROY EVERYTHING!*** WE DON'T BELONG THERE ANYMORE!

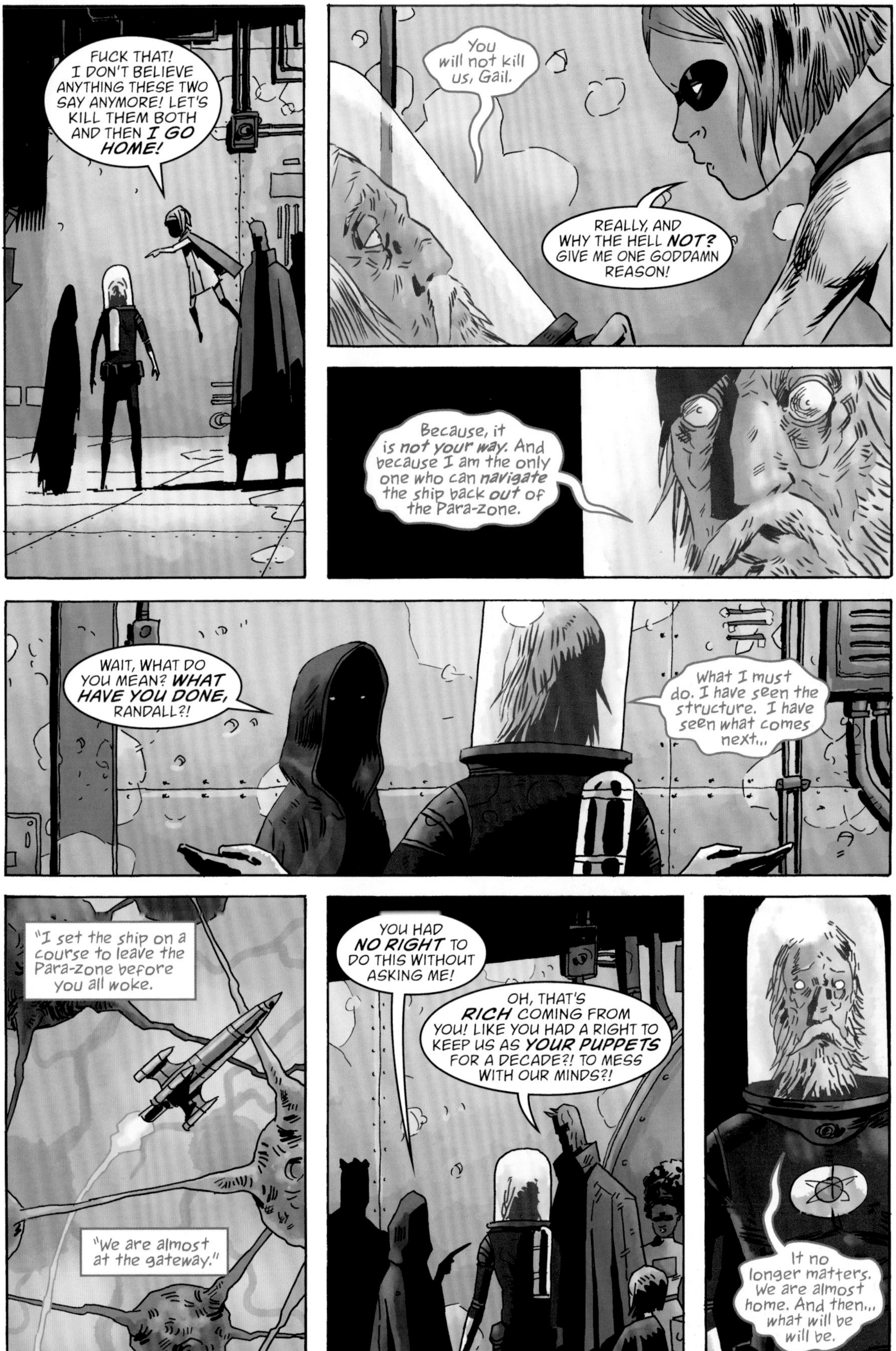
FUCK THAT! I DON'T BELIEVE ANYTHING THESE TWO SAY ANYMORE! LET'S KILL THEM BOTH AND THEN I GO HOME!
You will not kill us, Gail.
REALLY, AND WHY THE HELL NOT? GIVE ME ONE GODDAMN REASON!
Because, it is not your way. And because I am the only one who can navigate the ship back out of the Para-zone.
WAIT, WHAT DO YOU MEAN? WHAT HAVE YOU DONE, RANDALL?!
What I must do. I have seen the structure. I have seen what comes next...
"I set the ship on a course to leave the Para-zone before you all woke.
"We are almost at the gateway."
YOU HAD NO RIGHT TO DO THIS WITHOUT ASKING ME!
OH, THAT'S RICH COMING FROM YOU! LIKE YOU HAD A RIGHT TO KEEP US AS YOUR PUPPETS FOR A DECADE?! TO MESS WITH OUR MINDS?!
It no longer matters. We are almost home. And then... what will be will be.

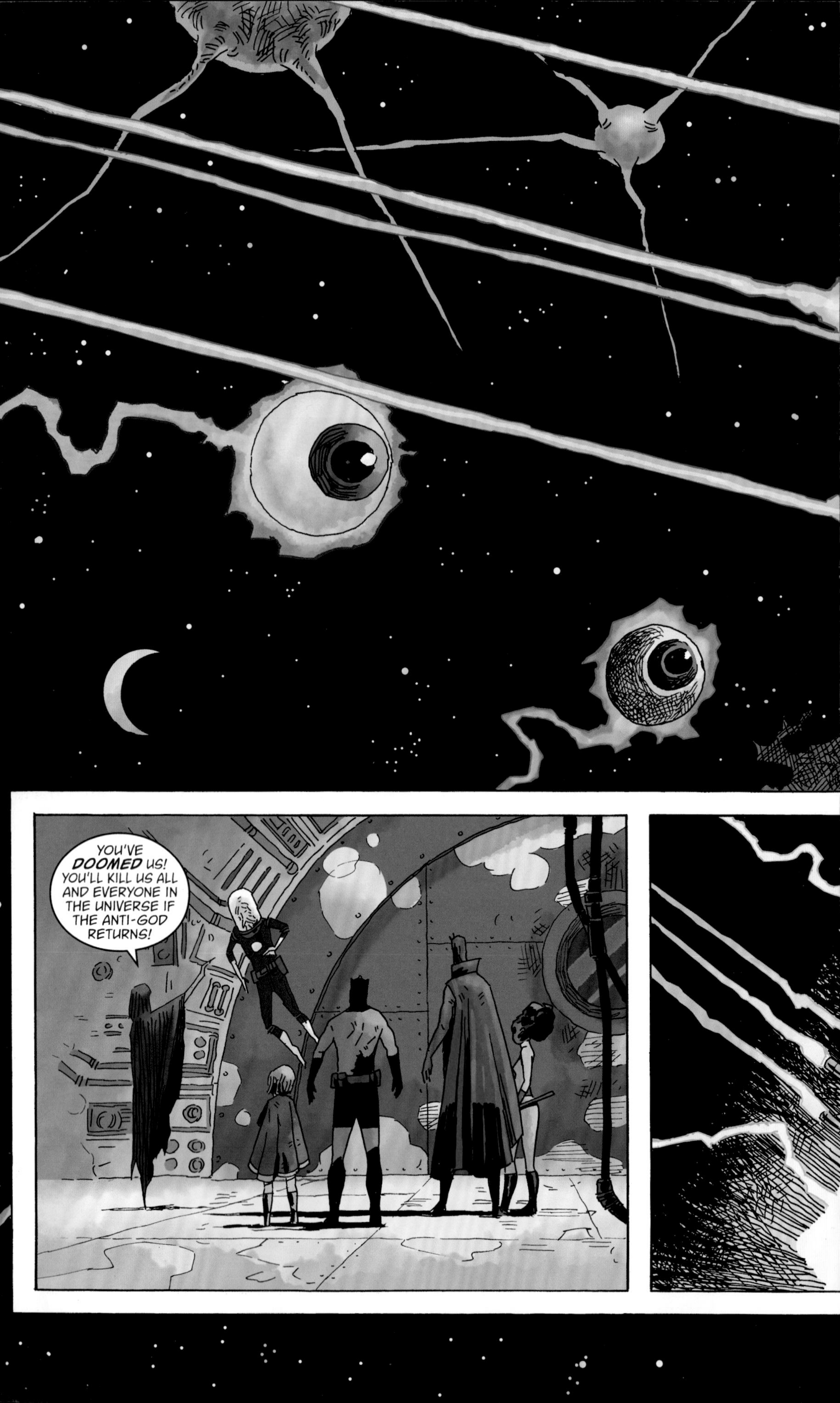
YOU'VE DOOMED US! YOU'LL KILL US ALL AND EVERYONE IN THE UNIVERSE IF THE ANTI-GOD RETURNS!

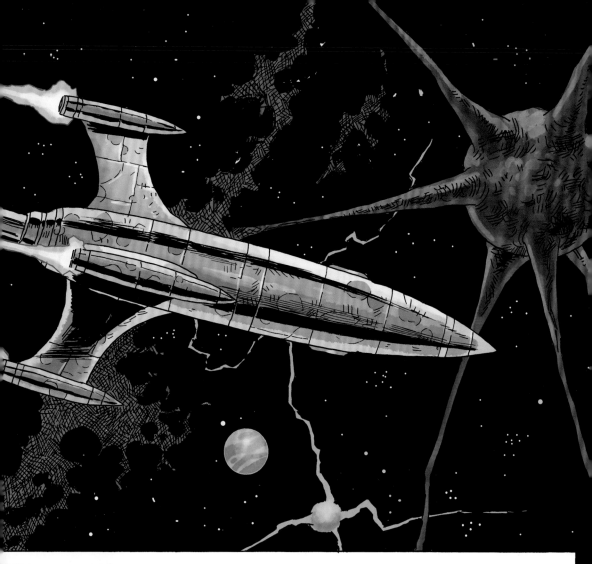

WH-WHAT'S HAPPENING?!

TURN AROUND! TAKE US BACK!

Too late, Abraham...it is done.

NO!

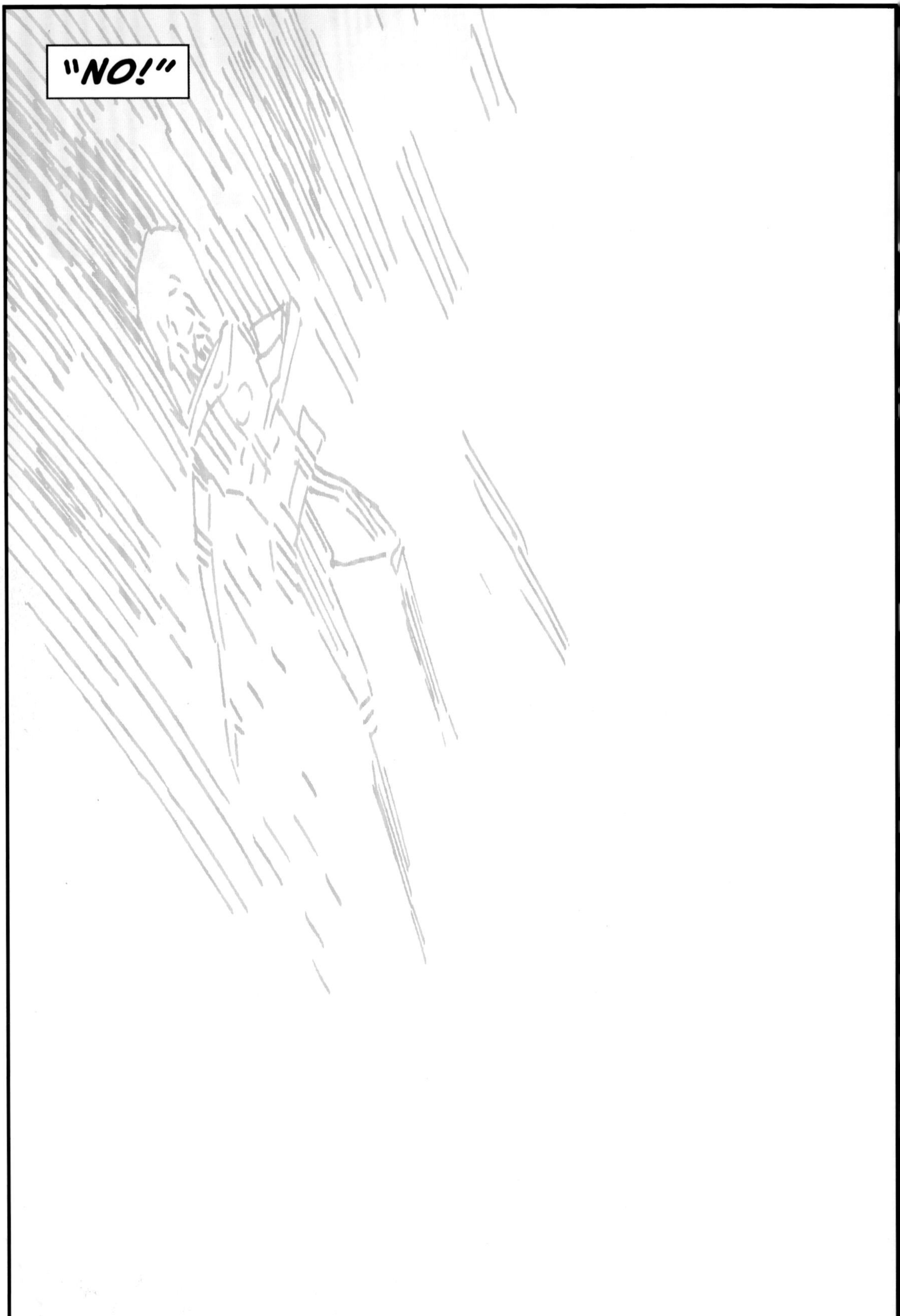
"NO!"

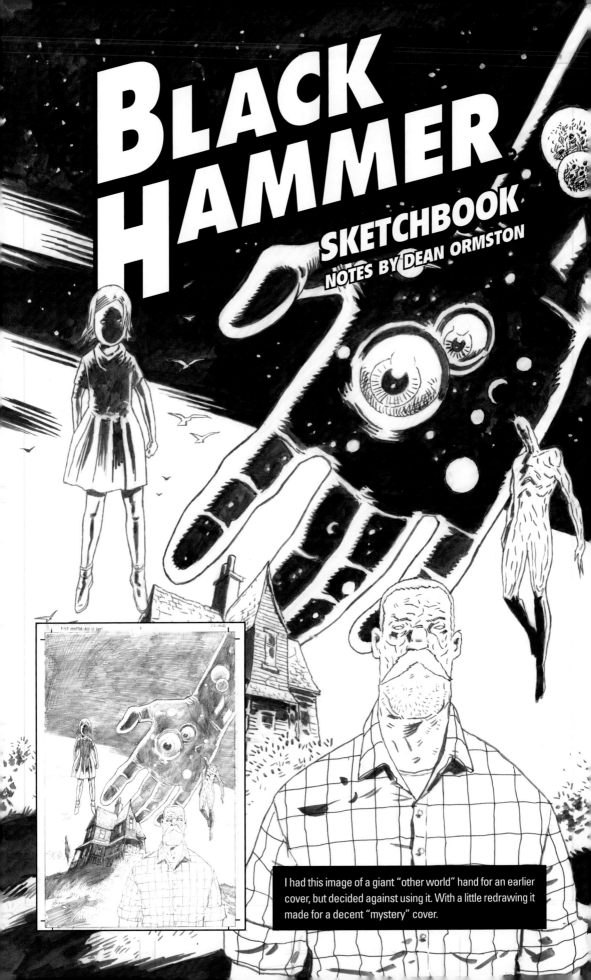

BLACK HAMMER

SKETCHBOOK
NOTES BY DEAN ORMSTON

I had this image of a giant "other world" hand for an earlier cover, but decided against using it. With a little redrawing it made for a decent "mystery" cover.

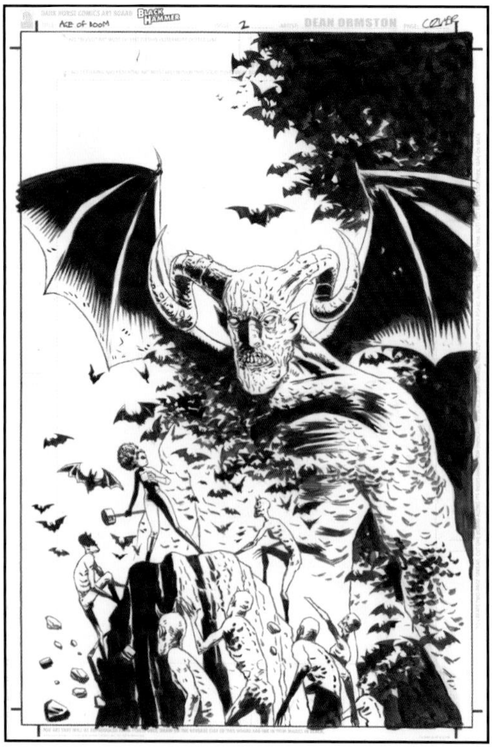
BLACK HAMMER
AGE OF DOOM
2
DEAN ORMSTON
COVER

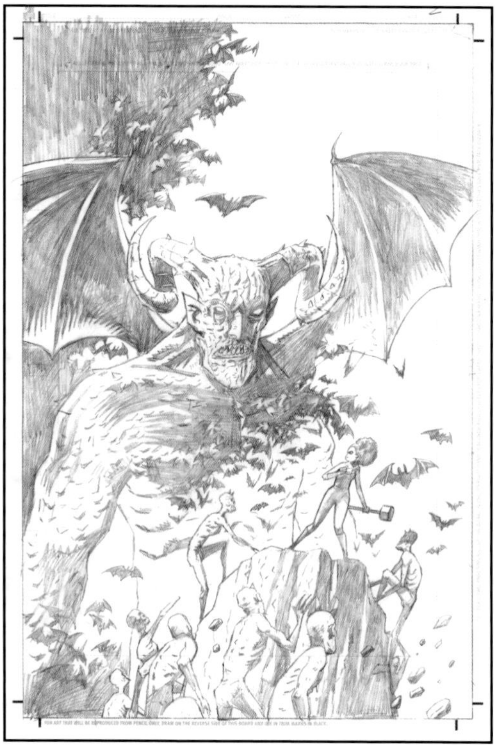

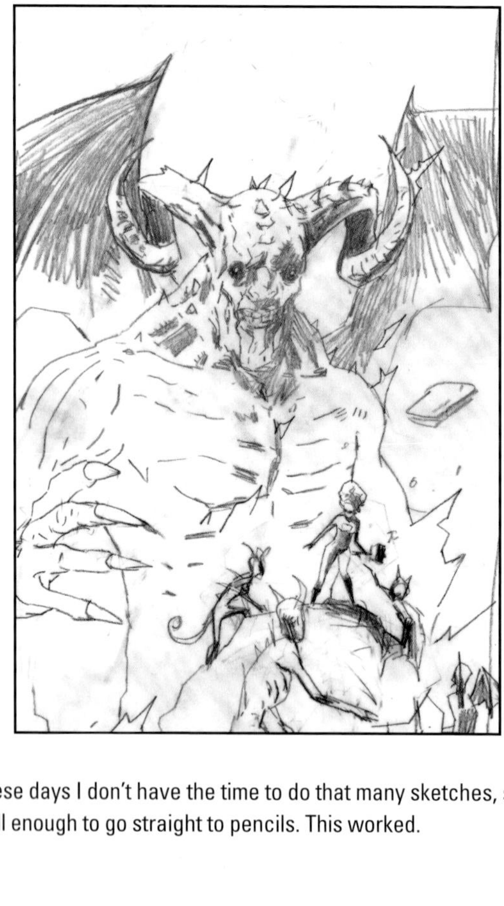

For most of my work these days I don't have the time to do that many sketches, so it's a great relief when a first sketch works well enough to go straight to pencils. This worked.

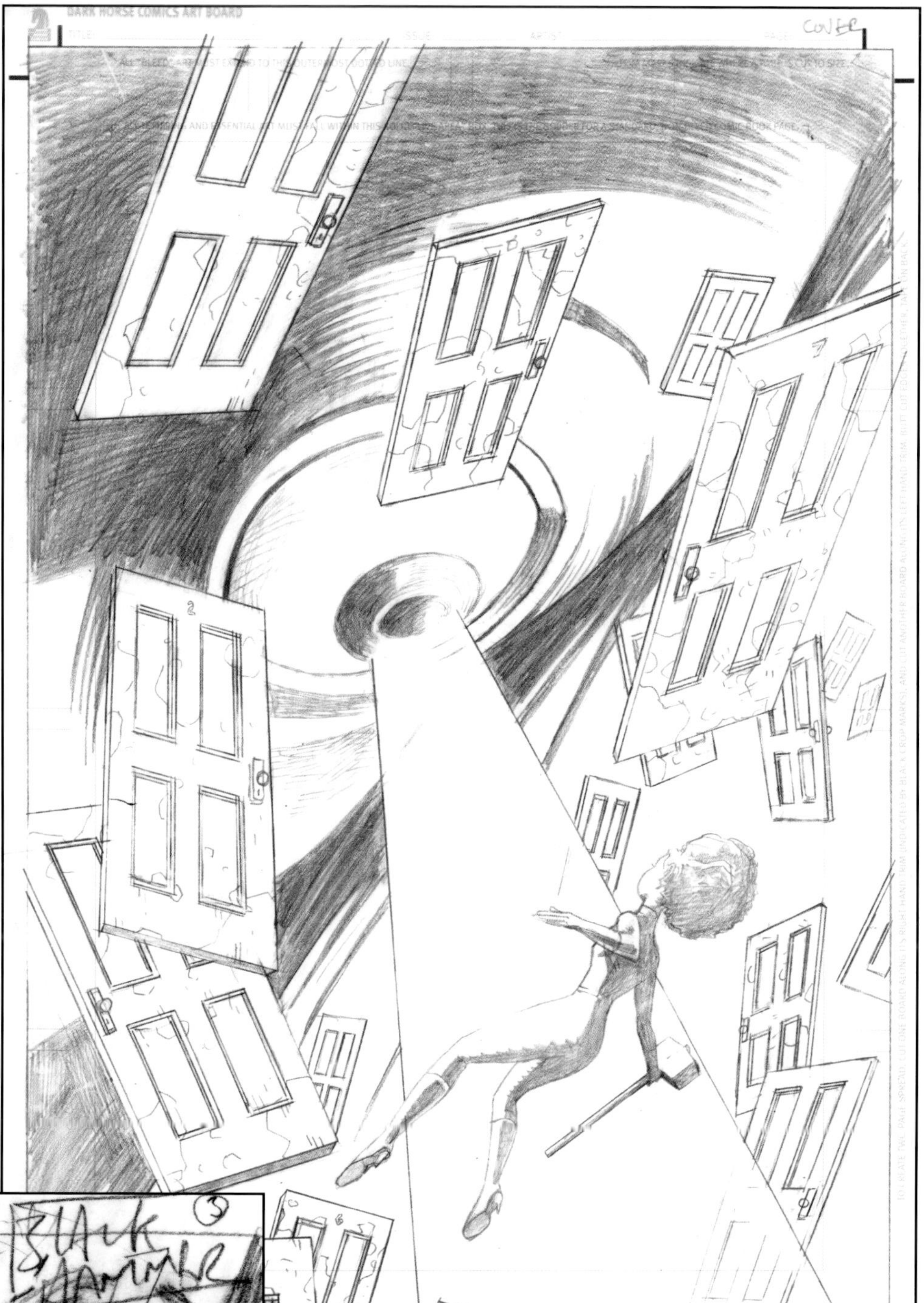
DARK HORSE COMICS ART BOARD
COVER
ONLY, DRAW ON THE REVERSE SIDE OF THIS BOARD AND INK IN TRIM MARKS IN BLACK.

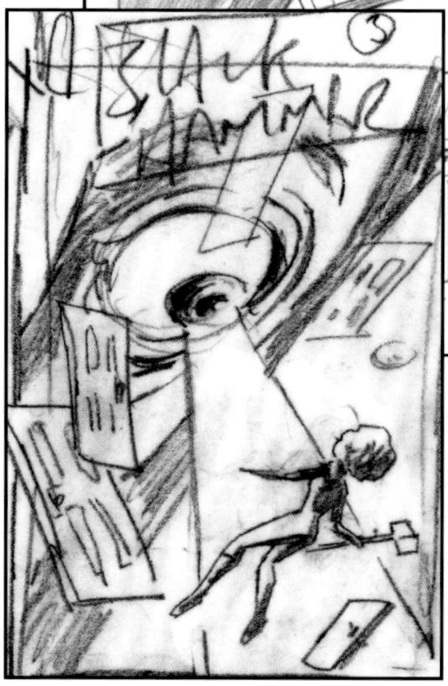

My main aim with this cover was to get a retro feel, so I took inspiration from Steve Ditko covers that he did for *Out of this World* and other Charlton titles. As with the previous cover, luckily for me the very first sketch had the simplicity and mood I was aiming for.

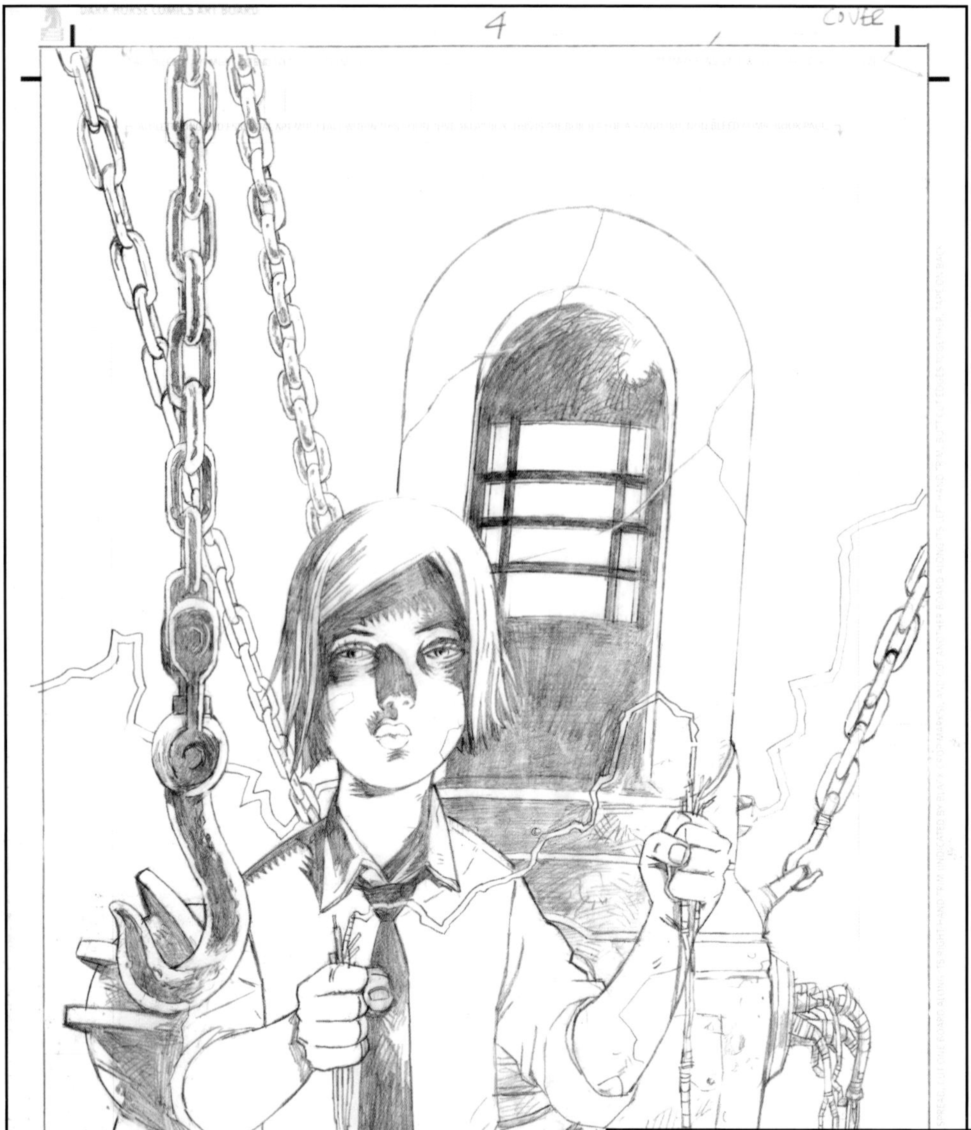
4
COVER

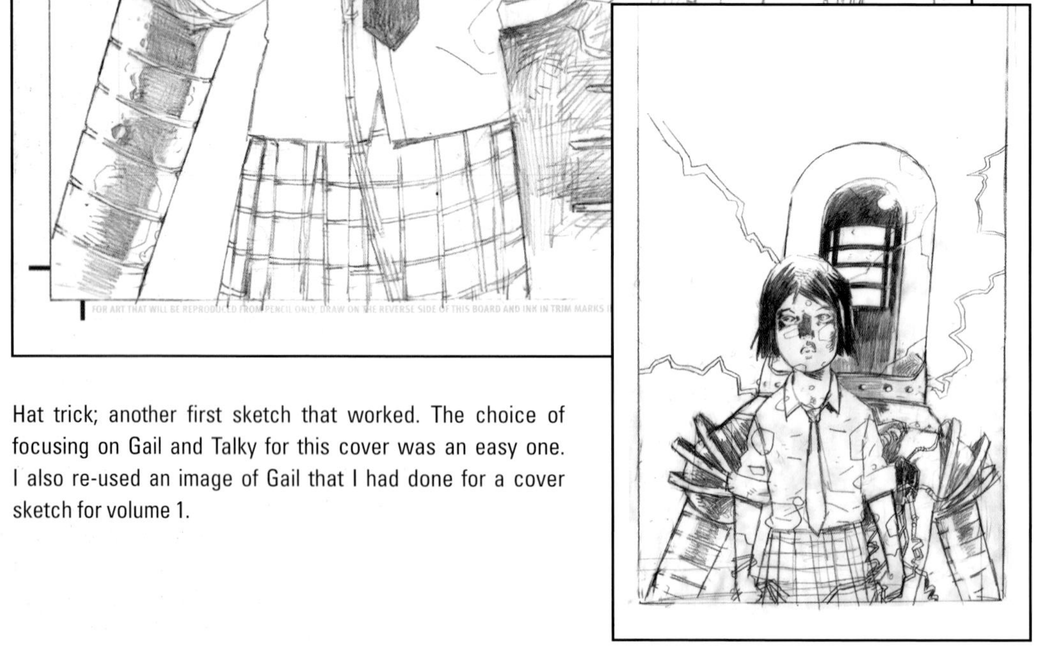

Hat trick; another first sketch that worked. The choice of focusing on Gail and Talky for this cover was an easy one. I also re-used an image of Gail that I had done for a cover sketch for volume 1.

The pace at which I can work is very compromised, it takes me almost twice as long to draw a page after a brain injury left my right hand physically impaired so on some pages I had help from Peter Gross who did rough breakdowns.

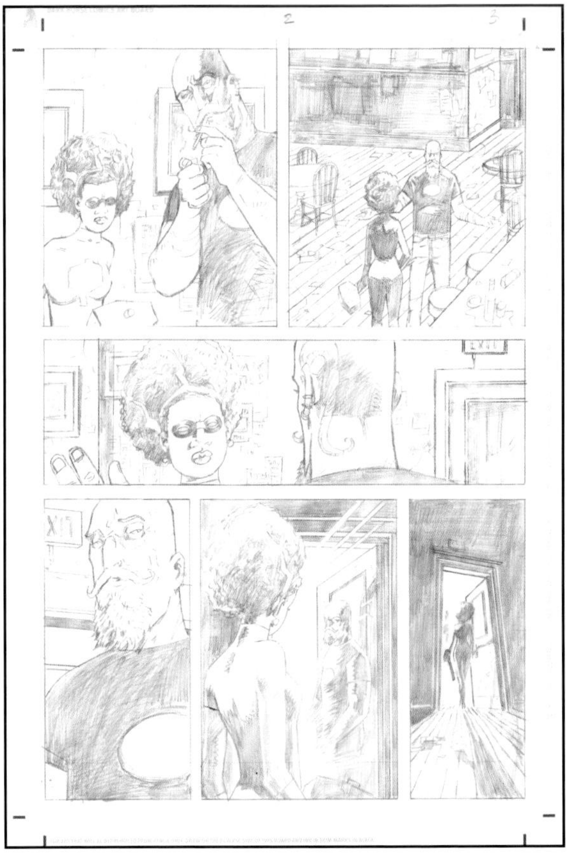

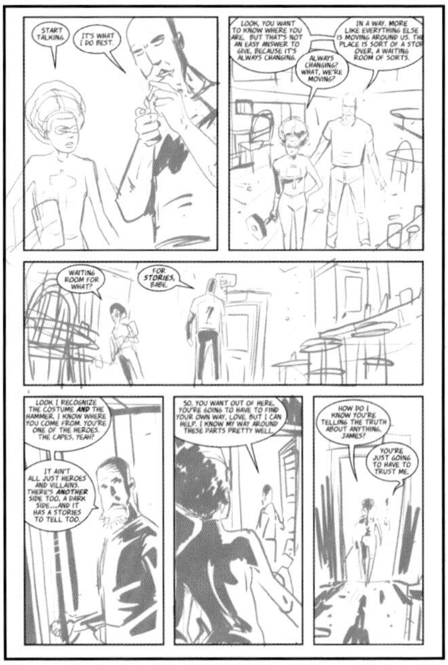

START TALKING.
IT'S WHAT I DO BEST.
LOOK, YOU WANT TO KNOW WHERE YOU ARE, BUT THAT'S NOT AN EASY ANSWER TO GIVE, BECAUSE IT'S ALWAYS CHANGING.
ALWAYS CHANGING? WHAT, WE'RE MOVING?
IN A WAY. MORE LIKE EVERYTHING ELSE IS MOVING AROUND US. THE PLACE IS SORT OF A STOP OVER, A WAITING ROOM OF SORTS.
WAITING ROOM FOR WHAT?
FOR STORIES, BABE.
LOOK I RECOGNIZE THE COSTUME AND THE HAMMER. I KNOW WHERE YOU COME FROM. YOU'RE ONE OF THE HEROES. THE CAPES, YEAH?
IT AIN'T ALL JUST HEROES AND VILLAINS. THERE'S ANOTHER SIDE TOO, A DARK SIDE....AND IT HAS A STORIES TO TELL TOO.
SO, YOU WANT OUT OF HERE, YOU'RE GOING TO HAVE TO FIND YOUR OWN WAY, LOVE. BUT I CAN HELP. I KNOW MY WAY AROUND THESE PARTS PRETTY WELL.
HOW DO I KNOW YOU'RE TELLING THE TRUTH ABOUT ANYTHING, JAMES?
YOU'RE JUST GOING TO HAVE TO TRUST ME.

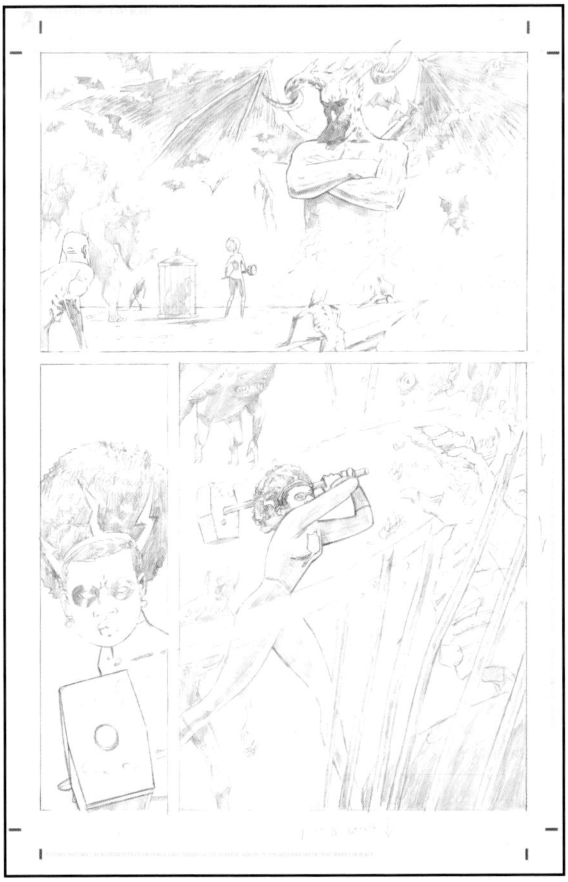

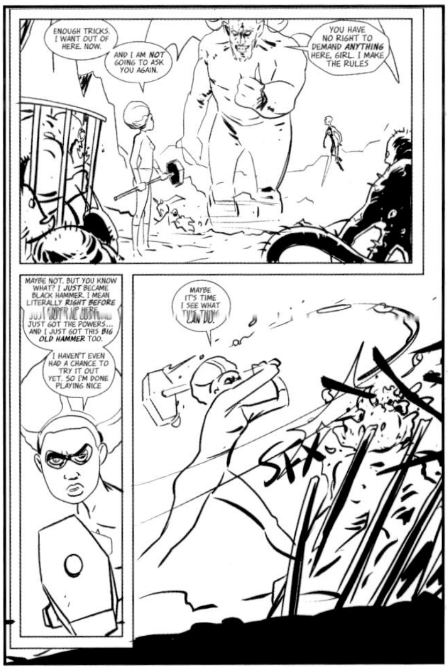

ENOUGH TRICKS. I WANT OUT OF HERE. NOW.
AND I AM NOT GOING TO ASK YOU AGAIN.
YOU HAVE NO RIGHT TO DEMAND ANYTHING HERE, GIRL. I MAKE THE RULES
MAYBE NOT. BUT YOU KNOW WHAT? I JUST BECAME BLACK HAMMER. I MEAN LITERALLY RIGHT BEFORE
JUST GOT THE POWERS... AND I JUST GOT THIS BIG OLD HAMMER TOO.
I HAVEN'T EVEN HAD A CHANCE TO TRY IT OUT YET. SO I'M DONE PLAYING NICE
MAYBE IT'S TIME I SEE WHAT
SFX

Here's another example of Peter Gross breakdowns and my pencils. I had worked with Peter on the Vertigo comic *The Unwritten* where he supplied breakdowns and I used them as a springboard for the finished page; I liked working that way. This is another page where I stuck pretty close to Peter's roughs.

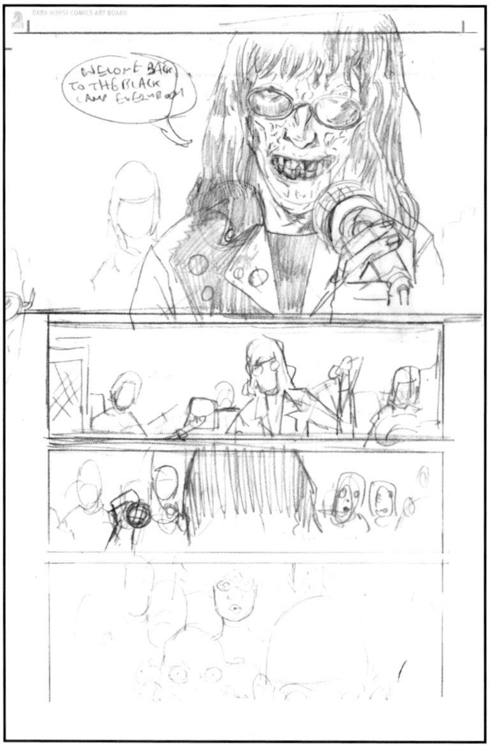
DARK HORSE COMICS ART BOARD
WELCOME BACK TO THE BLACK LAMP EVERYBODY

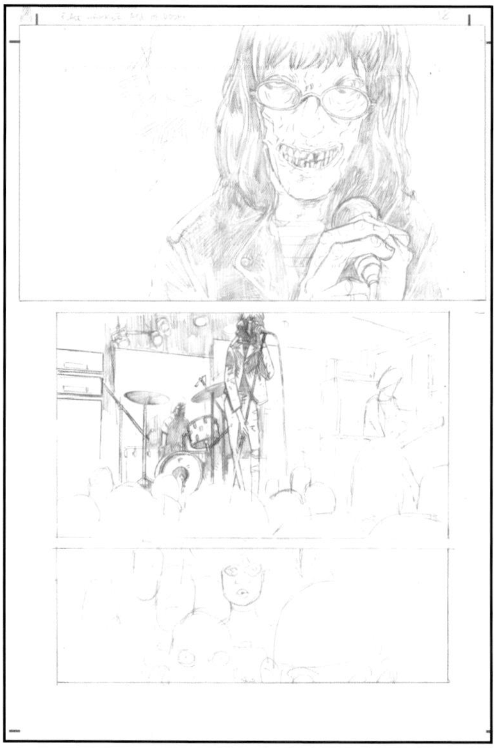

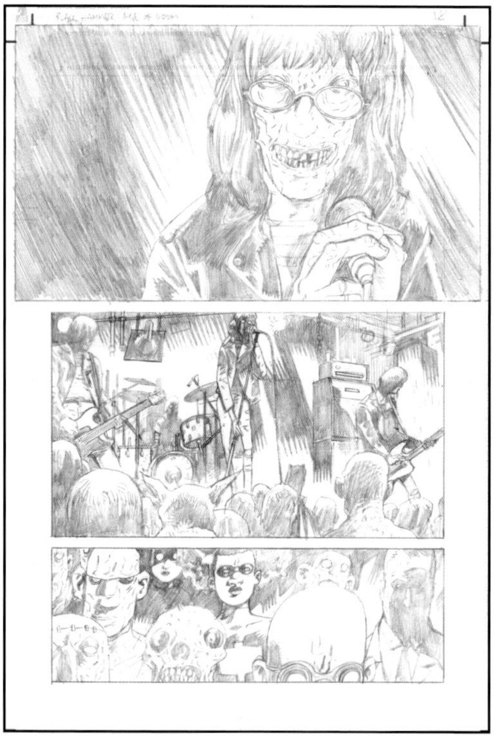

My rough pencils in progress and my finished pencils. One of the best things about working on a creator-owned book is the freedom allowed to indulge in one's own tastes, so I had good fun drawing an exaggerated, other world version of the Ramones. I figured Gail would be a huge Ramones fan.

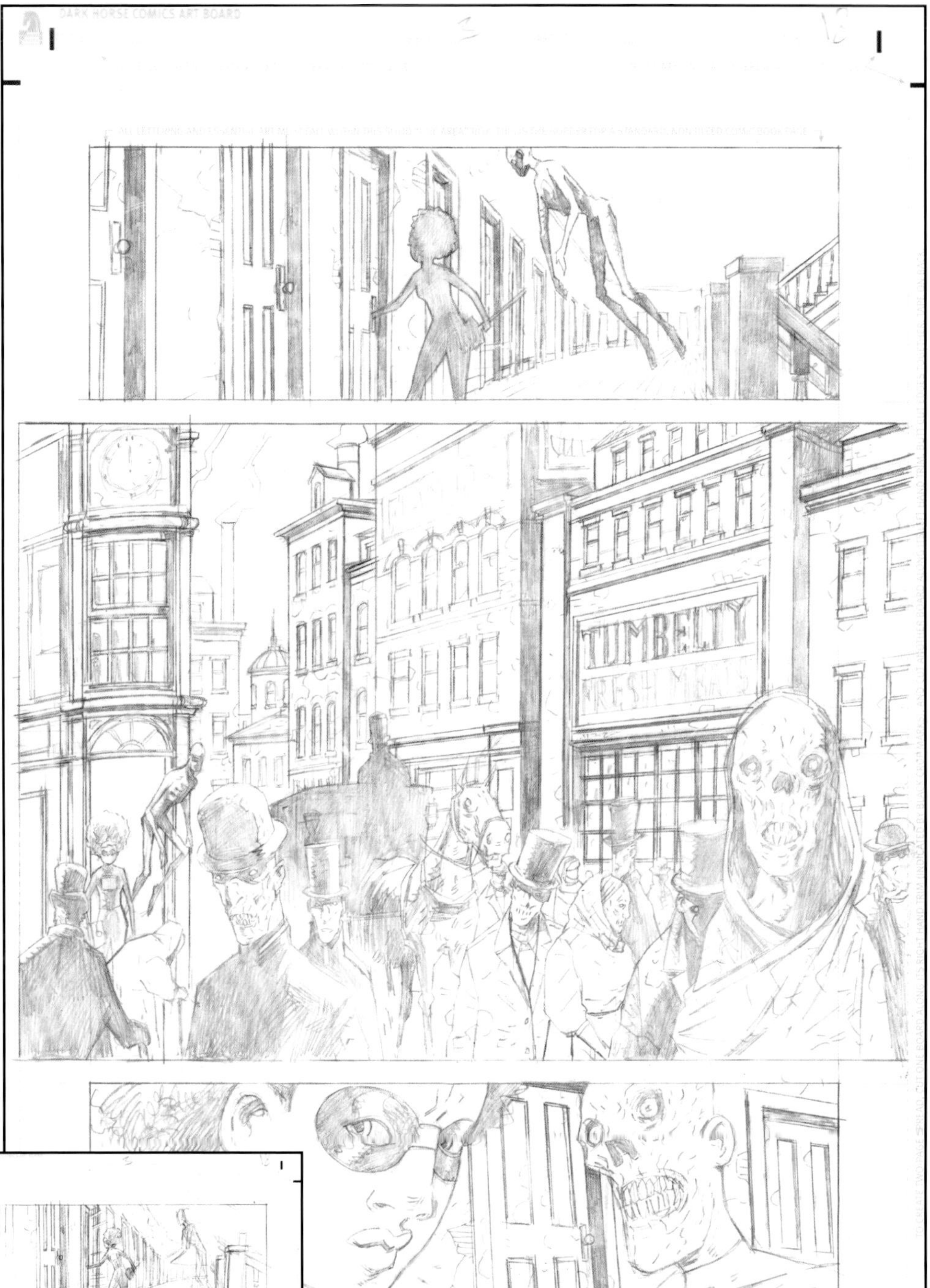
DARK HORSE COMICS ART BOARD
TUMBELTY
FRESH MEATS
DRAW ON THE REVERSE SIDE OF THIS BOARD AND INK IN TRIM MARKS IN BLACK.

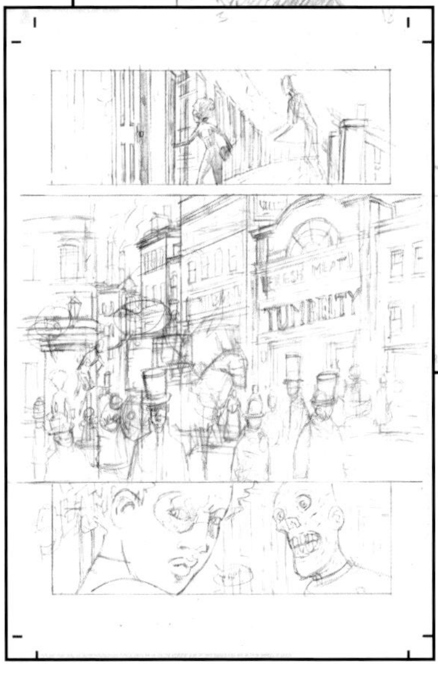
FRESH MEATS
TUMBELTY

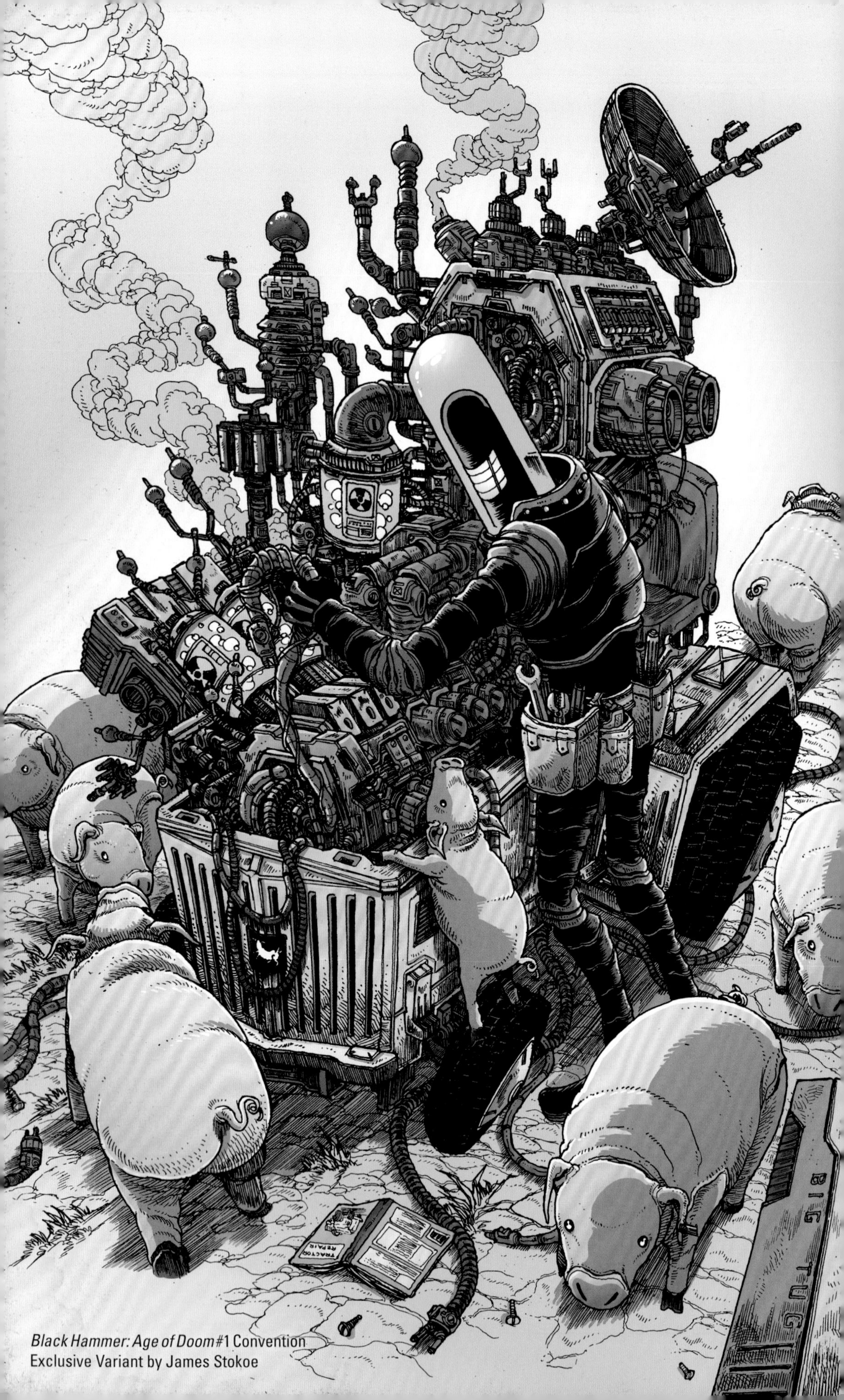
TRACTOR REPAIR
BIG TUG

Black Hammer: Age of Doom #1 Convention Exclusive Variant by James Stokoe

"If you think there's no room left in your life for another superhero comic, *Black Hammer* might just prove you wrong."—IGN

BLACK HAMMER™

ONCE THEY WERE HEROES, but the age of heroes has long since passed. Banished from existence by a multiversal crisis, the old champions of Spiral City—Abraham Slam, Golden Gail, Colonel Weird, Madame Dragonfly, and Barbalien—now lead simple lives in an idyllic, timeless farming village from which there is no escape! And yet, the universe isn't done with them—it's time for one last grand adventure.

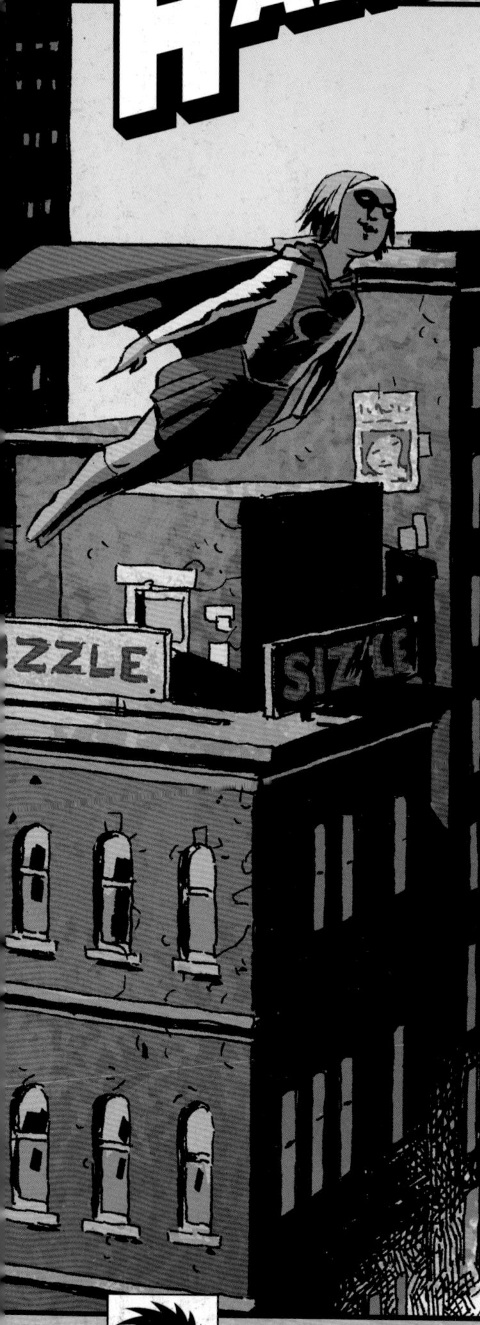

ZZLE
SIZZLE

BLACK HAMMER
Written by Jeff Lemire • Art by Dean Ormston

VOLUME 1: SECRET ORIGINS
978-1-61655-786-7 • $14.99

VOLUME 2: THE EVENT
978-1-50670-198-1 • $19.99

VOLUME 3: AGE OF DOOM
978-1-50670-389-3 • $19.99

SHERLOCK FRANKENSTEIN & THE LEGION OF EVIL
Written by Jeff Lemire • Art by David Rubín
This mystery follows a reporter determined to find out what happened to her father, the Black Hammer. All answers seem to lie in Spiral City's infamous insane asylum, where some dangerous supervillain tenants reside, including Black Hammer's greatest foe—Sherlock Frankenstein!
978-1-50670-526-2 • $17.99

DOCTOR STAR & THE KINGDOM OF LOST TOMORROWS
Written by Jeff Lemire • Art by Max Fiumara
This dual-narrative story set in the world of *Black Hammer* chronicles the legacy of a Golden-Age superhero wishing to reconnect with his estranged son, whom he hoped would one day take the mantle of Doctor Star.
978-1-50670-659-7 • $17.99

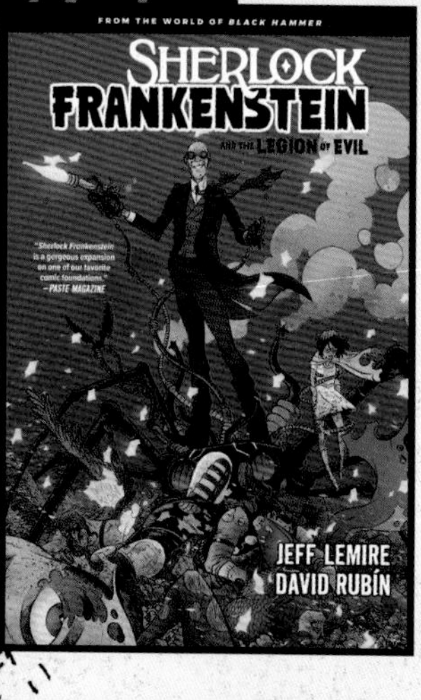

FROM THE WORLD OF BLACK HAMMER
SHERLOCK FRANKENSTEIN
AND THE LEGION OF EVIL
JEFF LEMIRE
DAVID RUBÍN

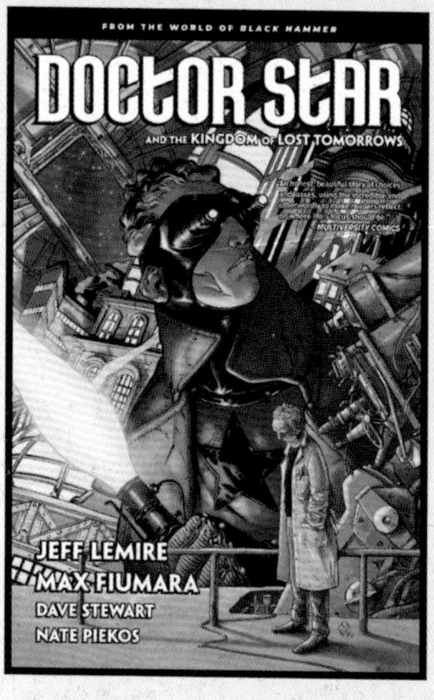

FROM THE WORLD OF BLACK HAMMER
DOCTOR STAR
AND THE KINGDOM OF LOST TOMORROWS
JEFF LEMIRE
MAX FIUMARA
DAVE STEWART
NATE PIEKOS

DARK HORSE BOOKS

AVAILABLE AT YOUR LOCAL COMICS SHOP OR BOOKSTORE

TO FIND A COMICS SHOP IN YOUR AREA, VISIT COMICSHOPLOCATOR.COM. FOR MORE INFORMATION OR TO ORDER DIRECT:
On the web: darkhorse.com • E-mail: mailorder@darkhorse.com • Phone: 1-800-862-0052 Mon.–Fri. 9 AM to 5 PM Pacific Time.

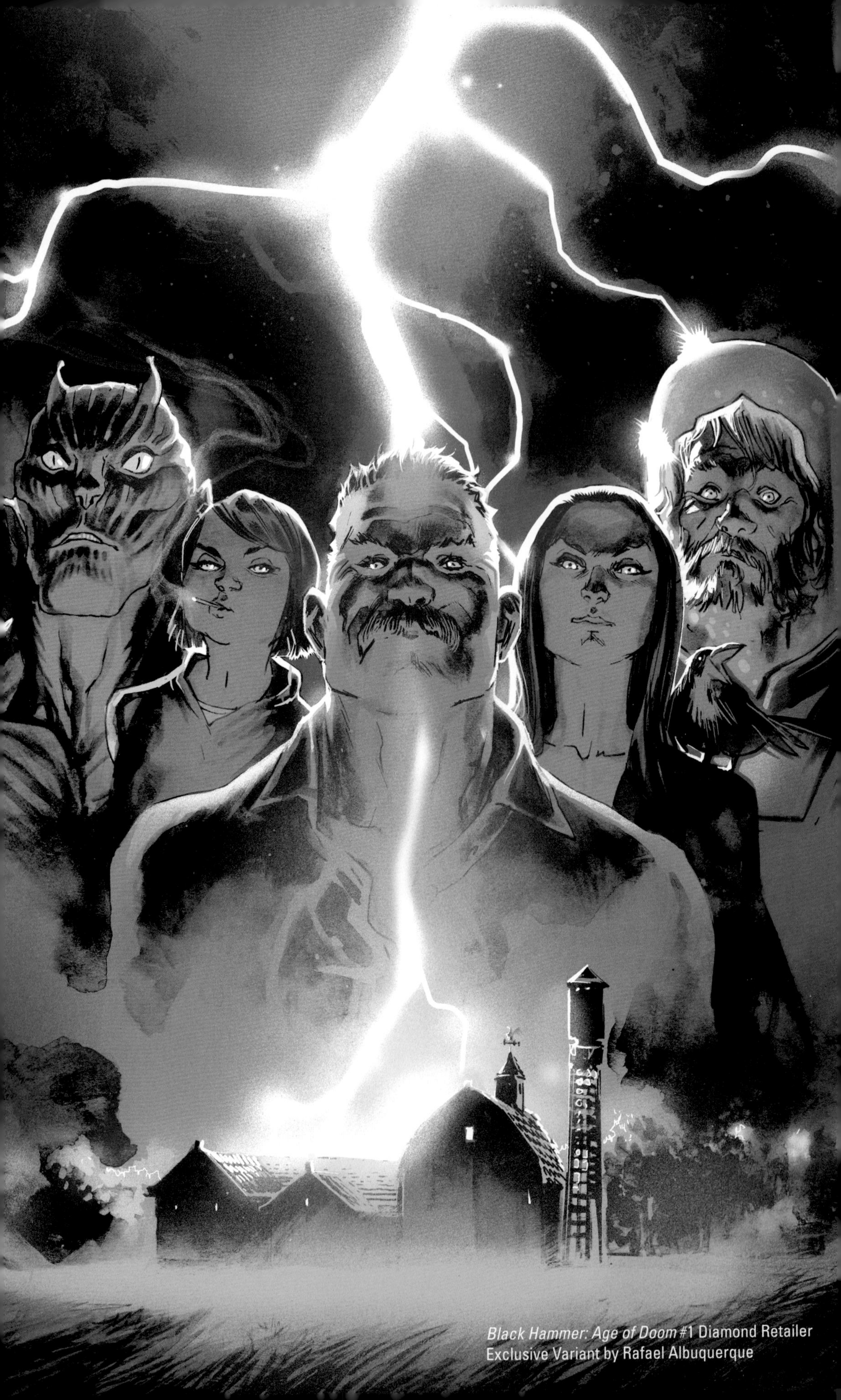

Black Hammer: Age of Doom #1 Diamond Retailer Exclusive Variant by Rafael Albuquerque